T0265919

what the trees see

A wander through millennia of natural history in Australia

Dave Witty

MONASH
UNIVERSITY
PUBLISHING

This book is dedicated to Pip & Eva –

I can't imagine life without you

Published by Monash University Publishing
Matheson Library Annexe
40 Exhibition Walk
Monash University
Clayton, Victoria 3800, Australia
publishing.monash.edu

Monash University Publishing: the discussion starts here

Dave Witty © Copyright 2023
Dave Witty reserves the right to be known as the author of the work.

All rights reserved. Apart from any uses permitted by Australia's *Copyright Act 1968*, no part of this book may be reproduced by any process without prior written permission from the copyright owners. Enquiries should be directed to the publisher.

Reasonable attempts have been made to locate copyright holders, and any potential infringement of copyright is accidental. Should any infringement be suspected, contact Monash University Publishing.

9781922633842 (paperback)
9781922633859 (pdf)
9781922633866 (epub)

A catalogue record for this book is available from the National Library of Australia

Cover design and typesetting by Peter Long
Author photograph by Brett Goldsmith

Printed in Australia by Ligare Book Printers

FSC
www.fsc.org
MIX
Paper | Supporting
responsible forestry
FSC® C011613

Contents

Introduction:
Ruins Green

Australia was different.

My experience of travel, as a child growing up in England, had been trips to Europe, cities like Paris and beach resorts like Benalmádena and Mallorca. The few memories I had were made from the rustic tones of buildings or the soft grey of delicate ruins. If asked to recall certain places, I would picture the grand architecture of Bordeaux or the winding medieval streets of Sicily. Paris is a city of columns; Munich one of turrets. Later, as a carefree traveller in my early twenties, I would visit Asia and bring back tastes on my tongue, my ears ringing with the charm of incessant traffic and boisterous conversation.

But my memory of those first towns I visited in Australia was not the architecture, the smells or the tastes, but the trees. Trees whose names I would not learn for many years: the hoop pines (*Araucaria cunninghamii*) and bunya pines (*Araucaria bidwillii*) of Brisbane, the lemon-scented gums (*Corymbia citriodora*) of Kings Park, the creamy white snappy gums (*Eucalyptus leucophloia*) of the Pilbara or the salmon-barked eucalypts of Kalgoorlie (*Eucalyptus salubris, Eucalyptus salmonophloia*). It was hard not to be enchanted by a continent where

80 per cent of the plant species are endemic. The trees changed as you passed from town to town. The differences were subtle to someone who, like me, could not distinguish an elm from an oak. But in a new country, with awakened eyes, these differences were exhilarating.

We lived in central Queensland for five or six years. My first job involved travel to towns like Dysart and Middlemount, Glenden and Mackay. One of the more frequent journeys I made was from Moranbah to Clermont. There was a rest stop halfway along, with views towards a hillock named Wolfang Peak. I would sometimes pull up there and switch off the ignition. Alighting from the car was always a curious sensation – passing from the artificial hum of air conditioning to the cloying heat of the lower tropics. It would be wrong to call the air silent. It was filled with the sibilant drone of cicadas and the aching cries of Torresian crows. Snakes passed through the grass. Orb spiders hung with gothic beauty from the trees. Yet there was a stillness here that suggested life existed in some form of permanent, semi-comatose state.

The trees by Wolfang Peak had thin, insipid trunks, and their leaves hung limply from the branches, as if they had landed in this rough, dry part of the world and, rather than adapting, had grown anxious of their surroundings. I had no idea yet about eucalypts. Had I been asked to guess how many species there were, I would have said sixty or seventy, a hundred at most. If someone told me the same species could grow stunted in one location but priapic in the next, I would never have believed them.

I would find out later the trees were mountain coolibahs (*Eucalyptus orgadophila*), red bloodwoods (*Corymbia erythrophloia*) and narrow-leaved ironbarks (*Eucalyptus crebra*), the ancestors of which took root here tens of thousands of years ago. The narrow-leaved ironbark is one of the more common eucalypts in eastern Australia, and *crebra*, the Latin name for the species, translates roughly as 'frequent' or 'abundant'. They provide a dark contrast to the silver-grey of the grass and the reddish-brown of the soil. When I first saw their blackened trunks, I presumed fire must have blazed through the landscape. In the forests of the Atherton Tablelands, they are large, forthright individuals, but here, in the grey haze of the Peak Ranges, they grow thinly, meekly from the ground. Squint in the heat and these trees make no more impression on the mind than flies on a windowpane: a ubiquitous yet unobtrusive part of the Australian environment.

'There can be no walk, no journey of any kind, more monotonous than one through the bush ... There is no association of the past connected with it. Your sight is never regaled with the "ruins grey" of some fine old fortress ... Imagination is at a standstill.' These words, quoted at the end of Robert Hughes' *The Fatal Shore* (1986), come from the pen of an English gold-seeker named John Sherer. It reflects how many early Europeans viewed the Australian landscape – 'dully-dead', a description Sherer uses later in the same passage. Whereas the tales of outlaws permeate the European forests, and the ruins of castles tell of escapades and tragedy, an indistinct blankness greets those new to the Australian bush.

§

For the narrator of Marcel Proust's *In Search of Lost Time* (1913), the taste of his aunt's *petites madeleines* dipped in lime blossom tea reawakens the spirit of his childhood.

I sometimes have these 'madeleine moments', the cascades of memories Proust describes, when a sensual trigger reawakens a former self. They can be welcome regressions, seizures of thought that allow a person to time-travel through memory. For me, when in central Queensland, it is not the weatherboard houses, the flyscreens or bullnose shades, but the sight of the trees, lank and wasted, that return me to my mid-twenties self in an instant. The haggard plains of Wolfang Peak were once capable of bringing my mind to a stop – dully-dead – and yet many years later, they are more evocative of that time than the houses we lived in or the people we knew.

To imagine trees and their histories is to think of time in a different way. The boabs (*Adansonia gregorii*) of the Kimberley, the bull kauris (*Agathis microstachya*) of Lake Barrine and the figs (*Ficus spp.*) of eastern rainforests have all lived venerable lives, some for more than ten centuries. Two thousand years is not uncommon for the trunks of Huon pine (*Lagarostrobos franklinii*), their root systems five times older, and there is one particular colony of King's holly (*Lomatia tasmanica*) in Tasmania's southwest estimated to have existed for more than 40,000 years. Compare this to the commonly planted Cootamundra wattle (*Acacia baileyana*), which will spiral from the ground, grow and look pretty, and then perish after a decade or two.

The same is true of landscapes. While time has been favourable to some, it has been unsparingly brutal to others. Certain areas have remained relatively stable during 60,000 years of human settlement, while others have been irreparably transformed, first through the fire regimes of First Australians and then, somewhat fatally, by the axes and chainsaws of European intervention. When one thinks of the effort involved in felling one tree, it can be hard to contemplate the brisk deracination of Australia's forests. Within hours of the First Fleet arriving, the sound of axes was already reverberating around Sydney Cove. Thomas Keneally likened the way the settlers bastardised the

4

land to that of a tree-eating insect. Trees that take hours to chop down take decades or centuries to re-establish. To get a sense of Sydney before European occupation is to look at John Lewin's painting of Castle Hill from 1806, in which the landscape is a patchwork of fields speckled with tree stumps every dozen or so metres. In the painting, the stumps are forlorn, appearing like tombstones, but imagine them growing again into tall, stately blue gums (*Eucalyptus saligna*).

At the beginning of his book *The Biggest Estate on Earth* (2011), Bill Gammage describes a manna gum (*Eucalyptus viminalis*) on Ellesmere station, south of Jericho in Tasmania. Its lower branches extend widely while its upper branches point to the sky. Its form is much like an artificial Christmas tree packed up for storage, the upper branches compressed while the lower ones have not yet been tapered in. This tree has existed for upwards of 200 years. For the first half of its life, the eucalypt, if we are to judge from its appearance, enjoyed clearance and space, but more recently it has been in competition with close-growing neighbours. There is only one explanation for this initial freedom: the tree survived as cool fires burnt the surrounding vegetation. The Palawa managed the land in this way not just to flush out prey but to assume permanent control over animals' movements. Grasslands, framed by areas of unburnt forest, were created by fire in the same way parklands are created today by fences and lawnmowers. Kangaroos and wallabies, lured by the promise of the short, lush grass and comforted by the shelter of the surrounding forest, would wander into this exposed amphitheatre only to be impaled upon the end of a spear.

There is a rather unbecoming mountain swamp gum (*Eucalyptus camphora*) close to Mansfield, Victoria, that shows the impact of a near-fatal incident, perhaps a flood, for its main trunk lies supine on the ground. The roots retain a weakened grip in the soil, but it has managed to revive itself, the branches growing vertically, like modified trunks. Trees are relentless adaptors. On any walk through a national park, it is not uncommon to notice these spirits of endurance, their twisted, malformed trunks sculpted by circumstance and weather. Wind is often the most revealing sculptor. The moonahs (*Melaleuca lanceolata*) of Churchill Island or the famous river red gum (*Eucalyptus camaldulensis*) of Geraldton wear their coastal burden distinctly, displaying every twist, turn and agony inflicted by the strong, salty, growth-retardant winds.

Irish novelist Edna O'Brien once said, 'When anyone asks me about the Irish character, I say look at the trees. Maimed, stark and misshapen, but ferociously tenacious.' Australian trees also reveal a lot about the Australian character, but they do so by virtue of their diversity. They can be tall and laconic like *Araucaria*, showy like the melaleucas and banksias, or enigmatic like the stunted trees of the mallee. A wattle in flower is a gorgeous treat, but when festooned with seed pods or struggling in the nutrient-poor soils of the outback, the same tree can become diffident. George Worgan, surgeon and passenger of the First Fleet, once applied the word 'delusive' to the landscape of Sydney. One may be taken at first by the vivid green lawns and purling streams, but closer inspection reveals rocky, sandy surfaces and swamps of impenetrable forest. The Norfolk Island pines (*Araucaria heterophylla*) that James Cook believed would make excellent ship masts turned out to snap like carrots under the slightest industry.[1] The dense, indifferent mangroves that inspired more fear than promise in European eyes had in fact sustained First Australians with food and medicine for thousands of years. For a description of the national character, 'delusive' is not an undeserving term. This a country where otherwise easy-going souls can be staunchly conservative, the derelict can be wonderfully literate and beauty can be found in the most surprising of human places.

Worgan was not the only early settler to find disappointment in the landscape. Many were sad to learn the riverbanks were not fringed with alders and willows, and the canopies of trees did not radiate with a lush Lincoln green. One settler referred to eucalypts as tiresome, shadeless never-greens. In a passage in her novel *The Secret River* (2005), Kate Grenville reimagines the thoughts of those first European settlers as they viewed their surrounds, writing: 'There was something about its tangle that seemed to make the eye blind, searching for pattern and finding none. It was exhausting to look at: different everywhere and yet everywhere the same.'

The long, spindly, falcate leaves of acacias and eucalypts were not the large, welcome, ovate leaves of the elm tree or common lime. Hanging vertically to avoid exposure to the sun, they looked lethargic in the cloying heat, limp and pathetic as they sashayed in the breeze. But over six or seven generations, this feeling of revulsion was exorcised and the strangeness of the trees, reviled by those first European settlers, became a source of comfort, even pride. Eucalypt leaves were sent to servicemen fighting overseas in the two world wars. The smell summoned feelings beyond words.

If we ask people why they enjoy nature, they may cite its beauty or its grandeur. They may romanticise it, eulogise it or enjoy its difference from urban life. Some learn their Linnaeus classifications and devote their energy towards the pursuit of identification. Others wish to understand the interplay between species, the fascinating relationships that may reveal themselves only upon careful observation. Tim Flannery, one of Australia's foremost environmentalists, says he observes nature in the same way one listens to an intricate orchestra. Where some hear only a drone of endless green, he hears an overture of sound. When John Sherer explored the Australian bush, he could not see the 'ruins grey' of old fortresses, but had he looked closer he would have seen old landscapes and old trees: scarred river red gums, their bark wearing the imprint of large canoes, or birthing trees, their bases hollowed out by vehement fires. These are the green ruins of Australia, trees that have grown for hundreds of years, members of dynasties that have dominated the landscape across geological time.

In the first episode of the BBC series *Civilisations* (2018), British historian Simon Schama reflects on the importance of preserving artworks from past cultures. Marauding, conquering tribes understand the power of these symbols, destroying them, toppling them in a quest for year zero. In Australia, this connection to the past is delicate, at best. It is drawn in ochre on the walls of caves, recalled in the stories of First Australians, and retained in the enduring trees of our landscape. To destroy these trees in the name of a residential estate or a highway is to topple some of the last remaining symbols of this history. 'What is the present except an endless chain of memories …?' asks Schama in the first episode. 'We are all the inheritors of those memories, and we look after them as best we can. All this, so we can pass on their revelation to the future.'

This book aims to explore what these trees can teach us about our past. In the hypnotic film *Ten Canoes* (2006), the narrator, voiced by the actor David Gulpilil, describes the story as 'growing into a large tree now, with branches everywhere'. This book is similar. Some chapters may unfold in an orderly direction, much like the straight lines of a Norfolk pine or the Leichhardt tree (*Nauclea orientalis*). Others may twist and curl like the branches of the snow gums (*Eucalyptus pauciflora*) on Victoria's peaks. Some readers may wonder why mangroves get a chapter while melaleucas get none, or why foxtail palms appear at the expense of banksias or grevilleas. It is a personal account as much as a botanical one, a story that has been shaped by my experiences and influences.

It is my hope that these chapters will encourage readers to see trees differently. Some might wish to view drooping she-oaks through a similar lens to the Wathaurung people, or walk through the streets of Perth and imagine the jarrah, marri and the orange inflorescence of the kaanya tree. Every day, hundreds of people amble past the grey ironbark (*Eucalyptus paniculata*) in the garden of St John's Church, Glebe, but how many have stopped to wonder in awe at its ancient lineage? How many have viewed its furrows and visualised the turpentine forest of pre-European Sydney, the blue skies enlightened by the smoke of Aboriginal fires, the air filled with the sound of brolgas and swift parrots? This is not Proustian, for it does not transport to a former self. But it does transport back to a world only faintly depicted by our secondary sources. It is a form of 'madeleine response' peculiar to the power of nature, a late Pleistocene moment, a window into the world of a previous geological epoch.

This is the goal of this book: to help illuminate, as other books have done for me, the insight, the beauty and the instruction of these living monuments.

Wadjemup

On my first day in Australia, Marian, my partner, dropped me off at her work, and I walked to the museum in Perth's cultural centre. To get to the Causeway, I crossed Taylor Reserve and McCallum Park, the city skyline beaming across the river. The trees on Heirisson Island were wind-ruffled she-oaks and contorted eucalypts. The other side of the river, by contrast, felt like a mix between California and the French Riviera. All along Riverside Drive, the asphalt is lined with a parade of fan palms (*Washingtonia robusta, Washingtonia filifera*) and coral trees (*Erythrina x sykesii*). Like many things in Perth, it seemed both wondrous and artificial. Far too orderly: it was obvious this was not an original landscape but a simulacrum of Western ideals. Fanny Balbuk, a Whadjuk Nyoongar woman known to her people as Yooreel, walked a similar route for much of the second half of the nineteenth century. She walked from Yoonderup (Heirisson Island) to the freshwater lake where the museum and gallery now stand. It was her songline. She would recite the names of the trees as she walked, careful not to trip over her words for fear of provoking the spirits. 'She knew every rock hole,' recalls Marie Taylor, a Whadjuk Ballardong Elder. 'She knew every stream. She knew every sacred site.'

Perth, before Europeans arrived, was an open forest of jarrah (*Eucalyptus marginata*) and marri (*Corymbia calophylla*), swamp oak (*Casuarina obesa*) and firewood banksia (*Banksia menziesii*). The reclaimed land on which Riverside Drive was built did not exist at this time, and views to the river were blocked by swamp paperbark (*Melaleuca rhaphiophylla*) and towering clumps of jointed twig rush (*Baumea articulata*). Yooreel knew the stories behind every tree. She knew to stay clear of the large kaanya trees (*Nuytsia floribunda*), trees now largely only glimpsed along the messy banks of a highway, as this was where the souls of the deceased camped before floating to their resting place over the sea. She collected ripe fruit from the zamias (*Macrozamia riedlei*) around the west end of today's St George's Terrace, large nuts known as baio, which had to be soaked in water and buried before being consumed.

These trees were soon cleared to make way for the buildings of Perth's centre. Government House was built on the grave of Yooreel's grandmother, and the lake where she had gathered crayfish and turtles was drained. The open landscape gradually gave way to one of weatherboard and brick, but to the day of her death, Yooreel continued to walk her songline. 'When a house was built in the way,' writes anthropologist Daisy Bates, 'she broke its fence-palings with her digging stick and charged up the steps and through the rooms.' Yooreel's connection with the land is a kinship so intrinsic to one's being, so intertwined with one's ancestry and spiritual belief, that each violation of the landscape is irreparably seared upon one's soul.

Before I left London for Australia, I read up on the flora of Australia in the most basic fashion, rote-learning unfamiliar names such as *Hakea* and *Callitris*. I was taken by the silhouette of the eucalypt and expected to see it everywhere across the city, imagining Perth to be a Jeffrey Smart painting superimposed upon a John Glover landscape. The gum trees as we drove from Perth's airport were a surprise: they were diminutive striplings. When Captain Stirling visited the Swan River in 1827, hoping to secure a location for a new settlement, he was stunned by the immense stature of the eucalypts on display. Jarrahs and marris grew in profligate abundance on sandy ridges. Tuarts (*Eucalyptus gomphocephala*) occupied the limestone-rich higher ground. Coming from a land in which a tree's girth indicated the fertility of the soil on which it stood, Stirling foresaw in these open forests thriving orchards and paddocks subsumed by row upon row of healthy vegetables. But his hopes were misplaced, and the Europeans were shocked to discover these giant, masterful trees had grown for thousands of years on some of the continent's least fertile soil.

Keneally's metaphor of settlers as tree-eating insects attacking the giant eucalypts, hungry and rapacious, can be seen in paintings of the time, which suggest that most of the remnant trees were gone by the 1860s. Jarrah timber was cut and put on ships bound for England where it would be laid vertically in blocks, paving the roads of the West End and central London.[2] It would take me several years after leaving Perth to discover the serendipity of this fact: the trees I imagined seeing in Perth once lined the roads I walked as a child.

Marian and I made a pact to get away from the city as much as possible, and that first year in Australia was one of unabashed exploration. Weekends were spent scouting the national parks of the Perth Hills and the forests north of Yanchep. We took time off work to inspect the eroded spires of the Pinnacles, and I have good memories of walking the precipitous trails of Kalbarri and Karijini. Our first big trip took us south through the forests of Pemberton, and our second took us north, up to Exmouth and Ningaloo, along roads that trailed into a magnificent emptiness as if we were chasing the promise of an endless horizon. At different stages in between these longer holidays, we made four, possibly five, trips to Rottnest Island.

I recall an art critic once describing the modern art-gallery visitor as a tick-box tourist. They view each painting, contextualise the work in their mind and then, once a succinct précis has been reached, enjoy a moment of quiet satisfaction. Serious inquisition is lacking because time does not allow it, and the memory of the first painting is lost as one moves impatiently onto the next. My approach to nature back then was similar. I consumed landscapes for their momentary inspiration. I was living in the instant, revelling in the majesty of a tree only to forget its existence when the faraway song of a bird captured my attention. My emigration, by virtue of 15,000 kilometres, had disassociated me from any trace of my past. And while I was consumed by this reverie of change, lost in the throes of almost constant discovery, I saw the future as a rather indeterminate idea. It, therefore, does not surprise me to think that, despite my many visits to the island, I viewed Rottnest only in terms of its present condition, a perpetual holiday resort, a playground suspended in time.

For the Nyoongar people, the island is Wadjemup. When someone died, their spirit flew with the wind across the water, settling on one of Wadjemup's trees, most likely a marro (*Callitris preissii*), once the most common tree on the island, or a booree (*Melaleuca lanceolata*), the tree that brought rain.[3] Wadjemup came into being when Waugal, the rainbow serpent, creator of hills, rivers and waterholes and protector of the Nyoongar, challenged the crocodile Yondock to a fight. In the violent battle that ensued, the giant tails of these spirits buffeted and carved up the land. A trench of water was created between the mainland and the three islands, Wadjemup, Ngooloormayup (Carnac Island) and Meeandip (Garden Island). This was an event European science would recognise as the ending of the last ice age, but for the Nyoongar, it was a story passed down from generation to generation.

Before the island was separated, the vegetation was similar to that of the mainland: tuarts and bull banksia (*Banksia grandis*), jarrahs and western she-oaks[1] (*Allocasuarina fraseriana*). The Nyoongar initiated regular burnings to manage the land and flush out prey, but when human contact ended and these human-made fires ceased, the marro took over. The European's name for the marro was the slender cypress-pine, so called because it resembled the upright cypresses of Europe. 'The finest wood in the world, from which the whole land was filled with a fine pleasant smell,' wrote Willem de Vlamingh, the Dutch explorer, when he viewed the trees in 1696. When botanist and explorer Allan Cunningham visited in 1822, a brief stop-off during his hydrographic survey of Australia's coast, he was amazed by the dominance of *Callitris*. The trees grew like a noxious weed across all but the most westerly part of the island, relieved only by the occasional tea-tree[4] or boree, with its billowy, wind-petrified crown, and weeping pittosporum (*Pittosporum angustifolium*), acacia-like, its orange fruits glowing beneath its thin, acicular leaves.

The decline of the marro was rapid, a case of death by a thousand fires rather than by a thousand cuts. Individual trees were cut down to fashion fence posts and build houses, but large swathes were burnt to make room for the sheep, horses and cattle. The marro, upon which the spirits of deceased Nyoongar invariably settled, disappeared from the island. No longer would souls fly across the water. Instead their bodies would be transported in chains, some of them buried where the roots of the marro once grew.

In this combustible environment, the summer-scented wattle (*Acacia rostellifera*) thrived, frantically suckering after each destructive blaze. The groves of *Callitris* and *Melaleuca* would make way for messy swathes of *Acacia*, and by World War I, it is thought that two-thirds of the island was overcome by wattle. The plant was ascendant for half a century before the quokka, protected from hunting in 1950, feasted vociferously on the young acacia shoots. In 1955, a fire blazed through the island and the wattle did not recover. Wadjemup, once a forested wonderland, became a place of interminable heath. Walk or cycle around the island today and you see a measureless blanket of prickle lily (*Acanthocarpus preissii*) and feather speargrass (*Austrostipa flavescens*).

The first prisoners arrived on Wadjemup in August 1838: Buoyeen, Goodap, Cogatt, Tyoocan, Helia and Molly Dobbin. There were ten men on board the boat: a constable, a corporal, two soldiers and six prisoners. The prisoners, weighed down by leg irons and chains, were burdened with the task of their own transportation. As they ploughed long, unwieldy paddles through the water, rowing furiously upon the orders of the constable, rain lashed against the sides of the boat and a sickness infiltrated their lungs.

There was only one family staying on the island at the time. The family had chosen this location because, according to a letter Robert Thomson wrote to the Colonial Secretary, they did not want to be 'expose[d] to the savage barbarity of the natives at so early a period of settlement'. The winters here could be cold and the summers harsh. Crops struggled to grow, and the sheep died of a strange illness within months of their arrival. Robert and Caroline Thomson must have reeled when they saw the chained figures disembark from the rowboat. After rowing for nine hours across torrid seas, the eyes of both prisoner and solider must have been deranged. Constable Welch was supposed to be the calm, measured figurehead of authority, but, desperate for shelter, he pleaded for Thomson's help. Reluctantly, Thomson showed them to a cave along Bathurst Bay.

Welch's diary entries reveal the starkness of those few days.

August 17th. Arrived at Rottnest. Got the provisions into a cave.

18th. Coe [one of the soldiers] *and the natives employed in thatching up the entrance of the cave.*

19th. Sunday. The natives got some roots and frogs.

22nd. Weather too bad to work.

The rain was merciless that night of the twenty-second. While the soldiers slept inside the cave, the prisoners huddled together by an open fire, chained to the trunk of a marro. Only the most dogged and resourceful could have escaped in these conditions. Harnessing the fire to burn through the tree, they released themselves, the clamour of their chains stymied by the fury of the wind. Taking Thomson's whaleboat, the prisoners rowed the nine hours to the mainland, only to capsize in the untamed waters near the coast. One prisoner, Helia, lost this battle with the sea. The others came ashore north of today's Cottesloe Beach, but they would be recaptured and sent back to the island. It was an inauspicious start to what would become one of the most deservedly reviled prisons in Australia, that would serve as a place of subjugation for around 3700 Aboriginal prisoners over the course of almost 100 years.

On our first visit to Wadjemup, Marian and I stayed in the Caroline Thomson Cabins near the lighthouse. I had no idea who Caroline was, and didn't realise Thomson Bay was named for her family. The Bathurst cave where the soldiers slept was a five-minute walk from our cabin. By a strange coincidence, we arrived on 18 August and left on 21 August, almost identical dates to the prisoners. The evenings were cold, the days refreshing, and the island seemed the most peaceful retreat. The thought that this outpost could have a bloodied history seemed inconceivable. We dived in the Crystal Palace reef, the water rife with vivid fish such as the moon wrasse and Shaw's cowfish. People cycled around the island in gentle delight. Quokkas idled across the heath.

Thinking back to that time, I seem almost like a modern (less poetic) Wordsworth wandering through the meadowed hills, oblivious to everything but the beauty before me. Other visitors were more attuned to the island's darker history. David Mitchell, the British author, recalls feeling the heaviness of a presence on Wadjemup, a sensation he has felt only a couple of times before: in the concentration camps of Poland and at the site of the Newgate gallows. For a friend of journalist Kirsti Melville, the experience was more direct. She woke up terrified in the middle of the night as her room mutated into a scene from *The Amityville Horror* (1979), blood running down the walls, the building convulsing with fear and ill temper. Her friend had no idea of the building's past – that up to ten prisoners would have once slept in this room. The prisoners were sometimes chained together at night, and in lieu of a toilet they would have defecated and pissed on the ground. Henry Vincent was a particularly cruel overseer. 'Kok-butt dwarda', the prisoners called him – the one-eyed dog. He is said to have used a blacksmith's tongs to pull out a prisoner's beard by the roots. On one occasion, he ripped a prisoner's ear off with his bare hands. On another, he killed a man by striking him forcefully with a set of keys.

The first time I became aware of Wadjemup's past, I was standing in the Art Gallery of Western Australia, viewing Sally Morgan's
painting *Greetings from Rottnest*. The top third is filled with silver gulls
floating on the breeze and tourists looking awkward in garish clothes.
Below them, underground, are what appear to be large Fabergé eggs.
Look closer and the egg-shaped vessels reveal themselves to be human
bodies. The skeletons are hunched, foetal, hopeless. Many of the
bodies were indeed found in this way, bent over in a seated position
in shallow trenches. Some of the prisoners died from mistreatment,
some from malnutrition, others from diseases such as measles and
influenza. It would be nearly thirty years before a ground-penetrating
radar revealed the extent of skeletons underneath Tentland, the
island's camping site. For decades, around 370 bodies had shuddered
with every tent peg hammered into the ground. It was, and still is, the
largest deaths-in-custody Aboriginal burial ground in Australia. Glen
Stasiuk, a Nyoongar man who produced the documentary *Wadjemup:
Black Prison, White Playground* (2014), was a teenager when he went
camping with friends on the island. Sick to the point of fever, he
had to be helicoptered back to the mainland. He would return a year
later only to become sick once again. 'It's worra,' said his Nyoongar
grandmother. 'It's menditj. It's a sick place.'

§

After only one year in Perth, we moved to the other side of the country, living in Queensland for seven years before moving to Melbourne.
By the time I revisited Wadjemup, more than ten years later, my life
had changed. I had a new travel companion and together we sat on
the beach at Yallingup, listening to the wind as it railed against the

ossified melaleucas. We walked around Elephant Cove with an apricot sunset behind us, and we soared among the crowns of giant eucalypts, ascending the spiralling metal rungs of the Gloucester Tree and walking 40 metres in the air, amid the crowns of giant tingles (*Eucalyptus jacksonii, Eucalyptus guilfoylei*). When we arrived in Wadjemup, we were exhausted. We lay on the white, powdery sands of the beach, closed our eyes and fell asleep to the sound of the ocean.

In the short time we had to walk around the island, I looked out for the figure of the marro, thinking that it would graciously reveal itself upon closer inspection. But it was not until we were leaving, as we passed some disorderly scrub on the way to the bicycle-hire place, that I recall seeing a couple of the trees. My memory of them is faint, and it is possible they exist only in my imagination. It felt like, were one to view them for too long, they could disappear quite readily into a vaporous haze. They live now only as ghosts across a landscape they once dominated. Were it not for the custodial Aleppo pines (*Pinus halepensis*) on Vincent Way, or the Moreton Bay figs (*Ficus macrophylla*) and Norfolk Island pines (*Araucaria heterophylla*) around the settlement, one could leave Wadjemup thinking the place was effectively treeless.

There was a time, not so long ago, when prisoners sat on the beaches of Wadjemup, weeping and looking across the water as they watched the smoke rise up from the fires their family members were lighting on the mainland. They were observing the same viewline as their ancestors, only they were witnessing it in reverse. For thousands of years, people had looked across the water to where the faint silhouette of Wadjemup formed from the shapeless blur of distant *Callitris*. They looked out to where their ancestors' spirits flew when they died – to an island that was sacred and unknowable.

While Wadjemup is finally acknowledging the leg irons and skeletons of its history, it has a long way to go before it achieves any sense of reconciliation. One advance has been the closing of the Lodge in 2018. The unwitting visitor no longer sleeps in rooms once designed for prisoners. It is an initiative of the Wadjemup Project, part of a broader process of truth-telling, ceremony and commemoration that has been developed by Whadjuk Elders and Leaders. And while the burial ground is currently marked by a discreet pathway, an upgrade has been planned, showing a place of remembrance and reflection, the perimeter demarcated by plantings of marro and booree.

Next time your eyes are diverted, during those early summer months, by the fiery orange glow of a kaanya tree by the roadside, think of those souls who rested in the crowns of these trees before commencing the ocean crossing to Wadjemup. And if, on your travels, you pass a marro, take the time to stop and admire its presence. Fewer than 200 years ago, when the clamour of steam engines could be heard on the other side of the world, the tree flourished on this quiet, respectful island, embracing souls as they drifted dutifully across the sea, waiting for their passage to be granted to the afterlife.

Gods of the High North

I had never felt vertiginous before, but it happened halfway through the ascent: the expectation I was going to slip, fall and plummet to the ground. My chest tightened. I could not tell if my body was in shock or suppressing the desire to hyperventilate. To lose my footing would be fatal, and, as if reminding me of this, my knees shuddered back and forth, wildly, ungraciously. I am not sure how far I got, maybe halfway, but at some point I gave up the climb, took a deep breath and turned around. There is a metal-link chain, anchored with steel posts, that runs through the centre of the rock like a monstrous artery. I clung onto it, lowering my body until I was squatting, my glutes almost touching the surface of the rock. My steps narrowed, my pace now a shuffle. When I finally reached the ground, I could feel my breathing amplified, as if someone had placed a monitor on my lungs, broadcasting their heavy rhythm to all the people watching my descent.

I feel ashamed now when I admit to climbing Uluru. The question comes up maybe once or twice a year. Each time I respond cagily. I have read since of a sign at the base of the rock that says: *Uluru is sacred in our culture. It is a place of great knowledge. Under our traditional knowledge climbing is not permitted. This is our home.* But if I saw it,

I chose to ignore its message. Shame, not regret, is the word that best describes the emotion, for I believe there are few scenarios where, at that point in my life, I would not have climbed the rock, beholden as I was to a logic that impelled me to explore, free of any principles. Beauty was there to be observed and processed. As with Wadjemup, the passive majesty of Uluru seemed to exist outside of real time, and I could no more imagine the initiated Mala men, travelling the same pathways as their ancestral beings, than I could envision the earth folding and buckling 400 million years ago, one aggressive sheet of crust rising perpendicular against the other, the leavened appearance of Uluru slowly weathering over time.

Historian Mark McKenna has compared the isolated grandeur of Uluru with the cathedrals built in the Middle Ages, soaring conceptions that towered over everything nearby, richly hewn edifices that coerced humans into states of humility. Stand at the base of the rock, looking up, and one is, according to nature writer Arthur Groom, 'like an ant at the door of a cathedral'. The simile has often been used as a means to deter potential climbers, for one would think twice about ascending the arched walls of a transept or climbing the altar of a church. But assigning a reverence to something requires empathy and understanding. And while this empathy can be present in the discourse, this does not always translate into practice. Not that the sacredness of the rock, its place within the multilayered paths of the Dreaming (Tjukurpa), is the only reason the climb is discouraged. There is also the despair felt by the traditional custodians, the Pitjantjatjara and Yankunytjatjara, when someone is injured or killed. Thirty-seven people died in the space of sixty-nine years, from 1950 till the climb shut down in 2019 – some from heart attacks, other from heat exhaustion, and a few from losing their footing and tumbling to the ground. *As custodians we are responsible for your safety and behaviour*, the sign continues. *Too many people do not listen to our message. Too many people have died or been hurt causing great sadness.*

After returning to Alice Springs from Uluru, Marian and I took a walk through the city, stopping by Todd Mall as we searched for a restaurant. I have a memory of seeing an ancient tree, a particularly prominent river red gum, slightly unruly in form, on the corner of Todd Street and Parson Street. It was an unusual juxtaposition, the messy sprawl of nature brushing up against the grid-like angularity of the shopping mall. I may have remarked on its beauty at the time, but I gave no particular thought to its presence, adrift in the breadth of asphalt and concrete. The story it has to tell is there for everyone to see, but it is a story that remains largely unspoken. It is the city centre's only surviving remnant eucalypt, the one tree that has resisted the careless sweep of development. 'Ahead of us was the winding Todd River,' recalls Doris Blackwell of approaching the town of Alice Springs (then Stuart) as an eight-year-old in 1899. 'The biggest trees we had seen in three weeks ... and in the middle distance was the small township we had waited so long and driven so far to see. It was ... a forest of gums.' Underneath the boughs of these sacred trees, the Arrernte shared their knowledge. They exchanged laughter and stories. Walk along the Todd River and one can still feel the languid pace of history in the tortuous trunks of ancient river red gums. But the city itself, with its shops, art galleries and geometric roads, is a paroxysm of modernity.

§

Around 150 kilometres to the west of Alice Springs, in the direction of Hermannsburg, is a tourist spot rather less famous than Uluru. Someone has written over the road signs along Larapinta Drive, crossing out 'Alice Springs' and replacing it with its traditional name, 'Mparntwe', and changing 'Hermannsburg' to 'Ntaria'. It is four-wheel-drive territory after the highway: red and grey sands, rocks and river crossings. The red heart of Australia, a place where the air beats a lethargic, almost imperceptible pulse. And while there are river red gums (*Eucalyptus camaldulensis*) here, they do not exude the same majesty as the lone survivor by Todd Mall. Plants in this environment tend to hide. Clumps of spinifex (*Triodia spp.*) and witchetty bush (*Acacia kempeana*) seem to fade into ambiguity. The ochre soils and wiry plants lull the brain into perceiving a savannah of unending monotony. Australia can be full of surprises, but perhaps this oasis is one of the most enchanting.

The genius of the Palm Valley palm trees is how they seem to soften the brutality of the sandstone by virtue of their daintiness and grace. Acclaimed painter Albert Namatjira captures this illusion in his watercolours, the faded mirage of the cabbage palms (*Livistona mariae*) and ghost gums (*Corymbia apparrerinja*) almost transparent against the burnt-red scenery, the rock discoloured from the oxidisation of iron-bearing minerals. The trees are like spectres superimposed upon a coarsened landscape. They are bohemians, lost in a crowd of ascetics. The older trees may be three hundred years old, but they reveal a deeper sense of time. 'It is as if you were stepping back about 50,000 years,' writes Penny van Oosterzee in her book *The Centre* (1991). It can take a while to adjust to the delicate colours. Look at satellite imagery and the small, isolated population of palms resembles a green caterpillar making its way along the surface of a craterous moon.

The river is vivified with the green shoots of spikerush (*Eleocharis geniculata*) and the common reed (*Phragmites australis*).

There is another refugee growing thousands of kilometres from its nearest relatives: the MacDonnell Ranges cycad (*Macrozamia macdonnellii*), a plant whose ancestry dates back to the time of the dinosaurs. Other trees include the rock fig (*Ficus platypoda*), wild orange (*Capparis mitchellii*) and the rare river paperbark (*Melaleuca trichostachya*). But far more common are the mats of couch grass (*Cynodon dactylon*) and tussocks of buffel (*Cenchrus ciliaris*). These grassy weeds have taken over the MacDonnell Ranges. Not only are they aggressive in their pursuit of land, they are also highly flammable, meaning fire now poses one of the greatest threats to the endangered palms.

The red cabbage palms of the centre are almost 1000 kilometres from their nearest relative, the Mataranka palm (*Livistona rigida*) of the Roper and Gregory rivers. They get their name from the red glow they exude at dusk as the sun's rays illuminate the fronds, which, during the course of the day, have become dusted with the surrounding red soil. These awkward trees, with their gangly, attenuated trunks, are not unlike the fan palms of Africa and the Americas (*Hyphaene spp., Washingtonia spp.*). Around 12,000 survive within an area of 50 hectares. The majority are in Palm Valley, but others grow in scattered populations along the tributaries of the Finke River. The days are exacting and rainfall is scarce, but the trees subsist on the shallow underground waters that pass through the Hermannsburg sandstone. 'If the rock could be wrung out, it would drip like a sponge,' writes van Oosterzee. Their refuge has been given the name Palm Valley Oasis, a title more befitting of a motel on the outskirts of Cairns or California. My reliance on Hollywood for knowledge has trained me to view palms as overwhelmingly coastal, not just the coconut palms (*Cocos nucifera*) of tropical shores but also the Mexican fan palms (*Washingtonia robusta*) of Venice Beach or the Canary Island date palms (*Phoenix canariensis*) of Santa Monica. And yet this is a false impression. Los Angeles, for instance, may be the city of palms as much as it is the city of angels, but the cotton palms (*Washingtonia filifera*) that have been planted along its streets, the only palms native to America, are sons of the dry interior. They persist within the gorges and springs of the Colorado Desert, and to observe them in the wild is to view a mirage in an unforgiving landscape. It is a reminder that nature relishes the chance to surprise.

Of the eighteen *Livistona* species in Australia, only the cabbage-tree palm (*Livistona australis*) of the eastern coast grows in rainforest, with the rest occupying landscapes as diverse as monsoonal forest and open woodland, riparian forest and savannah. The red cabbage palms of Palm Valley, so far inland, are an outlier, a romantic anomaly. It was assumed they were a relict population from the late Eocene epoch, when rainforest covered large swathes of Australia. As the continent dried during the late Miocene, the trees are believed to have died out, struggling against the waterless tide of aridification. The palms in Finke Gorge survived, fed by underground aquifers and sheltered from fire by the rocky fortresses that encased them. The trees are 'botanic remnants from millions of years ago, when Central Australia was lush with tropical forests', says one promotional website.

'Marvel at ancient Palm Trees from a long-ago tropical rain-forest era,' says another.

The assumption of Eocene beginnings was the dominant view for many years, and few would have realised the secret lay hidden within the writings of a Lutheran pastor from northern Germany. A photo exists of Carl Strehlow in his early twenties, around the time he moved to Australia. He is both youthful and weary, cherubic and severe, his lustrous hair combed with ascendant strokes. By the time he got to Hermannsburg, he had hidden those cheeks behind an austere beard and the young philosopher had become the pious, paternalistic sage. He became fluent in Aranda and Loritja, acting as an interpreter and preparing lessons and curricula for the local school. He copied down Aboriginal stories, earning the trust of Elders such as Loatjira, Pmala, Moses and Talku, sitting with them as they described ceremonies or performed sections of their songlines.

It was in Strehlow's first report of Hermannsburg, written at the end of 1894, that he mentions the myth of Palm Valley. 'There are beautiful 40- to 50-feet-high palms here surrounded by gum trees and acacias, and the herbs and flowers at their base release a sharp smell,' he writes, the words translated from his native German. 'How this palm got into the interior of Australia has not been established yet by science.' But he offers an explanation: 'According to the old heathen beliefs, the gods from the high north brought the seeds to this place.'

David Bowman, part of a Japanese Australian team analysing the *Livistona mariae* palms of the Finke River, read a translation of this letter over a century after it was written. He was struck by the serendipity of its message. The researchers had been analysing the genomic DNA of *Livistona mariae* and *Livistona rigida*, and they had realised it was not just the botanical features of these two species that were similar, but their DNA as well. If their conclusions were correct, the two species diverged somewhere between 15,000 and 30,000 years ago, a remarkable discovery, which dispelled any idea these trees diverged millions of years ago as relicts of a tropical forest. How the trees crossed from the northern coast to the centre was a matter of contention. Thirty thousand years ago, it would not have been possible for the seeds to have drifted along the waters of the Gregory tributaries into the Finke River, as these water systems became detached during the Pliocene epoch. Neither does it seem likely that fruit bats and birds carried the seeds into the barren wilds of the continent without excreting populations randomly along the way.

This is not the first time western science has caught up with the wisdom of Aboriginal lore. It has taken the invention of autosequencers and thermal cyclers to learn a truth that has been passed through the ages by the recitation of words. What we could learn of the Egyptians or the Babylonians if we had access to a similar stream of insight. The lineage of this knowledge, the memetic truths passed down through song and poetry, may traverse 1500 generations. At some distant point in time, a few families, maybe more, packed up their supplies and headed into the interior, placing the seeds of *Livistona mariae* into dilly-bags made, perhaps, from the woven strands of the palm's leaves.

We may never know why these ancestors made the journey, but there is a Creation story that offers us a clue. An old man, frantically rubbing together two sticks, creates a fire that burns uncontrollably through the bush. The man and his friends flee the fire, seeking sanctuary in the cool waters of the centre. There they remain, morphing into beautiful palms.

The millstream palm (*Livistona alfredii*), at least 800 kilometres from its nearest relative (*Livistona victoriae*) in the Bungle Bungles, may also have been transplanted through human travel, as may the cabbage-tree palms of east Gippsland, which, nestled in the beautiful surrounds of Cabbage Tree Creek, are around 200 kilometres from their nearest compatriots in Bega.

This latter species, *Livistona australis*, is the cabbage-tree palm most people would be familiar with. It is the most widespread of the *Livistona* species and also the most visible. It is planted along the tourist attractions of Circular Quay and Darling Harbour, guarding the Museum of Contemporary Art and the entrance to Harbourside Shopping Centre. The individual plants mimic large, ungainly public-address systems, their fronds acting as loudspeakers, conveying messages to the people below.

I used to think the palms growing near my home in St Kilda West were also *Livistona australis*. They have the same appearance – that of a 'gigantic mop', to quote the nature writer A.G. Hamilton. But they are exotics, Mexican fan palms to be precise, the trees of Sunset Boulevard and Beverly Hills. They both have horizontal ring scars, circumferential strips formed by the shedding of dead fronds. But the straighter, more columnar trunks of *Livistona australis* have vertical ridges, as if someone has thrust a knife into the top of the trunk and restlessly carved out a vertical line, the fissures forming as the dead outer tissue shrinks over time.

When the crew of the HMS *Endeavour* approached the New South Wales coast, the first trees they recognised were the tall, rangy cabbage-tree palms. 'The trees were not very large and stood separate from each other without the least underwood,' wrote botanist Joseph Banks in his diary entry for 27 April 1770. 'Among them we could discern many cabbage trees but nothing else which we could call by any name.' They were staring at Woonona beach in New South Wales, not far from Batemans Bay. The term 'cabbage palm' had been in use for a while to describe any palm where the terminal bud, referred to as the cabbage, could be eaten. Daniel Solander, one of the naturalists on the *Endeavour*, ascribed these New Holland palms to the same genus as the gebang palm, naming them *Corypha nuda*. The *Livistona* title came later, named by Robert Brown in honour of his friend Patrick Murray, the Baron of Livingstone.

The Eora used *Livistona* fronds as boughs for their shelters, or stripped and wove the leaves to create baskets. They would cut from the tree the so-called palm heart or cabbage, the long fibrous cylinder that originates in the heart of the stem and protrudes from the crown like a giant sword. This bud, its removal a guarantor of the tree's death, was chopped up and boiled in hot water or roasted over a fire. Aware of the implications of their actions, they selectively harvested the trees to ensure populations did not decline over time.

For those on the First Fleet, it was the tree's quality as timber that was highly valued. They used the trunks as wall posts for their make-shift huts, but, alas, they did not apply the same level of conservation. 'All were cut down within a year,' writes Robert Hughes on the rapacity of the early Sydney settlement. Cabbage-tree palms, the comely doyens of the Sydney landscape, were annihilated, unable to recover, their fragile outlines erased from the shore. Trees that had sustained generations were sacrificed for impractical buildings that were torn down decades later and replaced by dwellings constructed from brick and stone. The colonists had the opportunity to learn from the original inhabitants, to gain knowledge of the idiosyncrasies and benefits of the various trees, to learn which trees might recover from harvesting and which could be fashioned more readily for construction. Not to do so was, according to critic Ashley Hay, the most 'extraordinary blindness'. One could even describe it as negligent.

'As the woods were opened and the ground cleared,' writes British officer Watkin Tench, 'the various encampments were extended, and all wore the appearance of regularity.' One wonders how many

First Fleeters felt pangs of loss as, each morning, they arose from their camps and saw fewer cabbage-tree palms on the horizon. 'The absence of these trees has taken away much from the tropical character of Sydney,' wrote the poet and judge Barron Field, decades later.

Finding untouched stands in the wild can be a rare pleasure. In places like Cabbage Tree Creek they grow within rainforest; in others, like Myall Lakes, they form monostands, shutting out the necessary light for other species to survive and ensuring, in Ian Hoskins' words, 'the overall impression is one of a haphazard plantation'. Palms are citadels of liberty, expressions of botanical elation, and their creeping disappearance could not have gone unnoticed. The few *Livistona* planted in Sydney today are faint records of this landscape, pseudo-memorial plantings, living statues commemorating scenery that once thrived in the area. But beyond the visible extirpation of the landscape was an even greater loss, one we are reminded of as we read through the letters of ethnographers such as Carl Strehlow. We are losing a trove of ancient wisdom, a lingual cloud of knowledge accessible only to those who will listen or those entrusted with its secrets. We should practise the art of 'clear listening', says Tony Tjamiwa, an Anangu Elder who has consistently voiced his displeasure at those, like myself, who have climbed Uluru. It 'starts with the ears, then moves to the mind, and ultimately settles in the heart as knowledge'. These insights are our closest link to the past, words first spoken thousands of years ago, songlines that have been echoed through generations, stories that can never be unearthed. Their loss, like the guillotining of a *Livistona* heart, is irreversible.

Monarchs of the Woods

There is a story that connects three of the most valuable timbers of Australia: the bunya pine (*Araucaria bidwillii*), the hoop pine (*Araucaria cunninghamii*) and red cedar (*Toona ciliata*). It begins in 1823 as four former convicts, Richard Parsons, Thomas Pamphlett, John Finnegan and Jim Thompson, head out on a boat from Sydney Cove, their mission to fetch cedar from the Illawarra. It is a fact largely forgotten today, but red cedar was the Pizarro's gold of Australia's eastern coast. The tree, referred to as polai by the Dharawal and wudgie wudgie by the Bundjalung of the Upper Clarence, would grow to huge sizes within the rainforests of New South Wales and Queensland. It was remarkably buoyant, and the trunks, once felled, were roped together to form a temporary raft, then floated downstream where they could be collected and put onto ships. The timber was easy to work and the finished product was imbued with a luscious red tinge. Cedar cutters would spot the tree by virtue of its flaky, almost reptilian bark and the red leaves, which materialise at the beginning of spring. When European skills of identification proved inadequate, Aboriginal trackers, who could recognise the trees from hundreds of metres away, were employed as guides to locate the precious resource.

The first sign of trouble was when a strong westerly wind began to blow. At first, it must have seemed a case of taking down the sail and waiting it out, but the breeze and the rain became more violent. For five days, delirious, hysterical winds pounded the boat, lashing it, convulsing it, sending it out further into the ocean until eventually the shoreline disappeared beneath the bleary horizon. When the weather regained its composure, the boat was stranded, a lamentably small speck in an ocean of inexhaustible blue. The sailors, shaken by the episode, believed they had travelled in a southerly direction since leaving Sydney Cove, but their intuition was wrong. They had been blown several kilometres north and, in their attempts to reach Sydney, they were sailing further from their intended destination.

By the time the boat washed up on the eastern coast of Moreton Island, the castaways had been at sea for twenty-five days. Jim Thompson was so incoherent from the dehydration he believed he was at a family dinner in Scotland, shouting out parts of imagined conversation before passing away in his sleep.

The survivors' first task upon landing was to find water. When they finally found a stream, John Finnegan, his mouth detestably dry, lay prostrate in its channel and lapped up the water like a cat. As far as they could tell, they were somewhere along the New South Wales coast, many miles south of Sydney Cove. They could not have known by observing the heart-shaped leaves of the macaranga (*Macaranga tanarius*) or by noticing the eucalypts (*Corymbia tessellaris*) with their smooth trunks and dark, tessellated bases, that they were several hundred kilometres north, not south, of the Port Jackson settlement. When the local Joondoobarrie saw these wretched, pale humans, they took them in their canoes over to Minjerribah (North Stradbroke Island) and nursed them for several weeks. Were it not for

36

the grace and hospitality of the Joondoobarrie, the castaways would have perished. Given food, taken hunting and allowed to sleep in neatly crafted, igloo-shaped huts, the castaways enjoyed a rich life as convalescents, gathering yams (*Dioscorea transversa*) and fern roots (*Blechnum indicum*) and roasting them on open fires.

It was on an excursion north, an attempt to reach what they believed would be Sydney, that the castaways came across a large waterway. Perhaps Matthew Flinders had observed the mouth of this river when standing on the summit of Mount Beerburrum in the Glass House Mountains, but he had not walked on its banks or tasted its water. This was the first time Europeans had been within touching distance of the Brisbane River, and one can trace the foundation of Australia's third city back to this seminal, albeit forgotten, moment. Under the dark, brooding watch of the hoop pines – ancient trees completely unprepared for the oncoming ecological onslaught – the castaways trudged the serpentine southern bank in what must have seemed a hopeless appeal for a crossing, passing through today's Bulimba, Woolloongabba and West End before finding an abandoned canoe near Tennyson. Thomas Pamphlett, a strong, even-tempered man, was the only competent swimmer of the group. He fetched the canoe and steered his two companions across the water. After a short journey north, the travellers crossed Pumicestone Passage and settled upon Yarun (Bribie Island), where they were looked after by the Joondoobarrie with a kindness and generosity Chris Pearce would describe as superior to anything they may have known before. They ate mussels whose presence they divined with the soles of their feet. They slept in huts, built from long, slender wattles and covered in tea-tree bark. They feasted on periwinkles, molluscs, cockles, whelks and prawns. Parsons was ascribed the name Wandi, Finnegan was named Woonunga and Pamphlett was named Juan.

The idea to search for Sydney again had been Parsons' decision. Not realising they were headed in the wrong direction, the castaways toiled through insufferable heat. Pamphlett walked around 80 kilometres before the pain in his feet became so acute he could go no further, aborting his journey roughly in line with today's township of Maroochydore. Finnegan would continue on with Parsons, but he remained wary as the relationship between the two men was frequently abrasive. Back at Yarun, when Finnegan had allowed a firestick to extinguish naturally, the Viking-like Parsons, his two front teeth missing and his eyes constricted with rage, had swung at Finnegan's head with an axe handle. When Parsons drew a knife on him close to today's Noosa River, not even the tall stately columns of red cedars could remind him of their common purpose. Finnegan turned around and headed back to Yarun. He would see Sydney in a month. For Parsons, it would be over a year.

Abandoned but not overwhelmed, Parsons continued to trek north, the stubborn hope of reaching Sydney enough to power his weakening legs. At some point, possibly when the heat grew too fierce, the mosquitoes multiplied or the rainforest and mangroves failed to soften into sandstone scrub and banksia, Parsons realised his mistake and turned around. It was during the return leg, trekking the hundreds of kilometres back to Yarun, that he met members of the Kabi Kabi and accepted an invitation to join them at a bunya gathering in the Blackall Ranges.

As the years have moved on, bunya feasts have become symbols of a romanticised past, a time when humans fell into line with the rhythms of nature, when riches fell from the sky, and people, grateful for the annual donation, celebrated as a collective rather than as self-sufficient units. Across the Bunya Mountains and Blackall Ranges, the two locations where the tree grew in abundance, around 600 people might turn up on a normal year, but around 6000 would attend the triennial or quadrennial festivals. Children would hunt for pademelons and play games; marriages were arranged, stories exchanged, laws made, and goods, songs, dances and knowledge traded. Parsons became the first European to attend a bunya festival, twenty years before Ludwig Leichhardt and twenty-one years before Thomas Petrie. Describing the event years later, he would recall the hospitality of the festival-goers, the gathering of emu eggs and wild strawberries and the strange shape of the bunya pines.

It has been said that custodians, by tying a vine around their legs and hands, could scale a bunya pine maybe 40 or 50 metres high. Once at the top, they would take one of the large cones and examine it to see whether the seeds were ripe enough for consumption. From the sound of their call, the men and women on the ground would know whether it was a good harvest or not. It was a connection with nature that drove the significance of the occasion. As Elder Paddy Jerome described in an address he gave at Griffith University, the Bunya Mountains or Boobarron Ngumpin was mother, and the attendees were children attracted to their mother's breast. Attending the festivals, and reaping the natural harvest, they would magnify their spiritual strength, a strength that had impelled their culture for tens of thousands of years.

The castaways were eventually rescued by the Surveyor-General John Oxley, who was patrolling the northeastern coast, investigating Moreton Bay as a possible site for a convict settlement. Finnegan and Pamphlett were picked up in November 1823, the former near

Sandstone Point and the latter at Pumicestone Passage, his body daubed in red and white paint while his companions danced, shouted and waved at the foreign intruders. The castaways regaled Oxley with stories of their journey up the eastern coast, their difficulty in crossing that large body of water, and their eventual recovery on the island of Yarun. The next day, Oxley and Finnegan set out in a whale boat looking for the mouth of the large, labyrinthine river.

Theirs was a journey I inadvertently re-created on my first trip to Brisbane, taking the ferry from the suburb of Hamilton to the Eagle Street jetty and admiring the untidy mix of boxy riverfront houses and towering, banksia-cone-style apartments. Hoop pines no longer grow naturally along the river, but they are still a presence, their large, patchy crowns poking above the jagged Brisbane skyline. 'If you grew up in Brisbane,' says the author David Malouf, 'they very much established the horizon… [Theirs] is the shape that you see on the top of all the ridges.'

Brisbane, it can be easy to forget, was born on the banks of the jungle. The true wonder of modern Australia cannot be discovered in its architecture or its engineering, but is felt as one walks to the James Street markets or plays bowls in Norman Park and considers that these same areas were covered in near-impenetrable rainforest fewer than 200 years ago. I was there on a short visit from Perth. While Marian attended a job interview, I stayed behind in the hotel, somewhere near Albion Park, and took a ferry into the city, following Oxley's journey along the river. My thoughts wavered between imagined futures, each as unknowable and opaque as the next. For a while, I had been contemplating returning to England. But this fresh city, with its tropical air and bright inflorescence, the dewy sheen of rainforest trees reflected in the windows of holiday homes and riverfront apartments, so impressed upon me its magnificence, it was enough to convince me to stay.

It was passing under the span of Story Bridge, with what would be Custom House's solemn grandiloquence and Harry Seidler's Eagle Street buildings to the right, that Oxley, turning to his left, first encountered the hoop pine along this river.

Setting off the next morning, Oxley and Finnegan sailed close to where the castaways had discovered the abandoned canoe, and upon reaching Tennyson, slightly downstream from the present power station, they disembarked and explored the surrounding bush. For the first time in his journal, Oxley appears to inspect the hoop pine up close, discovering, 'that the tree we had hitherto taken for cypress is this new description of pine, from 100 to 140 feet high'. According to historian J.G. Steele, 'Brisbane owes its foundation to Oxley's enthusiasm for the hoop pine and the river.'

Less than a year later, Oxley would return with the botanist Allan Cunningham, a man driven by both romanticism and industry. They would pick up Richard Parsons along the beach near Skirmish Point and explore the waterway, which would subsequently be named in honour of the New South Wales governor Thomas Brisbane.

Cunningham was aware of the hoop pine from his 1819 exploration on the HMS *Mermaid*. He had seen the trees near Townsville and, like Robert Brown before him, had mistakenly recorded them as Norfolk Island pines even though the Norfolk's upturned tassels are quite distinct from the hoop pine's bushy appearance. As he drifted along the Brisbane River, he was disappointed to find the trees were largely inaccessible: 'Hitherto in our examination of this River, we have been only gratified with a distant view of the Pine.' But that was soon to change. At Pine Mountain, upstream of the Brisbane

River, he found the slopes and ridges to be blackened by the trees. Awed by their beauty, Cunningham described them as monarchs of the woods, writing in his diary, 'It was totally impossible not to halt a few moments to admire this noble tree.' Although named *Araucaria brisbanii* at first, the tree would later take on the name of its greatest advocate: *Araucaria cunninghamii*.

Shortly after Oxley and Cunningham returned to Sydney, Governor Brisbane visited the area and was impressed by the hoop pines he saw, sending a number of logs to Britain for assessment. The following year, 1825, Edmund Lockyer, described the tree as one of the most 'valuable articles in the Colony', so valuable 'the merchants of Sydney are not inclined to give any information on their profits'. Chopped down and transported to sawmills, the timber from Araucarian trees was used variously for flooring, violin backs, cabinets, carriages, bookcases, rolling pins, plywood, veneers and boat oars. Forester Peter Holzworth described the hoop pine as one of the finest timbers in the world. Between 1917 and 1920, as the natural stands decreased, almost 50 hectares of bunya and hoop pine plantations were established in Queensland, a disarming contingency given that almost 80 years earlier, wild populations of bunya and hoop pines were so dense they darkened the landscape.

In January 1842, two shepherds at Evan Mackenzie's station near Kilcoy handed out flour rations laced with strychnine to the local Giggarbarah and Woogunbarah, killing around sixty people. This was the same station that John Carne Bidwill had used as a starting point to search for what would become the type specimen of the bunya pine, its leaves and seed pods studied by Sir William Hooker and named *Araucaria bidwillii* in honour of its collector. A code of silence meant the tragic story of Kilcoy would not reach the Sydney papers until December that year, and by the time an official enquiry was launched in April 1843, the finer details had been washed away by the rains of the summer. Retaliation began shortly after when a number of tribes met at the annual bunya festival at Baroon Pocket and agreed to enact a coordinated program of revenge. An almost daily onslaught followed, with animals attacked and stations besieged. Counterattacks followed, with roughly ten Aboriginal lives taken for every European life. 'A conspiracy of silence' is the term historian Timothy Bottoms would give to the Queensland frontier. During the years of pastoral expansion, particularly following the deployment of the Native Police in 1848, it is thought that in Queensland alone, up to 50,000 First Australians were murdered.

The festival of the bunya would barely survive the nineteenth century. When English botanical artist Marianne North visited the Bunya Mountains in 1880, she was already referring to the festivals in the past tense.[5] Gatherings occurred in the Blackall Ranges up to 1910, but these were small-scale corrobborees, pale imitations of the great festivals of the past. The First Australians who settler Ruth Laverick recalls heading to the festival in 1880 were visibly shaken, saying 'no hurt, no hurt' as they approached her and asked for cigarettes. The last Aboriginal family moved out of the area in the 1920s, leaving behind a bark shelter near the top of Mill Hill Road.

The bunya tree is one of only a few species to be given individual protection under Australian law, but this legal breakthrough lasted for little more than eighteen years. When the proclamation was rescinded in 1860, bunya pines that may have existed for 200 or 300 years were felled, cut into logs, fastened into makeshift rafts, and sailed down the river towards Dunwich, where they were put onto a ship bound for Port Jackson. Trees that had served families for generations might have ended up as butter churns or broom handles, piano keys or matchsticks. It is this image that perhaps should be remembered as a memorial for the great bunya gatherings: the First Australians in Ruth Laverick's story, accepting a light for their cigarettes, oblivious to the thought that the match may have once been part of a magnificent tree on whose seed crop they had dined as children. Perhaps its well-being was entrusted to the custodianship of their father or their father's father. Were this to be true, it would reveal a sadness beyond words. No apology could make up for such an act of defilement.

Under the Norfolk Pines

The first time Marian and I returned to Perth, perhaps three or four years after we settled in Queensland, we were there for the wedding of two friends, people we had, over the years, come to cherish. As part of a clustered itinerary, we ended up driving almost every street of the inner suburbs, passing my former workplace and the shops where we used to buy groceries. But for me, the most vivid memory of that trip is sitting in the garden of a Fremantle brewery as the afternoon sun accentuated the Norfolk Island pines (*Araucaria heterophylla*) of Esplanade Park. That memory is one of brightness and cheer, the laughter from other tables rippling through the air. 'Under the Norfolk pines gulls bickered on the grass,' writes Tim Winton at the beginning of *Cloudstreet* (1991), as the children take turns jumping off the jetty. In the novel, the laughter, which felt eternal in that moment, would soon be replaced by tragedy. But if there was a sense of tragedy attached to my memory of that day, it was simply the inevitable attrition of time. As the years moved on, I saw less of those faces, until now, almost a decade later, I can barely recall who was there.

The Fremantle trees are possibly the finest collection of planted *Araucaria* in the whole of Australia: large, confident individuals with a symmetry of posture quite unlike any other tree. My friend imagines them raising their branches in a yoga pose, saluting the sun, a gesture not entirely inapt given their propensity to congregate along our coastlines. When Marian and I travelled around the world for a year, the Australian tree we saw the most was not a eucalypt. It was the Norfolk Island pine, projecting awkwardly above the tropical canopies of Thailand and Costa Rica, or gracing the roadsides and hills of central Europe. Our host in northern Spain could not believe they were Australian. 'They're a pine tree,' he told us bluntly. 'Like all pines, they come from the north.' But they are neither a pine tree nor a tree of the northern hemisphere.[6] Rather, they grow naturally on the Australian territories of Norfolk and Phillip Islands in the Pacific Ocean, 1700 kilometres from Sydney Cove. Seeing the trees at Esplanade Park in Fremantle was perhaps my first introduction to a 'madeleine moment', their dark, scaly leaves taking me to those first few weeks in Australia, when we lay on Cottesloe Beach, the sheer immensity of the tree's crown lifting our thoughts skywards, our aspirations ascending with every branch.

There should be a more specific term for 'childlike wonder', something suitably grand: a German portmanteau or a philosophical neologism. If there was, I would use it unsparingly when talking about *Araucaria heterophylla*. While the patterns of nature, the Fibonacci spirals and hexagonal columns, can often be inspiring, rarely does it produce such perfection as the Norfolk Island pine. Observing the sunlight stream through the tree's crown is a divine experience. The bold, well-proportioned branches, especially in the younger, more sprightly individuals, offer a lesson in trigonometry. They are Vitruvian trees. It would not be unsurprising to learn they were mass-produced in a factory from the design of an accomplished engineer. When confronted with towering eucalypts, I feel awe; in the presence of Norfolk Island pines, I feel wonder. Unadulterated joy.

In Australia, the Norfolk Island pine is so richly embedded in our culture, few people realise the tree does not grow naturally on the mainland. It has become a symbol of our holidays, the unmistakable silhouette of Australia's coastline. Winton, when asked to name his favourite trees in Australia, selected the Norfolk Island pines at Fremantle's Esplanade, the same trees that formed the backdrop to my afternoon spent drinking. 'A stand of these soughing giants,' Winton says, 'means the sea isn't far off ... Only the fiercest storm will make them sway, but the sound they make is something else. In a good storm a Norfolk Island pine sounds like it's about to blast off into space.'

When Marian and I emigrated to Australia in 2006, we deliberately staggered our arrival. She moved over first, and I remained in England for a couple of months, finishing up work and saying goodbye to friends. I still remember the postcard she sent me upon her arrival. On the front was a montage: one picture showed the serviced apartments where she was staying; another, the city skyline as viewed from Victoria Park; another, a small dog who went by the name of Benji. But the most prominent photo showed the upturned branches of the Norfolk Island pine. This was the Australian ideal, a tree that was as distinguished as it was tough. There are few views as distinctive as the black outline of a Norfolk Island pine against a flawless cerulean sky. It has all the expressive simplicity of a Japanese woodblock print. It is as powerful an icon as Max Dupain's *Sunbaker* (1937) or Charles Meere's *Australian Beach Pattern* (1940). And in the same way these images reveal a very constrained idea of the Australian character – white, tanned bodies leading healthy, carefree lives – the Norfolk Island pine betrays a rather Eurocentric vision.

The first time James Cook noticed *Araucaria* growing on an island, it was September 1774 and he was sailing past New Caledonia. After his adventures four years before in the *Endeavour*, he could not have been oblivious to the dangers of sailing too close to the shallow and craggy edges of the reef. Back then, Cook had laughed at the obsessive botanising of Joseph Banks and Daniel Solander. But now, on this second voyage, he was a different man, and he saw little issue with steering the ship dangerously close to the reef simply to inspect these odd-looking trees at closer range. Crew members prayed for their lives as, all through the night, gale-force winds shunted the vessel from side to side. His journal reveals his obsession: 'I was now almost tired of a Coast I could no longer explore but as [sic] the risk of loosing [sic] the ship and ruining the whole voyage … I was determined not to leave it till I was satisfied what sort of trees those were which had been the subject of our speculation.'

Later, the tree, *Araucaria columnaris*, its straight, erect form making it a symbol of virility in local lore, became known as the Cook's pine, and his name for the island would be the one it still bears today: the Isle of Pines.

A month later, the HMS *Resolution* was on its way to New Zealand for repairs when, sailing through the Tasman Sea, Cook noticed a rocky island, its cliffs adorned with a large tree that appeared superior to those on the Isle of Pines. Landing at the northwest point of the island the following afternoon, a place we now know as Duncombe Bay, Cook went ashore with his party of naturalists: the Lutheran pastor Johann Reinhold Forster, Johann's son George and the astronomer William Wales. They roamed this strange, hushed island for an afternoon, its hills and coastline covered with what seemed to be natural plantations of Norfolk Island pines, some more than

60 metres high. Elsewhere, the place was a jungle. Large tree ferns (*Cyathea brownii*) feathered the landscape. A species of wild flax (*Phormium tenax*) grew from rocky crevices. The leaves, similar to the New Zealand flax, could be fashioned into a ship's sail by a process of soaking, beating, disentangling and weaving. Some trees were so corrupted by the winds, their trunks were almost horizontal. White oaks (*Lagunaria patersonia*), trees we know today as itch trees or Norfolk Island hibiscus, grew as crippled shrubs along the coast, unrecognisable from the erect, pyramidal trees inhabiting the inland forests. It was a land of darkness and great beauty. The ghostly sound of the wind would whistle past the leaves and, in the mornings, the light of the sun would filter through the sea spray, a ray of hope, which by the evening would evoke an eerie, desolate beauty.

There were no human footprints, no evidence of campfires, no rudimentary huts – no signs whatsoever of human habitation. The last people to stay there, a Polynesian group little is known about, had abandoned the island around 500 years before. Birds – the Norfolk kaka and the grey-headed blackbird, the Tasman starling and the Norfolk Island ground-dove – skittered freely between the trees. In less than a century, these species would exist only in history books and museums. The island would become, in critic Robert Hughes' words, 'the worst place in the English-speaking world'. But for now it was a beautiful jungle, a special place, as Cook noted, for this could be the only island in the South Pacific where one might secure both mast and sail for the navy.

For historians such as Alan Frost, were it not for the revelation of this island and those trees, the convict settlement of Port Jackson may have been established elsewhere, maybe on the east coast of Canada or in the baking heat of western Africa. 'Might it not be,' asks Frost,

51

'that the Pitt administration hoped to obtain something in return – something, that is, more than the simple removal of criminals from Britain?' It is customary today, when considering these motives, to focus on Australia's geostrategic bearings and its potential for Asian trade, but there is an odd episode that does not sit well with this prevailing narrative. Barely a month into the colony, Governor Arthur Phillip ordered Lieutenant Philip Gidley King to board the HMS *Supply* with officers, marines and convicts, and sail more than 1500 kilometres east, towards the treacherous surf of Norfolk Island. The true motivations for this voyage have been lost over time. Potentially, the fortification of the colony against French encroachment was the primary reason. But, as Geoffrey Blainey writes in *The Tyranny of Distance* (1966), 'Britain's military strength and an increasing part of her commerce relied on seapower, and flax and ships' timber were as vital to seapower as steel and oil are today.' Norfolk Island was, in Blainey's words, 'key to the plan to send convicts to Australia'.

Two weeks after King's party landed along the southern stretch of the island, three men dug a saw pit and felled the first Norfolk Island pine, which would be used for the island's first building, a storehouse in the burgeoning settlement of Kingston. The timber of the Norfolk Island pine was excellent for burning and useful for erecting huts, but when put under the slightest bit of pressure, 'it snapped like a carrot'. Norfolk pine logs began to arrive in Sydney shortly after, and any hopes they would revitalise naval shipbuilding were quickly dispelled. European dreams once hung from its symmetrical branches, wrote environmental scientist George Seddon in his book *The Old Country* (2005), but in reality the timber was good only for the smallest sailing vessels. Of thirty-four trees to be chopped down on the island, twenty-seven were deemed defective. While the living tree is exceptionally strong and resilient to coastal winds, the grounded timber, once planed or worked, fractures easily. Short-grained, knotty and spongy, the timber was not suitable for all-weather conditions. The trees were deceptive, wrote Hughes, like the rest of antipodean nature. The navy was forced to look elsewhere, to the red pine (*Pinus resinosa*), which grew in abundance in the eastern forests of Canada, and to the large-leaved *Calophyllum* trees,[7] known as poon, which grew in Ceylon and the East Indies.

Today, more Norfolk Island pines decorate the beaches of the mainland than exist in the wild on Norfolk Island. How confusing it would be for a twenty-first-century James Cook to sail along the eastern coast of Australia and see the trees everywhere, their regimented lines in place of the shaggy rows of coastal scrub. For many of us, they are a beacon of reassurance. 'I've been damn grateful,' recounts Tim Winton, thinking of the times he has viewed them from the ocean, 'to see their angular crowns poking up from the moving horizon'. But these trees are not what they appear. Max Dupain's photograph of a tanned sunbather has framed our view of Australian perfectionism as calm, insouciant strength. But there is another photo he took two years later, *Banksias by the Sea* (1939), which shows a different, more rugged impression of the coast. The banksias grip onto the vacillating sands, their branches curled, as vicious sea winds harass them. Many of the Norfolk Island pines along our coast fight death, struggling under the weight of their age or battling the detergent-laced winds from the sea. Climate change has darkened their future, and the deadly fungal disease *Neofusicoccum parvum* has killed thousands of them along both the eastern and western coasts. For a symbol of stability, their reign may be humiliatingly short, perhaps no more than half a dozen generations. If time were an Araucarian tree, and human inhabitation of this continent the length of the trunk, then the Norfolk Island pine's supremacy could be no greater than the length of one branchlet.

Were we to step back in time, before Norfolk Island pines proudly commandeered the beach at Coolangatta on the Gold Coast, we might see a Bundjalung woman carrying her baby in a paperbark sheath, the natural sling unwrapped from the bark of *Melaleuca quin-quenervia*. Or were we to walk the Esplanade at Altona in Melbourne, we would see drooping she-oaks (*Allocasuarina verticillata*), so clustered they would give, from a distance at least, the blurred impression of a singular form. These anterior landscapes have disappeared. There is scant trace today of the dune scrub and eucalypts that once covered Warrnambool, or any trace of the spinifex-covered sand dunes that once defined Manly Cove and Cottesloe Beach. Across these coastal strips, Norfolk Island pines now stand as totemic guardians, symbols of strength and virility. Except for the sound of the wind droning through the branches, the trees are largely silent. Birds rarely settle in them.

The Rapa Nui people of Easter Island chopped down the island's trees in order to roll carved, basaltic boulders towards the coast. As a result, the population almost perished over the course of a few hundred years. The monoliths stood, imperious faces carved into their surfaces, but they did not save a population who had deracinated their entire land. Stability should be measured across millennia, not assumed across a few generations. As the gulls bicker under the shade of Norfolk Island pines, perhaps it is time to wonder what tragedy may be lurking in our own climate-stressed future.

The Wollemi Paradox

It is hard to think of a tree in Australia more famously endangered than the Wollemi pine (*Wollemia nobilis*). Within a few small groves, deep in the bosky heart of the Great Dividing Range, the species hides from the modern world. It is the wood sprite of the Australian forest, trapped between canyons in a liminal, hospice-like existence. When journalist James Woodford was helicoptered into one of these groves, a few years after the trees' discovery, he was, along with the other passengers, blindfolded with a tea towel to prevent him from observing their location.

For a few days in January 2020, those closest to the trees' conservation feared the worst. Under threat from the Gospers Mountain fire, one of the largest bushfires on record, the wild populations of *Wollemia* were on the verge of extinction. Almost two-thirds of Wollemi National Park burnt. Air tankers flew across the surrounds of the main grove, laying fire retardant between the trees and the fire front. Firefighters, winched in by helicopter, set up an irrigation system to spray water on the trees, returning to the scene each day to fuel the engine and operate the pumps. There was an ever-diminishing supply of water, whatever could be drawn from the two waterholes, which existed only as puddles along the bed of the creek. Buckets of water were jettisoned from helicopters patrolling the edge of the fire. When visibility became intolerable, the defenders waited anxiously for the smoke to clear. With fewer than 100 mature trees in the wild, the possibility of extinction was real.

The morning after the fire, Steve Cathcart, an area manager with the NSW National Parks and Wildlife Service (NPWS), was winched down into the gorge. A huge eucalypt had fallen and spread its embers, which meant Steve's first task was to move the burning branches away from the trees. He did this 'by hand', reported *The Australian*'s Greg Bearup. 'He then went around the bases of all the mature pine trees, kicking the hot coals away.'

There is video footage of NPWS staff as they traipse through the hoary wildwood several days later, examining the blackened trunks. Some of the Wollemi pines were hollowed out by the fire's heat, others killed, but the majority had survived. It was a miracle of perseverance. The image taken from a helicopter of the salvaged trees was reprinted in several newspapers, depicting a strip of joyous, luminous green running through a charred and devastated landscape.

My father has a Wollemi pine in his garden. He purchased the tree several years ago for £100 from the United Kingdom's official supplier, and now it enjoys a prominent place on the terrace, sitting in a pot beneath the bay windows of the living room. The term 'incongruous' undersells its placement within this suburban English setting. It stands roughly 1 metre tall and leans slightly to the left. In summer, the tree drinks around 20 litres of water a week, but somehow it survives, sprouting an abundance of male and female cones, the female cones bulbous and spiky, the male ones long and proboscidean.

Twenty-five years before my father purchased the tree, the species was believed to exist only as a fossil. The discovery of around 100 surviving trees in Wollemi National Park is comparable to the first sighting of the coelacanth or happening upon a Tyrannosaurus rex in an Arizona canyon. Were it not for rock-climber David Noble abseiling into a remote, sheltered gorge thirty years ago, the ancient curiosity that is the Wollemi pine, one of our few direct links to the age of sauropods and iguanodons, may have passed into extinction during the first months of 2020 without ever being observed by human eyes. It is a rather inscrutable tree. Poplars or willows can be expressive, the rustle and delicate murmur of their leaves as revealing as language. But this tree, with its knotty bark and barbed-wire branches, is aloof and disarmingly terse. I get a similar feeling with dracaena and cacti, finding it hard to imagine, when admiring their irregular forms, that these plants could be alive. It is even harder, if one accepts the idea of panpsychism expressed by German forester Peter Wohlleben and others, to believe they have any degree of sentience, no matter how removed it may be from our own. And yet, to someone observing from afar, in their moment of crisis these trees attracted the attention of perhaps the only species on Earth who may be qualified to assist.

By the time he discovered the Wollemi pine, Noble had climbed and abseiled around 400 of the Blue Mountain's 500 chasms. He had the look of a 1970s athlete, his body lean, his muscles sinewy. As James Woodford writes in *The Wollemi Pine* (2005), 'Even the best walkers who have hiked with Noble speak in awed tones of his fitness and pace, his ability to climb and his navigation skills.'

On 10 September 1994, Noble set off with two friends, looking for a canyon he had stumbled upon three months earlier. The explorers were familiar with the surrounding vegetation – coachwood trees

(*Ceratopetalum apetalum*), with their grey and distinctively ringed trunks, and yellow sassafras (*Doryphora sassafras*), bearing glossy, scented leaves. At some point, the dense vegetation began to open up and Noble noticed an unusual tree, the bubbly, furrowed bark reminding him of the breakfast cereal Coco Pops. Although he knew it was a special find, he had no idea how special. When he took a sample of the leaf litter to his colleague Wyn Jones at NPSW, Wyn asked him if it was from a fern or a shrub. No, he said, it was from a bloody big tree.

It is quite possible Noble was the first human being to ever view a Wollemi pine although we will never know for sure. 'Considering the detailed understanding Aboriginal people have of their country,' writes James Woodford, 'it is hard to believe that if the Wollemi pine had been known by a tribe that its presence would not have become important.' The trees were unlike any of the surrounding flora. John Benson, one of the first people to be taken to the canyon shortly after the discovery was made public, said it was as if an alien from outer space had been found sheltering from the outside world in a crevice where, until now, it had evaded interference. No one could guess at the genus with any confidence. There was a fear the trees might be weeds, maybe an *Araucaria* from New Caledonia whose journey to this canyon perhaps began in the pocket of a South Sea Islander and ended from the cloaca of a black cockatoo.

By October, Jones and Noble were in a private aircraft flying into the canyon. The helicopter hovered among the canopy, the branches shaking violently with the rotor-propelled wind. Jones reached his arm out of the window and snapped a female cone off at the stem. This was what they needed to determine its genus. If the cones were spiky, it was likely to be an *Araucaria*. If the ovule was free of the scale, rather than embedded, it was an *Agathis*.[8] The strange thing about the Wollemi sample was that it appeared to show character-istics of both. The cones were covered in small spines and yet there was a clear separation between the ovule and the scale. This was a new genus for the *Araucariaceae*, a rare moment when the plant world could welcome a newcomer to the taxonomic rank between species and family. It was a close match to a 120-million-year-old Araucarian fossil in the Cretacean fossil beds of Koonwarra, eastern Victoria, and it was a compelling explanation for the mysterious *Dilwynites* pollen grains, some as old as ninety million years, found across the eastern range of Gondwana. This was a tree that had emerged in the time of the dinosaurs. Its leaves may have been eaten by herds of muttabur-rasaurus or the armour-plated minmi.

On the night of Tuesday, 13 December 1994, journalist James Woodford went to sleep knowing the following day, when he awoke, his story would become a worldwide sensation. 'Only a few times this century,' ran the headline, 'has something so spectacular as the Wollemi pine turned up.' As the publicity over the coming days reached a frenzy, the researchers were bombarded with requests to obtain the tree, with one individual allegedly offering $500,000 for the privilege.

Using seeds collected from the wild, the horticulturalists at Mount Annan Botanic Gardens incubated the potential pines in a special nutrient solution until, roughly two weeks later, the first seedling began to sprout. 'It's the son – or seedling of the Jurassic Bark,' pro-claimed *The Japan Times*. The greenhouse that bore the fruits of this research was under tight security night and day. Propagation was not easy as it was a new genus to work with and seeds were difficult to come by. In order not to damage the few remaining trees in the wild, there was talk of purchasing a hot-air balloon from America to float above the canopy of the forest, but it was deemed too great a fire risk. There was even consideration given to training monkeys to climb the branches to retrieve seeds. It is testament to Dr Cathy Offord's team at Mount Annan that they were so successful in their mission to cultivate the species.

In 2006, *National Geographic* established itself as a supplier to the American market, offering to sell trees to its readers for US$70. A year earlier, the actor Kenneth Branagh had planted one of the first Wollemi pines to take root in Britain, at Wakehurst Place in West Sussex. David Attenborough planted another at Kew Gardens. These globetrotting trees were an insurance against the Wollemi's extinction in the wild.

It is now apparent that, as well as being able to reproduce sexually, the Wollemi clones itself, meaning a number of trees in the wild may emanate from the same root system, roots that may be many thousands of years old. This is not unusual in itself. Species such as the quaking aspens (*Populus tremuloides*) in Fishlake National Park, Utah, and Tasmania's King's holly (*Lomatia tasmanica*) are famous for cloning. However, it does mean one of the world's oldest surviving species may also be hiding one of the world's oldest living root systems, possibly more advanced in years than the 43,000-year-old roots of the King's holly.

The offset to cloning is a lack of genetic diversity within the species, a particularity that can make a species less adaptable to changing environmental conditions. It was thought the Wollemi pine was, in James Woodford's terms, 'one of the most conservative organisms that life has ever thrown up', although a second surprise came in 2016. Using the latest techniques in DNA sampling, a team of eight scientists compared the chloroplast DNA of different trees from the

Wollemi population and found subtle genetic variations, a sign of hope for the long-term survival of the species. Now, translocation efforts can focus on spreading this diversity around.

Reflecting on the Gospers Mountain fire, James Woodford wrote, 'It is hard, after this week, to consider the remaining original Wollemi pines as wild.' They are as dependent on human trust as the Wollemi in my father's garden. But the alliance is a precarious one, and humans can inflict damage as easily as they can assist. This is the paradox of the Wollemi: its saviour is also its would-be executioner. In 2005, one of the natural stands was infected with the root fungus *Phytophthora cinnamomi*, suggesting that, despite the best efforts to keep its distribution secret, hikers must have detected at least one of the locations. Fortunately, the trees have survived, but root fungus still looms as a potentially catastrophic threat. In the world of Wollemi pines, old trees dominate: strong, mature specimens that are nevertheless susceptible to fungal disease and insect attack. Young trees do not grow underneath the dark canopy, so they must wait for a giant to fall before enough light can advance their upward journey.

'Only one or two seedlings out of every hundred need to make it to maturity in order for the genus to survive,' writes James Woodford. It is this probability game that has allowed the trees to subsist on the brink of extinction for thousands, perhaps millions, of years, but now they are at the end of that line. They have flourished in the time of theropods, weathered colder periods and flooding, aridity and epic heat, but now they are one small misadventure, a disease or a human-authored tragedy, away from annihilation.

Wodyeti

At one of our rental houses in Mackay, I dug up the garden bed, a small strip of soil at the front of the lawn, and planted a young foxtail palm. And for a short time, it thrived, relishing the open aspect. For all its promise, though, and for all its nascent beauty, its life turned out to be exceedingly short. We moved out a few weeks later, taking up another rental on the other side of town, and the tree, deprived of regular water, failed to establish and wilted in the tropical sun.

In selecting the tree, I had been trying to re-create the front gardens we had seen in Moranbah, our previous home. Foxtail palms (*Wodyetia bifurcata*) were everywhere in Moranbah's newer estates. They were the pert, attractive plantings of front yards, precious adornments of the suburban ideal. In the older streets, golden cane palms, yuccas and banana plants grew messily in front of weatherboard homes. But in a town aggrandised by coal money, these flamboyant palms served as an attractive emblem of the brashness of new wealth.

I first heard the story of the foxtail while undertaking filming work in St Lawrence, a couple of hours south of Mackay. We were traipsing through marshland, amassing footage for a short tourism video on behalf of the local government. While we extricated leeches from our ankles, the cameraman pointed to a small tree. It was a foxtail, its trunk pale grey, the fronds bushy due to the spiralling arrangement of the leaves. It is hard to imagine, he said, looking at the palm's delicate form, that this tree had become commodified and exploited on a level equivalent to heroin or methamphetamine. Criminal gangs roamed the jungles of Far North Queensland to extract seeds from the tree and sell them on the black market. The scandal almost brought down the Queensland premier. And yet, he said, only a few decades before, the tree was not even recognised by European science, its existence known only by the local custodians of the land.

I found an interesting post online referring to *Wodyetia bifurcata*. 'This is the story of its discovery,' it began. 'In 1976 an Australian nurseryman who visited his aged mother in a retirement home on a regular basis, met an interesting old Aboriginal man that was also a resident of the retirement home.' According to this post, because his mother barely talked, the nurseryman would seek conversation elsewhere, and he soon became acquainted with the Aboriginal Elder, Wodyeti. The two enjoyed sharing their knowledge of plants, and Wodyeti told the man he knew where to find some of the most beautiful palms in the world. Wodyeti was 'the last of his line, holding a vast traditional knowledge of the palm's habitat', and he wanted to share this knowledge with his friend, and to see the palms once more before his death. Eventually, the man acquiesced to Wodyeti's repeated requests to visit the palms, and they both flew up to Far North Queensland, where they took a jeep into the heart of the jungle. Abandoning the car, they walked for what seemed like a whole day before they came across the trees that Wodyeti had described as the most beautiful he had ever seen. Taking a number of seeds with him, the man cultivated the trees back in Sydney, displaying them at garden shows, where he shared Wodyeti's story with those who would listen, well beyond Wodyeti's death.

It is tempting to believe apocryphal stories, especially when they have the appearance of a fairytale. But even if the setting and the characters were true, and even if the journey had occurred as described, the foxtail palm was already known to science by 1976. A year earlier, Bernie Hyland, a botanist with the CSIRO, had collected fruit remnants from the tree while on holiday, after noticing the trees seven years before when surveying Cape Melville with fellow botanist Peter Stanton.[9] Three years later, Hyland collected more samples from the tree, and these, along with leaves and fruit collected by the botanist Anthony Irvine in 1981, would enable the latter to declare the tree as monotypic, warranting a separate classification from the superficially similar genera *Archontophoenix* and *Normanbya*. In naming the species, Irvine used the following words: 'Wodyeti (Wad-yeti) … clearly intended for Johnny Flinders, the last surviving, male Aboriginal with traditional knowledge of the area.'

Johnny Flinders was a Yiithuwarra Elder who did indeed find himself in an old people's home towards the end of his life, not in Sydney but on Palm Island. And perhaps the nurseryman in the story could be a stand-in for Johnny's friend Peter Sutton, the professions of horticulture and linguistic anthropology becoming oddly confused. But while the details of the story seem unlikely, one could be swayed by the compelling allegory it presents. The most beautiful trees in the world survived for thousands of years under the custodianship of Elders such as Wodyeti. When he passed away, the trees, no longer afforded the same protection, were instead passed over to the careless impatience of capitalism.

§

The first time Peter Sutton met Johnny was outside the post office on Palm Island. Sutton was there as a student of the Australian Institute of Aboriginal Studies, conducting surveys by walking up to strangers and asking them where they were from or what words they knew from their ancestors' languages. He recalls the young people being 'puzzled, amused or made hostile at my interest'. Back in Canberra, his principal, Fred McCarthy, had taken out a map of Australia, pointed to the northeasterly tip and instructed Peter to survey the entire Aboriginal population within this area. For two months in 1970, the wide-eyed student travelled in his Commonwealth Land Rover between Cairns and Croydon, Townsville and Julia Creek, stopping at all the towns, cattle stations and Aboriginal reserves along the way, recording fifty-six hours of audiotape of more than seventy-five languages. 'Many of these languages were almost extinct then,' he recalls. 'The original Australian languages were becoming effectively extinct, in the 1970s, at the rate of about one a month.' Sutton returned on an almost yearly basis to the area. His friendship with Johnny grew over this period, the two becoming almost inseparable, sharing stories during the day, and drinks, cigarettes and jokes into the night. Their affection was such that Johnny adopted him into his clan, welcoming Sutton as a son.

For most of the nineteenth century, the northeasterly horn of Australia was untouched by European interests. It was a haven of windswept beaches, mangroves and melaleuca swamps, plains of tussock grass and small, messy patches of rainforest. Johnny was born around the turn of the century. He was, according to Sutton, 'an extremely lively man, with a lightning wit and views on practically everything'. His emotions, whether anger or elation, sadness or despair, were so immediate, so vital, it was hard not to succumb to their spirit. Johnny was part of the Flinders Island language group, his Country extending across what we know today as Cape Melville National Park, from Ninian Bay in the east to Marrett River in the west, a rugged country beset by fierce storms and sudden squalls. Johnny knew his Country as Yiirrku and the beach on which he was born as Ayamo. He learnt the stories of the Dreaming and he knew the places where his family were born, the trees under which they were received. To walk with him through the landscape was to be awakened by the spirits, to learn the stories hidden by the crown of the small-leaved fig (*Ficus obliqua*) or whispered through the roots of the spotted and orange mangroves (*Rhizophora stylosa and Bruguiera gymnorhiza*). Nature's generosity was everywhere on show. The trees displayed bright, glossy fruits. There were the delicious red berries of the wongi (*Manilkara kauki*), the drupes of the satinash (*Syzygium suborbiculare*) and the small, yellow fruits of the wild pear (*Persoonia falcata*). This was Johnny's land, the land of his ancestors. But it was not owned in a legal sense, at least not according to British colonial law. It was looked after and cared for, managed in such a respectful way that, for Europeans versed in the primacy of wheatfields and brick, it appeared undisturbed – terra nullius.

Peter Sutton describes a 'pincerlike pressure' making its way across the Cape York Peninsula at the beginning of the twentieth century. Gold mining followed the line of the Palmer River, cattle stations crept across the land and ships sailed the coast of Princess Charlotte Bay, their crew hunting for pearls and the coveted bêche-de-mer (sea cucumber). Johnny worked on a pearling ship for a time, as did his brother Diver, who drowned at sea during a cyclone. It was tough work.

The conditions were cramped, the food rations low and the dives often dangerously deep. By the late 1920s, many of the Yiithuwarra,[10] including Johnny, were moved onto the Lockhart Mission, where, in Sutton's words, they 'gradually died out or moved away'. Johnny would end up on Palm Island, expending the rest of his life in a displaced fog, unable to travel anywhere without the permission of the local sergeant, according to his nephew Tony Flinders. He was an exile without crime, stripped of his connection with the land which, from a young age, had instilled in him a greater purpose. When Sutton introduced himself outside the post office, the Aboriginal Elder had not seen his Country for almost half a century.

Sutton arranged a homecoming for 1974. Accompanying Johnny were his brother Bob and another relation, Mitchell McGreen. A recording exists of Bob, before they set off, talking to a pastor about the upcoming trip. 'I'm happy to go back and see my mother's land. But then again I dread. You know what will happen. There will be tears, because of seeing no sign of the people, only seagulls and dingoes running along the beaches.' The memories were harder for Bob because he had been taken from the beach at four years old by a policeman, smuggled onto a pack horse and despatched on a train bound for Cookstown. He could remember his father running after the horse, weeping, calling out for him, the outline of his son slowly disappearing. Bob had been holding a tomahawk when he was snatched and, on that return trip decades later, he found it in the sand, exactly where he had left it. In the intervening years the wooden handle had rotted away, but the stone was still intact.

It was describing this homecoming trip that brought Sutton to tears as he gave evidence as part of the Yiithuwarra's land claim. Sutton relates the morning they went to Ngurromo, also known as

Clack Island, a place where the power of the ancestral spirits is so strong it is dangerous even to sit the wrong way. People would venture over to the island to decorate the sandstone walls using pigments from the earth. Johnny was the last of his people to practise and have knowledge of this art. The crossing was rough and they were forced to disembark early, wading chest-deep in water towards the rocky shore while they balanced audio equipment above their heads. On land, the men stood in a circle and Johnny dusted each of them down with his sweat, requesting, in the imperative of his language, that his companions receive protection from the spirits.

Sutton visited Johnny a few times after that, the last being in 1978. As there was no accommodation available on Palm Island, they met at Townsville airport before driving up the coast to Babinda, Cooktown and Hopevale. Johnny was not the same man on this trip. He was tired and feeling his age. Whereas before, Johnny had been unrelenting in his desire to pass on everything he knew of his culture ('Have you got another book yet?' he used to say. 'We got to fill up another book'), this time he was content discussing the local gossip, his words soft and half-formed, at times almost unintelligible. One can hear Johnny's voice from those earlier days halfway through Lew Griffiths' documentary film *Dhuway* (1997). Slow and measured, his words arpeggiate up and down as he relates the story of Wakayi island. 'Itjibiya and Eelmbarrin were two brothers, Itjibiya the older,' he says in his language, his words lilting, almost breathlessly delivered. 'They speared a whale,' he continues. 'Afraid of the Whale's people, they ran north to the Flinders Island group. They camped at Ngurromo. Whale surfaced there in the south. He lies belly down. Belly down he lies.'

Johnny passed away in 1980. His death meant that Peter Sutton, a linguist born and raised in the tight, terraced streets of Port

71

Melbourne, was now the only living speaker of the Flinders Island language. Bob passed away in 1993, a few months before the land claim commenced. For their ancestors, the spirits of Bob and Johnny are still there, as latent impressions, vigilant souls, indelibly felt as one passes through their homeland. 'They may be deceased over there to you people,' says Bonnie Walker, Bob's granddaughter, 'but to us, they still live here in our hearts.'

And yet there is a form in which Johnny's name does live on: the genus *Wodyetia*, of which there is only one extant species, the foxtail palm (*Wodyetia bifurcata*).

§

Foxtails are the celebrity palms of Cape Melville National Park. They grow on the edges of the Melville Range, green, shaggy jester hats impaled upon long, slender poles. The trees jut out from granite boulders, rocks that have stockpiled in an almost unnatural manner, resembling dark, minatory mountains of rubble. Among this harsh, lithic scene, the trees themselves are a curious delight. The journalist Murray Hogarth calls the area a 'botanical Shangri-La'.

The story told to me by the cameraman that day, I realise now, was fairly accurate beyond a few minor details. For over a decade, seeds were harvested illegally from Cape Melville National Park with little resistance from the police. Smugglers strapped handsaws to long poles so they could sever the fruit stalks that grew beneath the crown. It was obvious when smugglers had been through an area because the ground was filled with the litter of these naked stalks. The fruits were picked off and thrown into hessian bags. The bags were then driven to the beach, where they would be offloaded onto fishing boats bound for Papua New Guinea. These were not opportunists but career criminals, their Landcruisers filled with shotguns and SKS assault rifles. Each tree yielded between 500 and 1000 seeds, and each seed could fetch between $3 and $5 on the black market. At its peak, around 700,000 seeds were being harvested in a year.

With the situation becoming untenable, Greg Wellard, a regional director with the Department of Environment and Health, entrusted the security of the palms to three rangers, one of them Johnny's nephew, a quietly spoken man named Tony Flinders. Another was Pat Shears, a Vietnam veteran, described later by Wellard as a Rambo ranger. On the morning of 11 November 1993, Tony and Pat travelled with fellow ranger George Monaghan to investigate a vehicle that had breached their barricade, a makeshift barrier of logs they had strewn across a known smugglers' track. The actions of that day would become the subject of a Criminal Justice Commission investigation that almost brought down the Queensland Government.

It still does not seem conceivable that these trees of the remote wilderness, so recently inducted into European science, would within a decade of their awakened state become embroiled in a political scandal. Interviewed for *Four Corners*, Pat, dressed in an Akubra and scrim net scarf, smiles wryly at the camera, happy to step into the character offered him by the ABC journalist: a real-life Crocodile Dundee. 'I think I remember saying at the time when I got back to Cairns,' he says, 'that there's more cartridge cases lying around Cape Melville than there was at the Battle of Long Tan.' Pat became either the hero or villain of the story, depending on one's perspective. He was working in treacherous conditions, where bullets were routinely discharged into the bay or into the bodies of feral pigs. He discovered the Toyota Landcruiser close to a stand of the foxtail palms, a shotgun

73

and chainsaw in the rear tray and two rifles in the cabin. Hearing the voices of its occupants through the trees, Pat assumed he was dealing with smugglers and, when he noticed the keys in the ignition, decided to seize the vehicle, leaving the alleged offenders stranded in the national park.

The six travellers, estranged from their car, would later claim they were taking photographs of the trees and, unable to see any signage, were not aware they had crossed into the national park. They were on a fishing and pig-hunting trip, so it was not unnatural for them to be in possession of a Winchester rifle, a Winchester shotgun and a Ruger .223 SL rifle. Being marooned within the wilds of Cape Melville could be a death sentence, but fortunately they had another car back at their camp site and were able to walk there in a few hours.

The organiser of the trip was Paul Barbagallo, a banana farmer from Innisfail who had become aware of the trees' location on previous trips. On one such trip, he was, by his own admission, part of a group who harvested more than 500 seeds. He was also the brother of David, the Principal Private Secretary to Premier Wayne Goss. By a strange coincidence that unleashed a frenzy of suspicion, David happened to be visiting nearby Starcke station at the time to scope out a media opportunity for the premier. When David and the premier's media director turned up at Cooktown Police Station and, according to Joan Sheldon, the deputy leader of the Opposition, 'acted improperly by intervening in a police interview' and 'intimidat(ing) Mr Shears', queries were raised as to the level of political pressure being exerted from the top. Expense documents were analysed to determine whether the trip was booked before or after the vehicle was seized. Phone calls were picked apart to ascertain the level of Goss's influence. Although the report rejected suggestions of a conspiracy as 'entirely without foundation', the Cape Melville Incident was a muddy period for those involved. Many felt that Pat Shears was hung up to dry in the baking, north Queensland sun. But, as one would expect from a barefooted Rambo, he withstood the assault and still works today as a ranger, mainly within the magnificent surrounds of Cape Tribulation.

Pat's diary entries are quoted halfway through the commission's report. Describing the morning of the Cape Melville Incident, he recalls Tony Flinders saying: 'We are frightened for our lives up here. Can't sleep of a night and there's a good chance of us being shot.' There's no law and order and we are withdrawing our land claim until National Parks cleans out these crooks.'

These are the saddest words of the report, hidden within the itemised chronologies and analysis of events. Tony was walking the tracks of his ancestors, the land where his father was abducted and where the spirits of Johnny and Bob remain. In interviews recorded as part of the land claim, he presents as a man whose every reflective turn is charged by an emotional flame, one that is stoked by the betrayal of his people. Describing the first time he visited Cape Melville, Tony said words could not express how he felt. 'There's nobody there to meet me, nobody there to greet me, nobody there to show me anything.' The disconnection could not be more abrupt. A landscape bristling with stories was now silent. In one generation, humans' intercourse with nature had changed, deference replaced with desecration, the botanical Shangri-La now overrun with criminals and assault rifles.

While the black market trade ended when commercial harvesting was permitted shortly after, the brevity of the episode has perhaps lessened the power of its instruction. The foxtail may be a popular plant, sold across nurseries and even at garden festivals, but few remember this story.

'Aampa aaku-l-wa aathi-y-ntu utakala uthi-ma-lada aampa. Aampa ngaladan aaku-ma warramu-ma,' says Johnny in the language of his ancestors. 'You see this land here: we won't give it. It's our land, where we will die.' He was partially right. In 1994, the Yiithuwarra won their land claim for Cape Melville and Flinders Islands, but they have still not secured native title. Their affinity with the land, the inextricable ties that bind them to this place, are not fully recognised. The labours of their ancestors is lost within the words, the convoluted parentheses, of legalese and statutory clauses.

The Leichhardt Tree

How the Leichhardt tree has survived is a mystery. How, in all its 200 or so years, has it not succumbed to the wild axe of human progress? When the blue gums fell and the jungle was torn from the ground, the Leichhardt tree remained. When the great cyclone of 1918 came through, the wind stripped its leaves but the trunk was not damaged. The tree persisted as, over the course of a century, the warehouses flourished around it. And when, in the 1980s, the Pioneer River Improvement Trust constructed a levee wall along the river, the tree's roots were avoided by a sharp dog-leg.

Somehow the Leichhardt tree, in its quiet, mysterious way, has demanded our protection, as if a transcendental power flutters above its crown. The tree endures as a guardian of the river, a watchful eye whose gaze may never cease. Perhaps its survival comes down to nothing more than its importance as a post, a trunk to tie ropes around. Its scientific name is *Nauclea orientalis*, which translates roughly as 'ships from the east'.[11] In what must be one of the few instances of binomial servility, during the second half of the nineteenth century it served as a docking point for ships arriving from the east, from places such as Solomon Islands and Vanuatu, New Caledonia and New Guinea.

Marian and I lived in Mackay for about a year. I remember this as a happy time, although, as I only later came to realise, every day of gentle contentment, with its ponderous rhythm, was one step closer to our relationship's end. Once a week, I used to run past the Leichhardt tree. Leaving my house along Ungerer Street, I jogged across the Forgan Bridge, passing Paxtons on my way to Sandfly Creek and Iluka Park. It is unusual for trees to be honoured with their own metal enclosure, so it was obvious this one was important. Each time I ran past, I would feel the soft current of its mystery.

The Paxtons building, a corrugated-iron warehouse with wooden steps and timber floors, is another historical artefact still standing along this part of the river, one of the few surviving links to the old port and the wharves. During the muggy summer months, Marian and I attended a yoga class on its top floor and mosquitoes would flit around us as we held *shavasanas* and *chaturangas*, the sun fading to pink in the distance. On the way to the car, we would see the black outline of the Leichhardt tree watching over us.

I'm not sure why we chose to return to Mackay after travelling for a year, but somehow fate had brought us back. That first week, I remember sitting in Bluewater Quay, having drinks under the tree's watchful shadow. We had arrived in Mackay after driving twenty hours from Muswellbrook in the Hunter Valley. The weather had been calm until we neared Rockhampton. By Sarina, the rain was torrential; fierce gusts blackened the windscreen, making it impossible to see. By the time we arrived, the pools of water were ankle deep. In most towns, people would speak of a downpour like this with fascination and quiet reverence, but here it was just another day.

Mackay has always attracted hardened types, and few came tougher than one of its early settlers, John Spiller, a gruff man with a long, shovel-shaped beard. For the first couple of years, Spiller lived in a grass humpy on the north side of the Pioneer River. He had been attracted to this area by the rich meadow grasses, which soared to heights close to those of a human – grasses so thick it was sometimes impossible for a horse to push through. Spiller enjoyed duck shooting on the lagoons near his property. On one occasion, while passing through a dense patch of reeds, his cattle dog was attacked by a crocodile. Spiller eyed up his target and, his hands nervous with excitement, raised his gun to his shoulder and put a bullet through the crocodile's head.

With the assistance of Percy Crees, Spiller grew fields of maize, cotton and sugar cane. Mackay had the right soils, the right temperature and the right rainfall to grow cane, but there was one thing it lacked: labour. Labourers would need to wake at dawn and finish with the dusk to clear trees and burn grasses, plough the land and plant crops between March and September.

On a Wednesday in mid-May 1867, the HMS *Prima Donna* sailed through the mouth of the Pioneer River with seventy workers on board, men from Solomon Islands and Vanuatu, from landmasses with short but mellifluous names: Epi, Mai, Efate, Togoa and Tanna. It is hard to know how those first arrivals felt. They were fit and healthy but looked uncomfortable in their new and unflattering European clothes. They were mustered onto the land and herded like sheep towards the primitive settlement. The significance of the occasion was not lost on a journalist at the time. It was an event, he wrote, 'fraught with the highest importance'.

We must remember, when imagining the scene, that Mackay was still scrub at this stage, a mixture of mangroves, palms, rainforest, gums and melaleuca. One only needs to go a few kilometres from the present township to walk the dusty paths of Reliance Creek National

Park and reawaken that riparian wilderness, the luscious vegetation that, fringing the banks of the river, would have greeted the South Sea arrivals. Here, the fronds of Alexander palms (*Archontophoenix alexandrae*), artistic and brash, radiate like pretty starlets against the lush, messy backdrop of the jungle. A green haze of swamp box (*Lophostemon suaveolens*) mixes with weeping paperbark (*Melaleuca leucadendra*). Vines of native grape (*Cissus oblonga*) and supplejack (*Flagellaria indica*) hang from the trees. In this environment, the Leichhardt is one tree among many. Part of the emergent layer, it sits above the forest canopy like a sentry, an arboreal watchtower. The garish fruits of the brush cherry (*Syzygium australe*) and the Damson plum (*Terminalia microcarpa*) fall amid the large, pulsing roots of the green fig (*Ficus virens*) and the wavering buttress roots of the brown tulip oak (*Argyrodendron polyandrum*). Birds skitter through the canopy. Sunlight stipples patterns in the leaves. The rustling of ground debris indicates a brush turkey walking by.

Approaching the area in 1860, close to today's township of Marian, one of the members of that first European exploration team, Andrew Murray, described the scenery as 'quite picturesque, with clumps of palms and other tropical vegetation, unlike anything we had previously seen'. Interspersed with this attractive jungle were large patches of grassland, beautiful specimens such as blady grass (*Imperata cylindrica*), kangaroo grass (*Themeda triandra*) and native sorghum (*Sorghum nitidum*). Murray, along with John Mackay, was part of that first European exploration team. The meadows he observed were not quite as natural as he may have thought. For thousands of years, the Yuwibara had burnt the ground, flushing out prey and nurturing regrowth in the nutrient-rich ashen soils. We can only guess the true number, but perhaps 1000 or 2000 people lived in the Pioneer

Valley when the first European settlers arrived with sheep, cattle and ammunition. Stone axes, many thousands of years old, with notches crafted into each side to create hand grips, have been discovered in the Mount Jukes area near Mackay. The Yuwibara ate the fruits of Damson plums, cocky apples (*Planchonia careya*), pandanus (*Pandanus spp.*) and the wrinkled, lychee-like spheres of the Leichhardt tree which, when ripe, have an astringent but not unpalatable taste. The large leaves of the Leichhardt tree were used for plates, and infusing its bark concocted a remedy for snake bite.

When John Mackay returned in 1883 to the town that bore his name, he witnessed a different place, the former hunting grounds redrawn as a monoculture of cane. 'Gazing round, I saw on a plot, familiar to me in days of yore as an area fringed with mangrove swamp, an embryo city with well-formed streets and stately buildings, while the background was studded with handsome villas, overlooking well-tilled fields of sugar-cane as far as the eye could see.' A town of 500 non-Indigenous residents in 1869 had grown to 700 people by the early 1880s. A quarter of the Yuwibara died from disease during this time, and around a quarter from calculated acts of slaughter. The small number of Yuwibara left by the early twentieth century would die in the influenza epidemic in 1919, and the last two Indigenous Australians in the town centre were taken to the missionary reserve on Palm Island in 1920. The numbers of Melanesians, meanwhile, had increased, and by 1880, there were over 2000 Islanders in the district, roughly three Islander males for every white male.

How quickly the numbers had escalated since those first seventy labourers arrived on the *Prima Donna*. This was the beginning of the pejoratively termed 'kanaka' labour in Mackay, a trade that would be stained by the epithets of kidnapping and slavery. Some would be killed in the ruckus and confusion of recruiting, and up to one-third of Islanders would die from disease. But these 'sugar slaves', through their hard work and tenacity, would ensure Mackay operated for decades as the capital of Australia's sugar industry.

As the men walked towards the Alexandra plantation, passing through the streets we now think of as West Mackay, they would have looked in wonder as strange, smooth-barked trees began to appear among the increasingly familiar trees of the rainforest. Similar to the scents and fragrances back home, the smell of the eucalypts would have seemed captivating, a light, menthol fragrance hanging softly in the dank and humid air. Some of these trees, those we now call Queensland blue gums (*Eucalyptus tereticornis*), would show patterns on their bark, watercolour shadings of blue, grey and brown. Others would be marble-grey, like the poplar gum (*Eucalyptus platyphylla*) and the Moreton Bay ash (*Corymbia tessellaris*), the latter with its blackened sock around the base. The labourers spent countless hours hacking down these trees, clearing the land for vast monocultures of sugar cane. The work was arduous and repetitive. They spent weeks blasting the hard, rocky ground to create holes for planting, and months were spent trashing, a process that involved stripping off the dry leaves at the top to admit sunlight to the bottom. Harvesting could be back-breaking work and, in the odious heat of the early afternoon, with the threat of the master's whip a constant worry, grief and homesickness would be ready emotions.

The etymology of the term 'blackbirding' has been obscured over time, but it is possible that somewhere, in the annals of slavery's history, someone compared the recruitment of slaves to the pursuit of catching blackbirds. It has been estimated that around 25–30 per cent of recruits were deceived in some way. Not all were forcibly abducted.

Some may have been lured with imaginary rewards. Others may have been ensnared by the false terms of service. The crimes would take place on isolated beaches, the footprints of struggle blown away by the overnight winds. The worst years for the Islanders were those first ones, where morality drowned in the rip currents of entitlement.

One can hold up a dictionary and argue it wasn't slavery, given that the workers received a salary and a fixed term of employment. But if not slavery, it was bondage. The wages were as low as one-fifth of an equivalent European worker. On average, the Islanders would serve three years – 'thirty-nine moons', as some used to say – and they would toil for around twelve hours a day. Certain accounts depict the workers as happy, but most present them as weary and sullen. Historian Noel Fatnowna, a descendant of Solomon Islands indentured labourers of the late nineteenth century, says sugar became a synonym for hard work, and Islanders around the dinner table would say, 'Hey, pass 'em hard work here.' Amid the confusion of foreign words and restless discomfort, there was only one rule in the cane fields: follow the lead, or the whip, of one's master.

The success of recruitment would often centre on the power of the lure. Beads, pigs, tobacco and tomahawks were used as gestures of reward, although the biggest drawcard was the firearm, something that would revolutionise the terms of intertribal warfare, which was promised upon completion of service. The ships were known as 'thief ships', 'kill-kills' and 'snatch-snatches'. The cramped conditions on the voyages to Australia led to outbreaks of dysentery, bronchitis and pneumonia. Many would arrive confused as to the terms of service, shocked to learn the length of their indenture. The luscious jungle that greeted those on the *Prima Donna* had been reduced to a solitary tree – the *Nauclea orientalis* – not much more than a decade later. For most of the nineteenth century, due to the absence of more formalised arrangements, ships would be tied to the firm, fissured bark of this tree.

There is a moving scene in the documentary *Sugar Slaves* (1995) in which Joe Leo and his wife, Monica, return to Pentecost Island in Vanuatu and walk along the beach where their relatives were kidnapped. A legend has flourished from this incident. Having to include the strange event in their own set of ideas, the Islanders assumed the recruits were taken to a nearby island, where they were murdered and cannibalised in an act of premeditated revenge.

But for every story of violent abduction, there are others of Islanders volunteering, some excited by the adventure, others wishing to escape tribal punishment and a few simply succumbing to the pressures of overbearing relatives or friends. It is believed the majority of blackbirding took place in those early years between 1865 and 1868, with a second burst when the trade moved to New Guinea in the 1880s. As historian Clive Moore suggested in an interview for *The Monthly:* 'Even from the 1860s, there were people going backwards and forwards between Queensland and the islands – sometimes two or three times. It's demeaning to the intelligence of the Islanders to think that they just waited on the beaches for white men in rowing boats to scoop them up for forty years, without figuring out how to make the system work for them.' Moore tells in his book *The Forgotten People* (1979) that he drove out to the site of the old Habana mill. His companion, Christie Fatnowna, pointed out the place where an eagle used to fly into the hut of his relatives. They would talk to the eagle, feed it, and in return the eagle would offer them messages from the islands. 'It's not just a legend,' he said. 'It did happen.'

Sorcery offered solace, but there was an even more powerful force, music, which provided both rhythm and relief for the Islanders. At the end of the working day, around six or seven in the evening, the workers would head back to camp where someone would unleash on a mouth organ and the others would sing or beat time with a piece of wood.

On Saturdays they would finish at four and, not having to begin work again until six on Monday morning, they met up with Islanders from other plantations and enjoyed sing-sings, feasts and fishing. They swapped stories of their island homes. Fights with other tribes were not uncommon. It was not an easy life. In Tracey Banivanua-Mar's book on the realities of the trade, *Violence and Colonial Dialogue* (2006), she recalls the story of Ueuega, a labourer from Moresby Island, who said that after he finished cutting each day, he would return to the house and weep. People kept track of their length of service by cutting a notch into a stick, one notch for every moon.

When I returned to Mackay for a weekend visit after a long absence, I walked down to Bluewater Quay. The Leichhardt tree seemed different from my memory of it. I stood in its shadow hoping it would speak to me, hoping that, like the eagle in Christie Fatnowna's story, it would bring me messages from the islands or from its nineteenth-century past. But its leaves were motionless. I recalled a poem written by a local, Dorothy Moffatt. The final lines are as pertinent now as when they were written:

Straight and strong in your youth you stood,
Beside the tidal stream.
Black men lay in your summer shade,
Lost in a torpid stream.
…
In the hustle and bustle of Life today,
Few spare a thought for you.

The Leichhardt tree reminds me of another solitary tree, one that has assumed almost fabled acclaim in the Australian narrative: the Lone Pine, the 'small ragged pine tree' that stood out on the Turkish coast 'very gauntly and conspicuously in that wilderness of stunted bushes'. With the frenzied chaos of war hanging heavy in the air, the visual sadness of this tree was inescapable. It stood like a hopeless statue above Anzac Cove, a natural memorial that pre-empted the cenotaphs and shrines that now permeate our battle-weary nations. This tree was orphaned with the same spirited industry that extirpated the landscape of Mackay. Many other Turkish red pines (*Pinus brutia*) had grown in the area before the war, but their trunks were repurposed as support beams and covers for makeshift, impromptu trenches. There could be no greater symbol for the transience of life, the mortality of endeavour, than the perseverance of this one vestigial conifer. Its survival was not just a warning of what was to come – it was a reminder of everything that had been lost and destroyed.

It does not take long, as one stands on Bluewater Quay, to realise the Leichhardt tree has borne the same symbolic burden as the Lone Pine. Stare at it for too long and an uneasiness slips into your veins. Within those blustery leaves, there is a sadness for the mistakes of the past; in the awkwardness of its branches is a warning. Today, the tree looks healthier than ever, bolstered by the decking and turf of the quay's redevelopment. It would be inconceivable for most walkers and cyclists to imagine that this pedestrianised walkway was once an area of dense, riparian rainforest; the Leichhardt tree, once surrounded by tulip oaks and paperbarks, Damson plums and supplejack, is a living relic, an orphan from another time. Where once it heard the hack and slash of European axes, the tree now hears the rattle of prams or the rhythmic thud of trainers.

Around 1000 Islanders live in Mackay today, many of them descendants of the 3000 or so workers who stayed in post-Federation Australia. Recognition has been a slow process. Noel Fatnowna, in an interview for Clive Moore's *The Forgotten People*, said, 'In death they didn't even want us … Today when I drive around the district, I know the exact places where our people are buried. Unmarked graves in cane fields, some with roads going over them today.' A gathering was held in July 2017 to recognise the 150th anniversary since the *Prima Donna*. There was no more fitting place to meet than by the Leichhardt tree. This was a moment to look back in celebration as well as sadness. Starrett Vea Vea, chair of the Mackay and District Australian and South Sea Islander Association and one of the people who spoke at the ceremony, sees the tree as a symbol of hope rather than a reminder of darkness: 'People don't want to talk about it. But as descendants, we're quite happy, we're quite proud of who we are and where we come from.'

At a time when statues of James Cook and Matthew Flinders are desecrated with hostile graffiti, when people call for monuments of the oppressed to counterbalance the imperial narrative, the Leichhardt tree provides a natural, unassuming tribute to the Islanders. Standing in its presence, one can hear the faint cries of the sugar slaves as they touch land for the first time, the dysentery pleas of the ill and the sobs of the imprisoned, the loud thrum of workers as they disembark and gather beneath its crown. Eventually this tree will pass away and these sounds will be subsumed by the endless lapping of water as it breaks slowly, laboriously against the metronomic pulse of the land. I wonder how a tree of such genial spirit can live with such darkness. But the tree makes no judgements. It is, and will only ever be, a passive observer.

A Mangrove Story

My memories of a place can often be biased in favour of one activity at the expense of others. In my memory, my time in Mackay was an almost endless series of jogs, which could not have been true, for running was only an occasional pastime, albeit one that gave me a great deal of pleasure.

My most common route extended east along the Bluewater Trail, following a concrete pathway that passed the Leichhardt tree before meandering through mangroves and open grass. Just before the confluence of Sandfly Creek and the Pioneer River, there was an unusual sculpture called *Mangrove Cap*. For a public artwork, it is in a strangely isolated location. I wondered how many people knew of its existence and, if they did, what they made of its awkward body: whether, like me, they viewed it as a headless arachnid or perhaps a tribute to the famous Philippe Starck lemon juicer. Fiona Foley, the artist who created the sculpture, drew inspiration from her childhood memories playing within the mangroves, finding turtle and dugong bones, and watching her family gather periwinkles, mud crabs and oysters. Made from weathered Corten steel and standing 9 metres tall, the artwork represents the roots of a red mangrove tree (*Rhizophora sp.*), the exterior deliberately rusting in the salty air of its environs. Sitting beneath it, the artist describes feeling herself underneath the transepts of a church. The sculpture is a testament to the spiritual power of sitting among the tree's enfolding and undisciplined roots.

During the late 1990s, hundreds of ghostly mangroves lined the banks of the Pioneer River, close to where Fiona Foley would erect her sculpture. The trees, dying or dead, rose like white angels from the mud, their alopecian branches a contrast to the luscious surrounds. Deformed pneumatophores had the appearance of strange fungi, and some resembled fat, surrealist, sculpted flowers, not unlike a John Perceval artwork. Norm Duke, one of Australia's chief experts on the trees, arrived in Mackay in 2002, and he and his research team traipsed through the areas most affected, taking soil samples. They noticed there was one mangrove affected more than the others, the grey mangrove (*Avicennia marina ssp. australasica, Avicennia marina ssp. eucalyptifolia*), and as more testing was undertaken, a correlation began to emerge. Areas with high levels of dieback coincided with soils recording high levels of diuron, a chemical used by farmers as a herbicide and by boat owners as an anti-fouling agent.

The grey mangrove, which has since recovered, and the long-style red mangrove (*Rhizophora stylosa*), the tree upon which Foley's sculpture was based, are the most common mangroves in Mackay, and they are also the most common in Australia, but in many ways they could not be more different. The former's canopy can appear welcoming, rounded, while the jagged, pointed leaves of the red mangrove are aggressive and harsh. The pneumatophore roots of *Avicennia* look like snorkels or stalagmites, whereas *Rhizophora* roots stretch menacingly across the ground, twisted and entangled, like pale corpses. Pure stands of the grey mangrove can be fairly open, whereas the long-style red grows in thickets, so dense they could act as a prison wall. They are from two separate botanical families, two separate orders, related only in as much as they are both eudicots, a scientific classification accounting for around three-quarters of flowering plants. Even human beings and elephants are closer on the family tree. And yet they are both referred to as mangroves, and for many, they could be the same plant. A layperson, someone who might not know an oak from an elder or a eucalypt from an acacia, would still, being aware of how close they are to the ocean, see the strange roots and the mud and identify both species as something called a mangrove.

We do not know the exact etymology of the word 'mangrove'. Possibly the term derives from the Malay word *manggi manggi*, or from the Portuguese word *mangue*. The breadth of its usage is somewhat unique in that the word can describe an individual tree, a collection of many trees, a community of plants or a community of organisms. One may, on walking through mangroves, pass ground-creeping plants like sea purslane (*Sesuvium portulacastrum*) and beaded glasswort (*Sarcocornia quinqueflora*), but these plants cannot be called mangroves. Only woody species, more than 1.5 metres tall and restricted to hypersaline environments, are deserving of the term. Some plants, such as the native hibiscus (*Hibiscus tiliaceus*), are not true mangroves because, while they tolerate salt, they can also establish elsewhere.

Mangroves are not without their beauty. I remember with fondness passing through mangroves on the way to the beach with a surfboard in Costa Rica, and river-cruising in Thailand with green, picturesque mangroves in the background. But this admiration is not widely held; for many, mangroves are considered outlets of smell and slime, mephitic factories, emitters of sulphur, the grey pits of purgatory in between the beach and modern life. Duke laments their reputation as the 'ugly ducklings' of the natural world, while the colourful underwater seagrasses of stretches like the Great Barrier Reef are the elegant swans. But this is changing, and champions like Duke, who runs the excellent Mangrove Watch website, are beginning to recolour the maligned ecosystem in the public's mind, turning it from a grey charcoal sketch to a fine, nuanced watercolour.

To visit the Daintree Rainforest is to see both sides of the mangrove story. When you follow the Marrdja boardwalk in Cape Tribulation, you step through a grey, vapid world. Your feet shuffle over the hollow, boggy landscape. The sound of pistol shrimp jolts the senses, strange snaps that precipitate a cold, disquieting shiver. Different species tend to occupy different tidal positions – *Avicennia marina* and *Sonneratia alba* are found near the coast; *Heritiera littoralis* and *Xylocarpus granatum* more upstream. It feels as if the trees have been exiled here, banished from the lush, species-rich rainforest only metres away. Roots litter the ground, particularly the distended arches of the orange (*Bruguiera gymnorhiza*) and red mangroves (*Rhizophora apiculata, Rhizophora stylosa*). Perhaps the most conspicuous species is the cannonball (*Xylocarpus granatum*), its grey-green patchy bark so defiantly khaki one might mistake it for army fatigues. The seed capsules, large, round and obtrusive, drop to the ground and shatter, sending seeds flying in the same manner that shrapnel might be released from a grenade.

Compare this to the beauty of a boat trip down the Daintree River, where over thirty species of mangrove take root along this one water system. Upriver, the wonderfully elegant *Bruguiera sexangula* grows, its lush yellow-green foliage overhanging the water, its resplendent crown hinting at the rainforest nearby. Brash flowers of purple-red adorn the leaves of the red-flowered apple mangrove (*Sonneratia caseolaris*), the trunks of this tree rising vertically like extensions of the tree's pneumatophores that punctuate the ground. The attractive holly mangrove (*Acanthus ilicifolius*), with its sensual mauve flowers, grows beneath its canopy. You may observe a satin flycatcher darting underneath a *Barringtonia racemosa*, a gloriously confident tree with thick, clubby leaves and seed pods hanging with poetic decoration. Its thin, wistful, myrtaceous flowers speckle the water. So, too, do the flowers of the native hibiscus, which flower in the morning and shed into the water by dusk. Sailing along the river is a serene and joyous experience.

The most frustrating thing is that, were the finest minds of public relations to discuss re-energising the reputation of mangroves, there would be no shortage of positive attributes to draw on. They are the overseers of the coast, protectors of riverbanks and shorelines. They regulate water, filtering out toxins from the industrial and agricultural run-off. They keep sand and mud in place, protecting the riverbanks and coastlines against erosion. They recycle nutrients, their dead leaves providing food for plankton, algae, shellfish and fish. They sequester around five times as much carbon as normal forests. They control floods. They mitigate the impact of storm surge. They are nurseries for young fish and a habitat for specialist species. And they provide food, fibre, timber and fuel to meet the needs of our human population.

Perhaps the most famous display of mangrove wood hangs in the Enlightenment Gallery of the British Museum. It is an elemong shield made from the timber of the red mangrove. When the museum's Department of Conservation and Scientific Research removed a thin sample of the bark, approximately 2 millimetres square and

2 millimetres thick, and put it under an electron microscope (which can provide higher resolution and detail than an optical one), they discovered that both the shield and handle were made from *Rhizophora stylosa*. This was a revelation, for the shield was thought to be acquired by James Cook and his crew on the shoreline of Botany Bay. If this was true, it could represent the first discovery of long-distance trade along the eastern coast of Australia. The nearest stand of red mangroves is almost 500 kilometres north of Botany Bay, around the mouth of the Macleay River. It is possible someone walked this distance many years ago, presenting the shield in exchange for something equally as prized. Or maybe several groups traded the shield, and it passed in a southerly direction until it reached the possession of a warrior named Cooman.

The first record of the shield's appearance was, according to Peter FitzSimons, 'the most iconic moment in our history'. Cooman and his younger companion came down to the rocks carrying spear-throwers and spears, their naked bodies decorated with white interlocking patterns. Earlier that afternoon, the Gweagal people, local to the area, had watched as a giant waterbird approached the shoreline, its wings billowing sails, the crew thought to be possums scrambling across its body. Cook's men had tried landing the day before, just north of present-day Wollongong, but there had been a strong southerly and a small landing boat had suffered in the surf. The water seemed calmer here. At some point, they lowered the landing boats into the water and a number of crew members climbed aboard to go ashore.

It was an unprecedented sight: boats of oddly clad men carrying long instruments, their bodies twitching with anxiety. Perhaps the Gweagal could feel the threat in the Union Jack flag. Perhaps the land trembled at the thought of this unsolicited burden of hungry, thirsty sailors. Botanical illustrator Sydney Parkinson recorded one of the expressions he heard in his journal: 'Warra warra wai.' It was a phrase repeated again and again, a phrase taken to mean 'go away' in the Dharawal language. For there was no greater insult than to turn up uninvited, expecting to trespass without any prior attempt at communion. But Ray Ingrey, a Dharawal man, says the phrase has another meaning. 'Warra' means 'dead'; he believes the men were shouting 'They are dead, they are dead', for they saw these Europeans as ghosts, spirits of their ancestors, apparitions who were returning unannounced from the dead.

Attempts at communication were unsuccessful, and when Cook ordered the boat to row closer, Cooman and his companion raised their spears, causing Cook to fire a shot over their heads. Around 40 yards separated the two groups. The younger man dropped his spears in fright, only to pick them up again. Cook fired twice, one of the shots striking Cooman on the leg, prompting the injured man to retreat to a hut more than 100 yards away. When Cooman returned, he carried extra spears and a large, oval-shaped shield: the elemong. More spears were thrown, stones as well, and when Cook fired two shots in response, Cooman threw one last spear before the out-weaponed, outnumbered defenders started to back away. Inspecting the nearby huts, Banks says they found around forty to fifty lances, some as long as 5 metres, which they removed and sequestered onto the ship. They also picked up a shield, the same one the Elder warrior Cooman dropped as he retreated.

The shield is, in the words of the British Museum, one of the most potent objects in their collection – 'symbolically charged', says former director of the museum Neil MacGregor, 'freighted with layers of history, legend, global politics and race relations'. Scrolling through my Twitter feed around the time of the 250th anniversary of Cook's landing, I saw a tweet from Jonathan Green, the host of ABC's *Blueprint for Living*. 'Cook was a remarkable navigator of extraordinary achievement,' he said. 'Cook's arrival here marked the beginning of a catastrophic encounter for Australian Indigenous peoples. I can't see how it is not possible to hold both these ideas simultaneously.' The tweet is accompanied by an uncaptioned photo of the shield, a large slab of bark with a hole in the middle. The hole was most likely made by a spear rather than a bullet, but the suggestion of the latter prevails in our collective consciousness, the image symbolising the violence and disarray of first contact.

Except history rarely ends with a full stop. It now seems that the shield in the museum's collection may not be Cooman's after all, despite MacGregor writing unequivocally of the historical connection. Nicholas Thomas, an anthropologist and historian at the University of Cambridge, has compared the shield with a John Frederick Miller sketch from 1771, the only primary evidence we have of the shield, and noticed several unmistakable deviations: the hole is in a different location, the ends are more rounded, and the curvature of the sides contrast markedly. Sometimes the symbolism can be more expressive than the truth, and as an emblem of that first encounter, the shield on display, with the suggestion of its penetration by gunfire, is an understandably compelling image. As an example of history's uncertainty, it is not quite so enticing.

Australia is particularly blessed with mangroves, and so it is fitting that this icon of conquest should be made from mangrove timber. Mangroves skirt almost one-fifth of the country's coastline, and more than half of all global species reside here. The Ian Fairweather painting *Mangrove* (1961–62) deftly conveys the dark, web-like beauty of these trees. Fascinated by the overlays and rhythms of nature, Fairweather used long brushstrokes to savage the canvas, layer propelled upon layer, the tangled chaos of *Rhizophora* roots embodied in paint. The result is an artwork that is at once putrid and beautiful. The calligraphic patterns capture the swirl of these vainglorious trees; the harsh strokes symbolise the Darwinian aggression of nature; the grey blotches approximate the mud.

I had a moment of Fairweather consciousness when I stared at a dense stand of red and grey mangroves at the northern end of Cairns Esplanade. The soft sunlight dappled through the canopy. Birds rustled the leaves. A varied honeyeater chirruped from somewhere within, but it was impossible to determine where. It was obvious a world existed within this thicket that was just as intense as one outside it. And yet, when I tried to view this activity, it was as if a deception took place. The crown was so dense and the roots so impenetrable, the more I looked, the less I saw. It was the Principle of Mangrove Uncertainty. Nature photographer Jeremy Stafford-Deitsch says the silence of mangroves 'has something ancient, something other, something separate about it'. We will never observe this mangrove microworld with the same clarity and respect as the varied honeyeater. It has an untouchable, unknowable beauty. A world of countless interactions that are hidden from human view.

Within this gothic morass of tree trunks and roots, there is a nutrient-rich playground for fish, molluscs, insects and crustaceans. A teaspoon of mud from the mangroves of north Queensland may contain more than ten billion bacteria. The noisome smell is a sign of health. As the bacteria anaerobically break down the debris, hydrogen sulphide is released into the air. There are crab burrows everywhere, the silty surface pierced by row upon row of furtive holes. Mud crabs break down leaves; hermit crabs shimmy in their pilfered shells; armies of soldier crabs sift through sediment for small particles of food, corkscrewing into the ground whenever they are startled by a predator. Mangrove snails hang off leaves on mucous threads, marine borers tunnel through trunks, and mangrove oysters and barnacles cling to the distended roots. Spiky sea urchins come on the high tide, scraping algae off the roots with their teeth. Turtles chomp on the almond-shaped fruit of *Avicennia marina*. Fish breed and seek refuge among the roots. It is thought that around 75 per cent of Queensland's total fish catch begin life in these mangrove nurseries.

For Aboriginal Australians, mangroves are an important source of food and medicine. Mangrove worms are extracted from the decaying wood of *Rhizophora* and *Bruguiera* species and longbum snails from the mud. Periwinkles are taken from the roots of *Rhizophora stylosa* and mud mussels at the base of the mangrove palm (*Nypa fruticans*). One wonders at what point someone realised they could take the seeds of the looking-glass mangrove (*Heritiera littoralis*), crush them into flour and create a treatment for diarrhoea. Or remove the outer bark from the rib-fruited yellow mangrove (*Ceriops tagal*), revealing a sticky inner bark that could be boiled and mixed with water to treat scabies, sores and infections.

The Aboriginal relationships with nature are about practising restraint and maintaining resources. An obvious dissonance exists between the way the First Australians understood sustainability and the manner in which the Europeans prospected, looking for any short-term, commercial advantage. The cabbage-tree palms (*Livistona australis*) were cut down in the first few years of settlement at Sydney Cove, and it is likely the same fate would have befallen the *Araucaria* of Norfolk Island had the trees proven more valuable as a shipbuilding timber.

In an interview for the ABC, Bob Randall, a singer and Yankunytjatjara Elder who grew up under the shadows of Uluru, described his view of nature: 'The tree cares for me, it gives me this food … You have a relationship of receiving something good from something other than your human mother … the tree, in a sense, to that child is another mother.' Kill the mother and the baby cannot survive.

There is a striking black-and-white photo taken by Sue Ford in the mangroves of Bathurst Island showing a woman resting while the roots of the mangroves appear to engulf her.[12] To my city-dwelling mind, it looks as if she is trapped. But Emmie Tipiloura, who is taking a break from hunting with a rolled-up cigarette in one hand, sits at ease among the trees, as if she has slipped into this scene and will just as easily slip out again. Only the cigarette and the clothes give a clue as to when in the last 60,000 years this photo was taken.

Stare at the photo for long enough and signs of life will start to infiltrate the dark surrounds. Ford was at Bathurst Island to run a photography workshop that had been organised by Emmie. When she exhibited these photos, she gave the exhibition the title *A Different Landscape*. It was a landscape that was superficially familiar, the same landscape she had grown up with – the same contours, the same colours – but now she viewed it through different eyes, with different preconceptions. These dark, dishevelled places were now something else. They were no longer to be feared. They were sympathetic. Tameable. Alive. A lesson in how prejudices can haunt our intuition.

§

It was November, the end of the dry season, when I travelled from Normanton to Karumba. The drive took me through the cracked, desiccated banks of the Mutton Hole Wetlands, past salt pans and the coarse, stunted woods of the Gulf of Carpentaria. I was expecting a Drysdale painting, the musty red of *Sofala* (1947) or *Walls of China* (*1945*), so I was surprised to find the scenery imbued with the soft, pastel shades of an Arthur Streeton. There is a pub in Karumba called the Sunset Tavern, which affords you a view of the beach. It is not the kind of beach that ends up on postcards. It is gritty and austere. Its sole resident when I was there was an eastern curlew, a shorebird that flies in from Siberia for the summer feeding. Beyond the beach is the far more attractive western bank of the Norman River, where a lush, verdant horizon of mangroves separates the bright tones of the sky from the sparkling waters of the sea. It is hard to imagine that only a few miles behind this pretty façade, Burke and Wills toiled across some of Australia's most uninviting environment.

Upon leaving the pub, I walked along the shoreline towards Karumba airport, reflecting on how much has changed in the last 160 years. It took Burke and Wills five and a half months to get from Melbourne to Karumba. It took me around fourteen hours. I walked to the airport not to board a plane, but to imagine the devastation that lay beyond the landing strip. For, around 15 kilometres between there and Brannigan Creek, several hectares of dead, ghostlike mangroves decolour the land; the trees have died but remain standing, their eerie, skeletal figures a haunting reminder of life's impermanence.

This was the same country Ludwig Leichhardt and his men passed through in 1845, sixteen years before Burke and Wills. 'Miserable land' is how one of the expedition's trackers, Charley, had described it. He had gone out looking for game and found only box trees and anthills. Riding through mangrove scrub the next day, somewhere near the present township of Normanton, Charley came to a white sandy beach with the ocean before him. This was the first time anyone from the group had seen the ocean since setting out from Jimbour station. But any sense of freedom it offered was a mirage. This country was tough: saltwater creeks and lagoons, sandy flats and boggy soil, tea-tree thickets and stunted mangroves. There was no easy thoroughfare, no intuitive direction.

A few days before, on 13 July 1845, Leichhardt describes in his journal the delusive effect of the 'cumuli' clouds, which had been amassing that afternoon: clouds that cast their shadow over the forest, creating the shimmering promise of water. If these clouds had a silver lining, it was that it was July and the weather was calm. Night-times were cold and the wind occasionally icy but, for the most part, the weather was pleasant. When Robert O'Hara Burke passed through sixteen years later, it was February, the height of the wet season. The rain was fierce, the ground boggy, and the mosquitoes were rife, flitting about like pestilent, bloodsucking irritants. But despite these travails, Burke and his party trudged on, dolefully and dutifully. Most days they would rise before dawn, retrieve the camels, prepare the packs and begin walking. Alan Moorehead describes the tedium: 'The world narrows in these conditions; one's boots have the disembodied fascination of a clockwork pendulum, weariness is subdued by the dull compulsion of the rhythm, and ground is not ground but simply distance to be put behind one. In this apathy of movement, this concentration merely upon keeping going, this coma of walking, any intrusion is resented and any call upon the mind is an effort.'

Burke had been given instructions to explore the country between Cooper Creek and the Gulf of Carpentaria. Others had explored to the west and to the east, but the area encompassing today's towns of Mount Isa, Cloncurry, Boulia and Bedourie was known as 'the ghastly blank' for good reason. There was an additional motive: no European had yet crossed from south to north through the continent's dead heart. The prospect of being the first to bisect the country had inspired a race. South Australia was financing John McDouall Stuart, an amiable but taciturn explorer whose great achievements belied his failing eyesight. Victoria was supporting an Irish police officer, Robert O'Hara Burke. But while the ghastly blank may have been a reasonable description for the inland bush, the Gulf itself was neither ghastly nor blank. While on the HMS *Beagle* in 1841, John Lort Stokes had remarked upon the monotony of the mangroves as he sailed along the coast. Four years later, Leichhardt, walking across the Gulf from Maramie to Borroloola, noted the boggy saltwater creeks, grassy swamps and forests of mangroves and melaleuca. Following a similar course eleven years later, Thomas Baines, as part of Augustus Gregory's exploring party, painted watercolours of the mangrove-fringed coast. Burke read up on these explorers. He would have known the Gulf was not an uninterrupted expanse of palm trees and white sand.

Reading of the expedition today, it is hard to move beyond the caricature of Burke, the policeman who lay in an outdoor bathtub waving to gold diggers, naked but for a helmet upon his head. Burke is a figure of ridicule, as impulsive and stubborn as previous explorers were cautious and reasoned. He is the man who got lost between Beechworth and Yackandandah. He is the dishevelled, careless bachelor who, according to one acquaintance, stuck to his walls scraps of paper with comments such as: 'I cannot keep any record in a systematic manner, so I jot down things like this.' But he was not without virtue. His respect as a policeman was such that when he left Beechworth, the community petitioned him to change his mind.

When he farewelled the citizens of Castlemaine, around six weeks before the expedition departed, the overflow from the crowded hall was so vast, people were queueing up outside, jostling for a view. A toast was raised to celebrate his 'cordial demeanour, urbane and frank manner, and numerous sterling qualities'. But perhaps his chief characteristic was his determination. Imbued with a sense of higher purpose, he would not let anything prevent him from being the first person to cross the continent. Scientific endeavour would not hold him back, nor unregulated curiosity. He was a man with a chance to prove a point, a single-missioned, single-minded leader.

Ludwig Leichhardt was the antithesis of Burke. Whereas Burke was fuelled by ambition, Leichhardt was driven by curiosity. Henry Turnbull, who accompanied the Prussian on his failed second expedition, described him as having an observant eye, one that could unlock secrets. He was a subscriber to Schopenhauer's philosophy, where the interests of the state should be subordinate to one's natural inquisition, but he was not an instinctive leader. Shy and introverted, he had an awkward manner. 'He was rather given to melancholy at the highest pitch of pleasure,' describes Patrick White of Voss, his Leichhardt-inspired character.

When in July 1845 Leichhardt's party was near the present locality of Yagoonya, on the eastern edge of the Gulf, they came across a large, sandy plain dotted with stunted tea-trees. There was a species of Hakea, most likely *Hakea arborescens*, which he recognised as one that grew near saltwater. The sand, too, was encrusted with salt, and beyond the plain the party could see a dense green line of mangroves. Walking on, following a creek to the mouth of a 'fine salt water river', they felt a sense of relief: 'The first sight of the salt water of the gulf was hailed by all with feelings of indescribable pleasure ... Brown's joyous exclamation of "Salt Water!" was received by a loud hurrah from the whole party.'

After travelling south for nine days, they set up camp by a water-hole not far from present-day Normanton. On 18 July, they explored the area, passing through plains of grevillea forest and thickets of tea-tree, until: 'About five miles from the camp, we came to salt-water inlets, densely surrounded by mangroves, and with sandy flats extending along their banks, encrusted with salt. Charley rode through the dry mangrove scrub, and came on a sandy beach with the broad Ocean before him.'

Leichhardt and his men had achieved what every twentieth-century Australian, disorientated and in a strange place, had sought to do. They had located the beach.

When Burke approached the Gulf in the summer of 1861, he was almost six months into his expedition. The entourage that left Royal Park had been whittled down to four: Burke, William Wills, Charles Gray and John King. They were exhausted, beaten down, tortured by the dull rhythm of their feet. Sarah Murgatroyd, the writer who retraced their steps around 150 years later, describes the site of their penultimate camp (Camp CXIX) as mournful and drab. The suffocating, fetid heat does nothing to prepare one for the coldness of its welcome. Dismal and listless during the dry months, the site was a quagmire by the time the explorers arrived, beset by a pattern of constant drizzle interspersed with heavy rain, turning the grey, helpless soil into a sickly, glutinous slime. But, despite its austerity and isolation, the surrounds can be momentarily lifted by the jaunty, infectious song of a pied butcherbird, the golden flash of a yellow honeyeater or the grandiose, balletic flight of the brolga, a bird English writer Alan Moorehead described as the most beautiful living object in Australia.

It was decided Burke and Wills would set out to find the north-ern coast while Charles Gray and John King stayed behind at Camp CXIX. Turkeys, kangaroos and emus roamed nearby. Saltwater croco-diles lurked on the banks of fishing holes. Gray and King each had a Bible and a prayer book, and occasionally they would read sections to pass the time. King, a diminutive man whose life had been marked by poverty and illness, had made it this far thanks to his composure and determination. Charles Gray was of different stock: almost thirty years King's senior, he was a 'stout hearty man', an ex-sailor whose arms were covered in tattoos of mermaids and anchors. Neither Gray nor King would see the blue infinity of the Gulf's water, nor would they lay down and feel the soft, glorious comfort of sand on their weary limbs.

Edward Jukes Greig's *Arrival of Burke & Wills at Flinders River 1861* (1862) is a vivid evocation of the moment Burke and Wills, looking towards the river's mouth, get their first glimpse of the Indian Ocean. Burke, dressed in red, takes off his hat and points to the water. Wills, walking stick in one hand and the reins of Billy the horse in the other, crouches down to take in the glorious vista. One can imagine the joy they felt touching sand for the first time. 'We made it!' Wills would say as the two exhausted explorers lay down on the beach, beneath a Union Jack stabbed proudly in the ground.

'There is something you must do for me. When we get back,' Burke would say to his second-in-command. 'When I return. When my name is on everybody's lips, we will marry. I have her promise.' He is referring to the woman he loves, a sixteen-year-old actress called Julia Matthews. 'And I want you there ... At my elbow. My best man. Do I have your word on that?'

'You have my word.'

But they had a lot to do first. They had two months' travel to Cooper Creek, where supplies awaited them, and yet they only had rations for a month. How Wills must have been cursing Burke's words to William Brahe the day before they departed: 'We should be back in three months, four at most.' Wills was playing cricket at the time. The Scotsman Thomas McDonough had bowled him out, knocking away the leg stump, but King, who was umpire, had ruled it a no ball and ...

Wait. These two images, Burke and Wills at the beach, McDonough playing cricket, they are the productions of fantasy. They are sourced not from diaries but from the imaginations of director Graeme Clifford and his screenwriter, Michael Thomas. To watch the 1985 film *Burke & Wills* is to revel in a joyous beach scene which, far from being historically accurate, was invented for the screen. The explorers may have been first to cross the continent, but John McDouall Stuart was the first to dip his toes into the Indian Ocean. There was no sweeping vista of the Gulf, as Jukes Greig had painted, only a sad, withered landscape, bleached of colour and sapped of inspiration. William Wills, the boy who could reportedly complete Hampton Court Maze in ten minutes, the man who stayed up late reading books on mathematics and astronomy, found himself vanquished by the northern coast. His faith in both God and authority had been tested. He would be dead before the end of June.

Read through the many books and articles on the expedition and the blame is almost unanimous.

'Mangrove swamps blocked the way,' writes Moorehead.

'Burke's hopes of reaching the sea were dashed,' describes journalist Tom Bergin, 'as he found himself blocked by mangroves and flooded plains.'

For critic Michael Cathcart, a 'fantastic tangle of branches and aerial roots, rising from the mud like living stalagmites, stood between the two men and the ocean'.

The mangroves were 'impenetrable', says *Australian Geographic*. The explorers were forced to turn back, writes Annabel Venning in *The Daily Mail*, 'unable to penetrate the tangle of trees' of 'the thick mangrove swamp'.

The explorer John McKinlay suffered a similar roadblock fifteen months later when he was exploring the country around the Albert and Leichhardt rivers, 80 kilometres to the west. Enlisted by the South Australian government to look for signs of the missing explorers, if successful in this mission, he was instructed to leave Cooper Creek and head north towards the Gulf. Hearing the news that Alfred Howitt's search party had found King still alive and the others dead, McKinlay travelled north, discovering that the closer he got to the Gulf, the harder the travelling became. On 18 May 1862, McKinlay and his men arrived at a fine mangrove creek with water lily in bloom. They attempted to reach the coast the next morning but, for the second time in three months, an exploring party was denied the honour of an ocean view, their progress hindered by mangroves and boggy flats.

Following the line of the Little Bynoe River, Burke and Wills were roughly 5 kilometres short of the coast when they aborted their northerly route. It is hard to know the exact position because the records are not explicit. David Hillan, a retired surveyor who knows the area from fishing trips, used Wills' survey notes, aerials, modern maps, GPS receivers and a number of helicopter trips to determine the most likely location for their makeshift final camp along the Bynoe, Camp CXX. After erecting a small memorial close to the site, Hillan walked what he perceived to be the most efficient route towards the coast, avoiding the mangroves lining the river and the creek, before reaching what he termed the last sandhill. Had the explorers been able to levitate 10–12 metres above the ground, they would have seen, around 5 kilometres in the distance, the endless blue of the ocean. And had they, with angel wings, been able to fly above the sandhills and boggy flats, they would have landed on the soft, welcoming surface of the beach.

Hillan's quest is illuminating. He managed to avoid the mangroves and instead walked in a northerly direction, maintaining a course which, to some degree, bisected the salt plains between the Bynoe and Norman rivers. For those of us less adventurous, the walk between Karumba and Karumba Point gives a rough idea of the terrain. It is one of vast tidal salt flats stained with a blood-red carpet of shrubby samphire (*Tecticornia halocnemoides*). Mangroves are common, the orange burnish of the rib-fruited yellow mangrove clearly visible against the green of the club mangrove (*Aegialitis annulata*) and the soft silvery glaze of the northern grey (*Avicennia marina ssp. eucalyptifolia*). But their presence is patchy. There are no thickets or forests. We must look instead for a different culprit, the ground itself, the heavy rains whipping up the land into a marshy and mucilaginous slime. When Dave Phoenix, president of the Burke and Wills Historical Society, attempted to re-create the journey in 2008, he encountered the same problem. Three times he left Camp CXIX to reach the coast, and each time he was beaten by the rising tide and flooded rivers. His feet would sink, his body would weaken, and 5 kilometres would appear like an eternity. Reimagining those last northerly steps of Burke and Wills, author and journalist Peter FitzSimons writes: 'It is not the mangroves ahead that trap and block them, it is the gravity that sucks them down.'

Today, mangroves are in the news for a different reason. In 2016, Norm Duke surveyed Australia's northern coastline by helicopter. For around 1000 kilometres, from the Roper River in the west to Karumba in the east, blanched, anaemic trees replaced what was once a beautiful green belt of mangrove fringe. A video shows the view from Duke's helicopter as he flies along the stretch of coastline north of Karumba, not far from where Burke and Wills were blocked by the impassable swamp. Grey, petrified tree stands next to grey, petrified tree, dense thickets of death with the occasional green outlier clinging to life on the muddy banks of the shore. The ethereal trees are motionless, skeletal – arrested while fleeing a disaster they could never outpace. Occasionally a bird, maybe a corella, flutters past, a reminder of the brief, evanescent beauty of the area. The video continues for seven minutes. The noise of the helicopter blade evokes the Vietnam War; the footage, of helicopters transporting soldiers over freshly napalmed forests. This may not have been war, but these micro-ecosystems of life had very quickly transformed into cemeteries.

The first report had come in at the end of 2015. By early 2016, reports were arriving regularly from local tour operators and those conducting bird surveys. In May, at the Australian Mangrove and Saltmarsh Network Conference – an annual get-together of researchers, policymakers and industry stakeholders – attendees shared photos of the unfurling tragedy. Through conducting their own aerial surveys as well as studying others' satellite imagery, Norm and his team would discover that, across this remote, often forgotten expanse of coastline, around 7400 hectares of mangroves were dead. Duke had previously described the mangroves along Australia's northern coast as some of the least altered in the world. Yet here they were, this enchanting strip

111

of pre-anthropogenic nature, quietly exiting stage left, slipping away without a sound.

In June 2016, the Northern Territory government supported the first investigative survey. Duke and his team recorded the coastline from Roper River to McArthur River. They flew past Karumba in October, beginning close to the airport and travelling north up to Brannigan Creek. In November, they monitored the shoreline around the Albert River, the same expanse where Augustus Gregory had waited all those years ago for his ship to arrive with provisions. By the end of these surveys, they had covered around 600 kilometres of coastline. They found that key species were devastated: grey mangroves, red mangroves, yellow mangroves.

Over the next four to five years, the roots rotted, further destabilising the sediment and eroding the banks, creating an exponential tragedy for the organisms that depend on their existence. It was, to quote a media release from James Cook University, 'the worst incidence of climate-related mass tree dieback that has ever occurred globally'. Images from the survey are explicit: the green of life and the grey of death run in layers, like ecological strata. This was one of the most interesting findings from the survey: the stretches of mangroves around estuaries and rivers, where the trees had access to freshwater, were for the most part unscathed, presenting the team with one of the few clues they had to go on. The dieback had also followed a severe drought and four years of below-average rainfall. The mangroves, Norm Duke realised, had died of thirst.

Sitting on the beach at the Sunset Tavern, sipping a schooner of draught beer, I try to imagine the level of destruction a few kilometres to the east. How bitter is the realisation that these trees, lauded as one of our strongest protections against rising seas, could themselves become a victim of climate change? Almost two years on from those first reports of death along the northern coastline, there are still thousands of dead trunks, waiting, as if by some miracle, to be resurrected. I cannot view them myself; they are inaccessible by foot. But if I chartered a bi-plane at the nearby Karumba airport, I would soon soar above their petrified cadavers. It is the isolation of mangroves that has meant they have died in silence, far removed from our eyes. Clustered in dense, impenetrable stands, their decline was swift. According to Peter Wohlleben, trees scream when they are desperate for water, ultrasonic cries caused by vibrations along the length of their xylem. For how long were these mangroves screaming before that first report came through?

On my way back to Cairns airport, I listen to a news report of tourists taking Instagram selfies in front of the jacaranda blooms in Sydney. Those working to protect mangroves can only dream of this level of admiration for the trees. Before I flew to Melbourne, I stopped by Chinaman Creek, following the track down from the western end of Little Spence Street. The Cairns city centre is about a kilometre away, but here, one can imagine how the area may have appeared before Europeans dropped concrete on the sand dunes and swales. Hidetoshi Kudo, known to his friends as Mikey, would come here often with his field book and play a game called mangroving. His aim was to tick off as many mangrove species as he could within a radius of the Cairns CBD. On one particular day, he was looking for the red-flowered black mangrove (*Lumnitzera littorea*) on the recommendation of one of his naturalist friends, Brian Venables. Crossing the bridge, Mikey left the cycle track and began to explore a grassy verge. Here, the Arcadian beauty is disturbed somewhat by the powerlines and the smell of discarded rubbish, but there are mangroves everywhere – red, grey, yellow, black. Once past the pylon, Mikey stepped into a cloistered microworld of mangrove ferns (*Acrostichum speciosum*) shooting from the craggy knee roots of orange mangroves (*Bruguiera gymnorhiza, Bruguiera parviflora, Bruguiera cylindrica*). It is here he found a tree displaying some rather unusual flowers. According to his field guide, this was a Haines orange mangrove (*Bruguiera hainesii*), a species researchers were aware grew in Singapore, the Malay Peninsula and Papua New Guinea – but until now, not in Australia. This was the largest individual specimen, but it was surrounded by several smaller ones.

The finding was extraordinary. This was an area routinely walked and surveyed, and yet somehow, almost fifty Haines mangroves, one-fifth of the world's known population, had gone unnoticed.

The findings show how much we still have to learn about mangroves, these forgotten forests we have ripped from our coastline. I had imagined the mangroves near Karumba, these legendary fortresses, to be immutable, and so it was shocking to watch Norm Duke's footage and see these trees expunged in vast numbers, their white, ashen branches mockingly erect like the white crosses of Ypres and Normandy. If Burke and Wills could view the footage now, if they could hear the screams of these mangroves, their sympathy would be monumental. 'For water such as you would not even taste,' remarked Wills in a letter to his sister after the explorers had been travelling for sixteen weeks, 'one smacks [one's] lips as if it were a glass of sherry or champagne.'

Survivors

There is a tree that exists quietly on the corner of Tanswell Street and Dowling Court in the Victorian goldrush town of Beechworth. It is a but-but (*Eucalyptus bridgesiana*), a gargantuan tree, so consumed by galls and wounds it resembles the scraggy, tumescent trees depicted in fairytales. The setting could not be more bizarre. In a residential street more accustomed to the delicate trunks of Callery pears (*Pyrus calleryana*), the tree is an outlier, a swollen anomaly. One might summon the poem 'Municipal Gum' by Oodgeroo Noonuccal:

> *Gumtree in the city street*
> *Hard bitumen around your feet*
> *…*
> *Here you seems to me*
> *Like that poor cart-horse*
> *Castrated, broken, a thing wronged*
> *Strapped and buckled, its hell prolonged.*

The tree has lived for around 300 years and, while it is only 23 metres in height, the width it has grown to is obscene. Few people know of its existence; unless you live down these streets, there is no particular reason to be passing.

Almost 1500 kilometres further north, growing along the edge of the Brisbane Botanic Gardens, is a forest red gum (*Eucalyptus tereticornis*), referred to up here as a Queensland blue gum, a relic from a time when the streets of Brisbane were clothed in rainforest rather than clogged with people in board shorts and thongs. I first observed it while taking the ferry along the Brisbane River, disembarking at the Eagle Street terminal and walking towards the Edward Street entrance of the gardens. Every time I visit Brisbane, I call by the tree to see how it is faring. Around 250 years ago, this Queensland blue gum was beginning its life on the banks of the river, leaning away from the rainforest canopy to grab whatever light it could attain. Now it seems out of place among the power walkers and yachts.

The but-but and the blue gum are survivor trees. Fading palimpsests from a soon-to-be-forgotten world. Stoically, they live on in almost every Australian city, often concealed or so cushioned within their suburban setting that they cease to be truly noticed. Not far from the centre of Perth, presiding over a shopping centre car park in Armadale, is a jarrah (*Eucalyptus marginata*) that may be as old as 700 years, its flexed, muscular branches reminiscent of the 1000-year-old oaks of English meadows. It has survived the threat of removal and, so far at least, a ringbarking attack with a meat cleaver, the pernicious act committed not long after its preservation was guaranteed by the local council.[13] And amid the hilly streets of Glebe, where exotic crepe myrtles (*Lagerstroemia indica*) mix with jacarandas (*Jacaranda mimosifolia*), there is a reminder of the forgotten Sydney landscape: a grey ironbark (*Eucalyptus paniculata*) hiding along the fence line of a Victorian church, the pathways of the church's garden decorated with pretty Chinese windmill palms (*Trachycarpus fortunei*). For a tree that is around 170 years old, it is disappointingly slight. It is only 16 metres tall. The reddish brown of the trunk, set against the luscious green of the foliage, is not dissimilar to the two-tone contrast of the messmate (*Eucalyptus obliqua*), common to the forests of Tasmania and southeastern Australia. The tree is a part of the turpentine-ironbark family, which dominated the drier, shale-capped ridges around Sydney, a sole survivor of a community that stretched from Glebe to Auburn in the south, Ryde to Glenorie in the north. The second-hand bookshop opposite contains many detailed books on the Aboriginal and European history of this country, and yet none of those words, no matter the elegance of their description or the strength of their facts, can inspire one's imagination with the same intensity as this lone vestigial tree.

My obsession with these survivors began in Adelaide. I was with a friend, staying in a modest hotel at the western end of Hindley Street. I had been single for three months, existentially lost as one is after the breakdown of a twelve-year relationship. Marian, the person who shared with me those first impressions of Australia, our affections back then interwoven with the same unending threads of curiosity, was no longer a part of my life. Waking up most mornings with a hangover, I would force myself to venture outdoors, finding in nature a diurnal panacea. Someone gave me a reference book on Australia's vegetation and a field guide for birds. I bought some binoculars and began exploring, often getting in the car with only a vague idea as to where I would drive. Our main reason for visiting Adelaide was to go to a gig and enjoy the night-time vitality of the Fringe festival, but one morning, perhaps three days into the trip, we decided to explore the surrounds. We must have read about the historic Glenelg tree in a brochure, but as we made our way there on the tram, we had no idea what to expect. While we weren't imagining bushland, we were surprised to find the tree nestled in the corner of a children's playground. The state of South Australia was allegedly declared by the side of this tree a few days after Christmas in 1836. When it was young, the tree blew over in a storm, causing its crest to fuse with the ground and form an arch around 5 metres tall. And while the tree, thought to be a river red gum (*Eucalyptus camaldulensis*), died in 1907, its ossified trunk has remained as a memorial to European settlement.

When I returned to Adelaide several years later, I tracked down a pair of remnant South Australian blue gums (*Eucalyptus leucoxylon*) in Statenborough Street, Erindale, both wearing their age with a quiet dignity, the most southerly a paragon of sufferance Hans Heysen would enjoy painting. A few kilometres further north, a mallee box (*Eucalyptus porosa*), remnant of the once arid landscape, can be seen from Jeffcott Road as it guards the twelfth hole of North Adelaide Golf Course. It is an outsider now, among the sugar gums and casuarinas. Stare at the tree for long enough and, as difficult as the transition is, you may be able to picture the streets of North Adelaide and Prospect covered in mallee scrub, with bilbies and bettongs running between cypress-pines (*Callitris preissii*) and desert senna (*Senna artemisioides*). To recreate a similar experience today, one must drive a couple of hours north to the wildlife sanctuary at Yookamurra.

I now had an obsession: the pursuit of ancient trees. In those initial few months after the break-up, as a means to get through, I planned trips to view these survivor trees, often with the knowledge they were unlikely to eventuate. Exercising the imagination was a reliable substitute for booking holidays I could not afford, and I found myself travelling, metaphysically at least, along the Strzelecki

Track to Coopers Creek and the Great Northern Highway up to Derby and Broome. In between, I made genuine trips to places such as Townsville and Mackay, Adelaide and Warrnambool, and in December of that year, I went on a camping trip to Canberra, stopping along the way at Cootamundra and Rutherglen, the Chiltern forest and the Strathbogie Ranges. The trip was partly inspired by the Ned Kelly tree, a mountain white gum (*Eucalyptus dalrympleana*) hidden down a trucking road within the Toombullup State Forest, and the Major Mitchell tree, a river red gum located beneath a bridge on the road into Wangaratta. But it was also born from a wish to explore Canberra, a place I had passed through with Marian and craved to revisit ever since. I arrived there on Christmas Eve, stopping by the war memorial and national gallery before settling into my motel for a decent night's sleep.

The following morning, I got in the car and drove to the suburb of Ainslie, in search of the Corroboree Park yellow box (*Eucalyptus melliodora*), a tree that is around three times the age of the city. It was the first time I had spent Christmas on my own. The city was deserted. For an hour or so, I sat in the presence of this tree, trying, without success, to experience something akin to the 'overview effect' – a state of awe inspired by the appreciation of beauty, as the astronauts viewing Earth from space for the first time were said to experience. Cognitive shifts of this magnitude are not straightforward, and, perhaps unsurprisingly, whatever revelatory thoughts I was trying to induce did not lend themselves easily to this moment. I was unaware at the time of the site's history, and I had no real affinity to the land. It was naive of me to think I could appreciate the tree's centuries-long life in the same way the astronauts could appreciate time from the perspective of space.

The tree is not particularly attractive, emerging from the ground in three disparate trunks. The base of one of these trunks has eroded over time to reveal a tortured face, the mouth stretched in fear as if conscious of its own mortality. Yet it has weathered and withstood the trials of time. It is a haggard survivor of the yellow box and red gum (*Eucalyptus blakelyi*) woodland that once crisscrossed large stretches of Canberra before the landscape was ambushed by asphalt and bricks. For thousands of years, this area was an important meeting place for the Ngunnawal, and there is an account, from a girl in the 1880s, of the tree's crown sheltering an Elder as he addressed his spellbound audience. Today, Corroboree Park is a place where people play tennis and walk their dogs, a green sanctuary within a residential setting, but on this particular morning, when everyone was inside waking up to Christmas stockings and presents, it was remarkably serene. Yellow boxes and red gums still grow together in large patches around the city, most notably Red Hill and Bruce. That afternoon, I drove around the suburbs looking for survivors, the largest of which was a monstrous, multi-trunked Blakely's red gum standing on the corner of Lycos Street and Kinloch Circuit.

I do not think it tenuous to say there are similarities between the way trees act as narrative signposts within Aboriginal songlines and the way trees can, on an individual level at least, conjure up memories and emotions from the past. Songlines are information pathways that interlace the continent, maelstroms of knowledge that encompass arts, philosophy and science, customs, law and the natural world. As one walks, one sings – the melody stimulating one's memory – and natural landmarks such as trees can function as a visual heuristic, a trigger point for stories that explore a multiplicity of subjects and lessons for life. 'Just as we see stars when we gaze at the night sky,' explains Marcia Langton, 'Aboriginal people perceive the spiritual presence of Elders in the landscape as what has emanated through time since the ancestor died.' In a similar if less culturally resonant way, a familiar tree can, through the power of its suggestion, reawaken a past mindset for an individual, rekindling the values held at the time, the thoughts offered on a range of subjects, the music heard, the friendships pursued. Trees can act as madeleines that add layers to an individual's narrative, rekindling ideas that one may have forgotten were it not for nature's gentle reminder, allowing one to interpret the past anew.

The Heide tree, a large river red gum close to the art gallery's main entrance in Victoria's Bulleen, has shown me this suggestive power. It is a wonderfully solid individual, standing on a promontory not far from the crumbling milk shed that stored Sidney Nolan's Ned Kelly series after he absconded from Melbourne. It is said to mark the convergence of five different songlines, and a visible scar shows where a strip of bark was removed, most likely with an axe, in order to fashion a small canoe. During those first few months after my break-up, I visited the gallery many times, always passing by the tree and standing calmly before it, like a parishioner before a shrine. To walk past it now is to reacquaint myself with that time, when my thoughts were an amorphous mess of affirmations and half-ideas.

§

The friend who accompanied me on our excursion to the old Glenelg tree called me up one morning almost a decade later and said he had something to show me. It was during the middle of Victoria's first major lockdown, when people were confined to their homes and only one hour of exercise was allowed each day. Restricted to a 5-kilometre radius, our walks usually took us to Albert Park Lake, where we observed the progress of young ducklings and cygnets, or to St Kilda Pier around dusk, where we saw penguins washing ashore or hundreds of little black cormorants flying overhead. But on this occasion, we met at the Fraser Street tram stop, and by the time we started walking, I had guessed we were headed to the Ngargee tree. I had jogged there several times over the preceding months, often stopping for a few minutes to enjoy the serenity of its presence.

When we got there, we walked up to its trunk and felt the coarseness of the bark. We imagined the structures of modernity fading slowly before us, time playing out in reverse, open woodland recolonising the brash apartment blocks, the smoke from campfires replacing the grey fog of the exhausts. It may be the ruffled manner of the tree, the way, when one looks superficially at least, the trunk appears dead, the leaves draped across the branches as if great clumps have washed there in a flood. Or it may be the obvious signs of its age. Whatever the reason, the tree suggests the wisdom of a dying sage. Messages shoot frantically across the hyphae of its roots and water ascends briskly through its xylem, yet it exhibits a semblance of calm, an effortlessness that is illusory, reminding me of the metaphor of the placid duck pedalling furiously underwater. My friend said, 'Can you believe how much this tree must have seen?'

I had thought the same thing many years before, while walking through Hickson Road Reserve, looking across to the ferries of Circular Quay, the Opera House appearing quaint in the distance. Just to the right of the sails, standing on a rise heralding the start of the botanic gardens, were what appeared to be two trees growing in close proximity. Survivor trees. The Bennelong twins. The trunks of these trees, smooth and polished, rose like marble columns, their dignified branches curling upwards as if they were the capitals of Corinthian columns. Growing in relative isolation, standing out against the sky, they seemed to me as bouffant candelabras, graceful and calligraphic, pre-Raphaelite in their beauty. Gum trees can be shaggy and unkempt, but the Bennelong twins could be type specimens for the elegance of the eucalypt. Pouring down the trunks of these forest reds is a grey-silver sheen. There is not a branch or a leaf that lets down their considered appearance. Their presentation is immaculate.

According to science writer Bob Beale, they are the country's 'most important historic trees', the only living witnesses to the landing of the First Fleet. Over a period of 300 years, they have watched a peaceful cove, notable for its 'campfires and flimsy canoes', transform into a city 'utterly engulfed by a towering world of concrete, glass and steel, the two sides of the harbour bridged by steel'. These trees are forest red gums. The Dharug call them burringora or yarro. According to Beale, they germinated in the early 1700s.[14] Few people notice these trees growing on the crest of Tarpeian Lawn, for their eyes are instead directed towards the sails of the Opera House. In a parallel history, the rock on which they stand would have been quarried. In another, their trunks would have been hacked down in the Depression years by drifters sleeping rough in the Domain gardens. Their survival is a miracle.

Most trees throw me back to a particular moment in my life, but some, like the Bennelong twins, recount a progression of events. I was a single man, recently unmoored, when I first observed them – a heavy mind walking through the sharp glow of a strange city. By the time I revisited Sydney, ascending the steps to Tarpeian Lawn, I was cradling the hand of a new love. And when I observed them for the third time, some years later, as my parents, visiting from England, soaked up the radiance of the Opera House, I carried in my pocket the half-written vows for our wedding. The Bennelong twins have come to symbolise to me the strength of love: two companions who have not wavered in their intimacy or surrendered to the slow deterioration of time.

It is not a modern indulgence to ascribe symbolism to the shapes and folds of trees. For thousands of years, ancient peoples have noticed messages in the curvature of branches, spirits in the galls of damaged trunks. The first time I showed the Bennelong trees to my new lover, we stood beneath their crown and looked out towards the harbour, the water soundless and calm. Tourists flittered about beneath us, but not one person looked up to these ancient survivors. The Bennelong twins are a reminder that elegance can be found not just in human architecture but in nature as well. They bear the scars of quiet endurance. Somehow, in one of the most populous sections of Australia, they have gone unnoticed by our collective gaze.

When the Wattle Starts to Bloom

It is disconcerting when you discover that you have an emotional connection to Napoleon. At least for a few seconds, the two of us shared the same involuntary discomfort. Soft, seductive acacias have reawakened in us memories of a past love.

For me, the experience began in the Victorian town of Daylesford. Marian and I were helping out on a small property for a few weeks, tending to a vegetable patch and pumping water into a primitive dam. Bushfires were passing through Bullarto, a short distance away, and one of our jobs was to spray the grass around the dwelling. The hose would hang limply as the water fountained out, evaporating as it fell. There were very few trees growing nearby – I recall a few cherry plums and some hawthorn, a hedgerow of cypress and the occasional eucalypt. There was also a small grove of fruit trees beside the vegetable patch, covered in netting to protect the fruit (rather ineffectually it turned out) from the onslaught of lorikeets and rosellas, currawongs and cockatoos. Among these trees, there was one that stood out. Its feathery leaves were so diaphanous they almost became invisible in the glistening light. It was the only tree that didn't bear fruit. An ornamental addition, unfurling from the ground in such a meek and delicate way. The leaves were a glaucous grey, a colour so rare in actual trees and yet so common in the ground-hugging plants of the coast.

'What tree is this?' I asked the owner.

'A wattle,' he said. 'Some kind of wattle. Don't ask me for the name.'

The tree was enchanting. From a distance, the leaves appeared thick and bushy, receding into an almost formless blur. But up close, they revealed themselves. Soft, bipinnate feathers as if exquisitely incised by an artisan.

After Daylesford, our next long-term home was Mackay. Although neither of us ever said it out loud, at least not at the time, our relationship was already beginning to unravel. While it is possible Marian had some foreknowledge of what was to come, I remained blithely unaware.

For those last few weeks we lived in Mackay, Marian spent most of her time travelling to Melbourne, where she had secured a promising, well-paying job. I drove our belongings down to Melbourne in our trusted sedan. The night I arrived, I wandered down to the Yarra River and sat on a bench, looking out towards Alexandra Gardens. It must have rained because I remember the aroma of lemon-scented gums, the restorative smell of those citrusy leaves. A feeling came over me. It was not quite a shudder I experienced – more an incursion of weight. Suddenly I knew we were going to break up. Like a tree dying from within, our fate was sealed; we just hadn't seen it.

In the end, it was a quick termination, twelve years of devotion disentangled in a fortnight. I moved out of the flat and, overnight, we went from confidants to acquaintances who barely spoke, two people leading disparate lives.

It was on a bus ride with some friends heading out towards one of the race events in Kyneton, several weeks after we had broken up, that I was reminded of her. The bus stopped outside a front garden in Daylesford, and there, growing beside a Hakea and a Callery pear, was the same species of tree we had seen in that orchard. Immediately I was reacquainted with the emotions of that time, subsumed by those same transient thoughts. The tree was a madeleine. I once again became that former self.

It would take me several months before I discovered the name of this feathery apparition, its ghostlike visage acting as a gateway to another time. When I visited libraries as part of my studies, instead of concentrating on whatever conundrum of urban planning demanded my time, I would find myself riffling through the reference books on Victorian flora, hoping to recognise in one of the pictures the distinctive form of this tree. Without knowing the tree's name, I feared its memory might warp over time, its silver-grey foliage morphing into larger, greener leaves, its cloudy, precious appearance maturing into a deep, formless blur. But the tree was not Victorian at all. Eventually, I discovered it again while passing through Cootamundra in New South Wales. The trees were growing at a stop-off called Migurra Reserve, a dusty walking track off the side of the highway. I can't recall whether I saw the name on a sign near one of the trees or in a brochure, but I finally had the answer I had been searching for: *Acacia baileyana*, the Cootamundra wattle.

I met Pip around this time, someone who would change my life. We met in a queue, waiting for a soul night, unconsciously plagiarising my parents, who had met at a soul gig almost fifty years earlier. Our first few dates centred on music, drinking and food, but at some point, I invited her to the Melbourne Botanic Gardens, where the titan arum (*Amorphophallus titanum*), famous for its smell, was in flower. It was our first diurnal activity. For Christmas, she bought me a leather-bound notebook that I could use to record my observations in nature. Our first trip was to the Edithvale bird hide, our second to Croajingalong National Park. Eventually we would go overseas, visiting Japan, where a magical, Murakami-like walk would take us to a shop named Uguizu, a small and personable boutique selling textiles and crafts. There, growing outside the frontage, almost dreamlike in their beauty, were four exquisite Cootamundra wattles.

Napoleon's tree was a Sydney golden wattle (*Acacia longifolia ssp. longifolia*), although both he and Joséphine would have referred to it as a mimosa, one of a number of Australian mimosas that she grew in the gardens of Château de Malmaison. It is a more forthright tree than the Cootamundra wattle. The leaves are greener and more angular, but the golden flowers they produce, small lanterns of inflorescence, are just as majestic and divine. When Joséphine gave visitors a personal tour of the grounds at Malmaison, she shared the scientific names of plants she had introduced to Europe. Regular visitors noticed repetition in what she would say, but others were impressed by her knowledge and devotion. For her, this newly acquired pastime was a source of delight. No longer was she the uncultured naïf who was shamed by her first husband, Alexandre. No more was she the provincial who knew nothing of opera, science and manners. Learning to mix with the nouveau riche, she had lost that grating accent. Her voice had softened, developing, as biographer Kate Williams writes, 'a husky, slow tone of voice that became one of her chief attractions'. There were few more flirtatious than Empress Joséphine.

'Malmaison' translates roughly as 'evil house', a rather disparaging title and one hardly befitting for such a grandiose home. For Joséphine and Napoleon, the estate was a sanctuary, a refuge from the exigencies and vicissitudes of life. 'Nowhere, except on the field of battle,' recalls Napoleon's old friend Louis de Bourrienne, 'did I ever see Bonaparte happier than in the gardens of Malmaison.' The estate was once a working farm with vineyards and verdant lawns, but after being seized by the revolutionaries, it had lain neglected and unkempt for years. Under Joséphine's auspices, the estate flourished, the closest post-revolutionary France came to fantasy. There were celebrated artworks in the galleries and a menagerie within the grounds. One's tour might be interrupted by a kangaroo hopping by or dwarf emus grazing alongside a cassowary. Joséphine became obsessed with plants, decorating the grounds with species of camellia, lobelia, dahlia, peony and over 200 varieties of rose. Botanical knowledge was the latest amusement of the enlightened, and, as a result of Banks' collecting on the HMS *Endeavour*, Australia was the country du jour for those interested in exotic flora and fauna. It is said Malmaison hosted most of the eucalypts known at that time. Prickly tea-tree (*Leptospermum juniperinum*) grew alongside swamp paperbark (*Melaleuca ericifolia*). Wattles bloomed lemon yellow. There was the green wattle (*Acacia decurrens*) and the prickly moses (*Acacia verticillata*). There were even species that were rare in their natural habitat. The awl-leaf wattle (*Acacia subulata*), which grew along the dividing range between Lithgow and the Pilliga, was named after a type specimen in Malmaison. The downy wattle (*Acacia pubescens*), one of the first acacias to be cultivated in Europe, had been almost obliterated from its natural range as the Europeans moved west of Sydney. But perhaps the most lustrous was the Sydney golden wattle, its leaves golden green and its flowers shining like bright, ornamental lanterns.

In the many paintings of Empress Joséphine, her smile is coy and elusive. Draped over her shoulder might be a muslin or cashmere shawl, one of about 500 in her wardrobe. When she laughed she covered her mouth with her hand, a coquettish and coy affectation, but one that served to hide the carious state of her teeth, the drawback from eating too much sugar on her parents' cane plantation in Martinique. Joséphine's affection for the rude, fidgety general was as mysterious as Napoleon's idolatry for her was overt. But amid the arguments and tears, there were moments of mutual affection. While Napoleon was vanquishing Rome, he would write capricious letters to his wife. 'I don't love you an atom,' he would declare in the morning, hurt by her refusal to reply, but by the afternoon his mood would be changed. 'I hope soon, darling, to be in your arms. I love you to distraction.' He feared she was having an affair, and he had every right to be suspicious. Her nights were spent in the company of Hippolyte Charles, a lieutenant with dashing good looks. Napoleon would respond to the affair by punishing his wife, taking mistresses and revealing, in lurid detail, the intimacy of their sexual activities. But they stayed together due to mutual need. Napoleon was not comfortable around other people, and he was only too aware how his wife dazzled in social company. She had a knack for making people feel at ease, as engaging as Napoleon was boorish.

Yet as each year passed, Joséphine's allure was waning. There was one thing Napoleon craved more than both sexual and military conquest: a male heir.

Napoleon and Joséphine divorced in 1809. 'To you, to you alone, I owe the only moments of happiness I have tasted in this world. But, Joséphine, my destiny is not to be controlled by my will,' he explained. 'My dearest affections must yield to the interests of France.'

Unable to provide her husband with a male heir, Joséphine accepted her fate. The night of their divorce ceremony, they both wept as she slipped into his bedroom and embraced him. She devoted the remaining years of her life to her two passions, art and botany, enjoying a retiree's life at Malmaison. By 1814, her health had deteriorated. The medical cause was most likely pneumonia or diphtheria. Her maid suspected it was grief.

The following year, Napoleon was exiled to an island more than 1000 miles from the coast of Africa. When he observed St Helena for the first time, his heart sank. 'I should have done better to have stayed in Egypt,' he remarked as the blackened, baleful rock rose into view. Volcanic activity had formed this vertiginous landmass over seven million years ago, and time had not softened its appearance.

Most of the island's buildings were located in Jamestown – a strange assortment of villas and cattle sheds nestled together at the cleft of a valley, as if the dwellings had rolled there in an avalanche. While his permanent lodgings were being prepared, Napoleon stayed out of town at the Briars with William and Jane Balcombe. He would get on well with one of their daughters, Betsy, a fiery and somewhat impudent thirteen-year-old. She had expected to meet an ogre, a giant with 'one large flaming red eye in the middle of his forehead, and long teeth protruding from his mouth, with which he tore to pieces and devoured naughty little girls'. Instead, she encountered a man who relaxed in her company, no longer fortified by the seemingly erratic defences of arrogance and anxiety. Not that he was oblivious to his fearsome reputation. When Betsy pointed out a young girl who was scared of him, he approached the girl from behind, touched her hair and pulled hideous faces, howling like a savage dog as the girl screamed.

Napoleon, in his letters, makes no secret of his lassitude on St Helena. He would lay maps across the floor and recalibrate lost battles with red and black pins. He would stare at the clouds as they passed over the mountains, wondering why life had led him to this hopeless impasse. Tedium was a natural precursor to reflection and he thought often of Joséphine, the most elegant, affable and charming woman he had ever met. 'I truly loved her,' he would recall while on St Helena, 'although I didn't respect her. She was a liar and a spendthrift but she had something that was irresistible. She was a woman to her very fingertips.'

After a couple of months, Napoleon moved out of the Briars and settled at Longwood, where he stayed until his death. He passed the time gardening, dressing in a hunting waistcoat and a broad-brimmed straw hat. The elaborate sunken pathways he designed concealed him from the English sentries. The flower beds, planted with roses and strawberries, were neatly arranged in direct contrast to the Rousseauian wildness of Malmaison. Among the pear trees and willows were bedded two Australian plants: the golden everlasting (*Xerochrysum bracteatum*) and the Sydney golden wattle. According to art historian Eleanor P. DeLorme, Napoleon introduced the Sydney golden wattle to St Helena to remind him of Joséphine and the grounds of Malmaison. Journalist Terry Smyth even suggests Napoleon 'brought golden wattle with him from Empress Joséphine's garden', as if he quickly harvested some seeds while the Prussians and British drew closer in their pursuit. But in fact the Sydney golden wattle, known to locals as the Botany Bay or Port Jackson willow, had been growing on St Helena for decades. In his *Tracts Relative to the Island of St. Helena* (1816), Governor Beatson refers to Botany Bay willows growing in the governor's residence from January 1810. The species' arrival may even have been earlier, for there is a nameless mimosa species growing in the St Helena botanic gardens in 1789, according to an early inventory of the site. Beatson writes, 'There are no trees that succeed so well on this island as the pineaster[15] and a mimosa, which is usually called the Botany Bay willow. They grow on the poorest lands, withstand the southeast wind, and thrive in the most exposed situations.' There is even a William Burchell water-colour from 1807, stored in the archives of Kew Gardens, that shows a tree growing by Longwood House with the annotation in pencil: 'mimosa longifolia or botany bay willow'. It is possible Lady Holland, an admirer from England, introduced the golden everlasting to St Helena when she sent Napoleon seedlings of the daisy-like plant with its heliotropic flowers. But while this may be true, she cannot be held responsible for Napoleon's acquaintance with the Sydney golden wattle. Walking one day on the island, he would have noticed those delicate yellow flowers and allowed himself to imagine the halcyon days of Malmaison. In that short, passing moment, he likely felt the same wistful sadness as I did when I viewed, from the elevated perch of the bus, the Cootamundra wattle growing in a Daylesford garden.

The Balcombes left St Helena for England when the poor health of Betsy's mother became a concern. Saying goodbye to his precocious friend, Napoleon took out his handkerchief and wiped the tears from Betsy's face, telling her to keep the mouchoir as a symbol of their friendship. 'Look at those dreadful mountains,' he said, 'they are my prison walls. You will soon hear that the Emperor Napoleon is dead.' It was true. Napoleon's health declined over the next three years as he suffered from severe catarrh and swelling of the gums. He would die on a camp bed in the salon of Longwood House, his vest stained with bloodied spit and his words almost nonsensical.

Visit the island today and one will see the hills around the Briars illuminated by the lush Lincoln green of the Sydney golden wattle, the ground dusted with the impish wisp of the golden everlasting. They have dispersed like weeds, unusual bursts of gold among the endemic gumwoods (*Commidendrum robustum*, *Commidendrum rotundifolium*) and tree ferns (*Dicksonia arborescens*), and the plains besmirched by lantana (*Lantana camara*) and prickly pear (*Opuntia spp.*).

Three hundred years ago, perhaps a few thousand people would have been familiar with the tree, all of them untitled experts in botany who could have told you when the flowers bloomed and what this meant for seasonal hunting. They ate the seeds and scrunched up the leaves, lathering them in water to make a soap. They made spears, boomerangs and axe handles from the wood, and it is possible they traded these artefacts with other groups along the coast. In less than three decades from the year the First Fleet arrived in Sydney, this tree was noticed by the world's most famous general on one of the world's most remote islands on the other side of the world, familiar to him from his wife's garden in France. As a means to describe an age of tumult and exploration, imperialism and enlightenment, there may be few more emblematic symbols.

Interestingly, there is a footnote to this story. While Betsy lived a restless life, travelling between Sydney and England, her youngest brother, Alexander, purchased land near today's township of Mount Martha in Victoria, a property called Checkingurk, which he would rename The Briars. He tried his hand at viticulture, ran sheep and constructed a number of buildings, including the homestead, which today attracts thousands of visitors. The creek, which runs from the property for about 2 kilometres to Port Phillip Bay, became known as Balcombe Creek. If Alexander walked to its confluence, as he almost certainly did, he would have seen growing among the rhagodia (*Rhagodia candolleana*) and the native spinach (*Tetragonia implexicoma*) a small tree called the coastal wattle (*Acacia longifolia ssp. sophorae*), a regional subspecies of the same tree Napoleon planted on St Helena. The tree is different only in the thicker, stockier phyllodes and the seed pods, which twist in messy spirals. Along the sand dunes of the peninsula coast Alexander could indulge in his own madeleine moment, a return to his time on St Helena.

§

The Cootamundra and Sydney golden wattles both embody the fleetingness of beauty. As the flowers of the Cootamundra fade, they turn from a rich lemon to a grimy yellow, one that is tainted with cinnamon-like hues. And the Sydney golden wattle, when not in flower, can be an impersonal tree, its leaves offering no expression. These wattles, like the silver (*Acacia dealbata*) and black wattles (*Acacia mearnsii*) common to the southeastern coast, are pioneer species, opportunists, quick-growing acacias that live fast and die young. They seek out any opportunity to sucker and spread across disturbed land, particularly areas that have been ravaged by fire. The seeds can lay dormant for up to forty years, protected by a hard, impervious coating called a testa. Exuding from each testa is the aril, a fleshy expansion of the seed, which is different for every species. For the one-eyed wattle (*Acacia cyclops*), the aril is an orange colour and it wraps around the entire testa like a twisted churro. For black wattles, the aril is white, scrunched and not dissimilar to a judicial wig. As the alkaline ash of a fire coats the soil, fertilising the ground, and the first rains come through, softening the testa, the seeds are able to germinate. Cleared areas of land become dishevelled swathes of wattle overnight.

WHAT THE TREES SEE

The first tree to grow after the devastation of Hiroshima was a silver wattle, sprouting through the cracks of the pavement a couple of months after the blast, at a time when people feared nothing would grow for many years. As the city regained consciousness amid the stench of dead bodies in the rivers, the fog of cremation in the air, it seemed as if life would never again bless this ruined landscape. More than 90 per cent of buildings were gutted or reduced to rubble. Utility poles leaned crooked in the streets. A number of trees survived the bombing, trees known in posterity as *hibakujumoku*, but new life recoiled from this strange, Cimmerian world. The Japanese surrendered nine days after the bombing and still nothing grew. A typhoon ripped through the city over one month later, washing some of the residual radiation into the sea, but there was still no sign of emergent life. And then, around two months since the dropping of the bomb, the bipinnate leaves of a silver wattle appeared through the cracks of the pavement. Other plants began to grow, and weeds such as the sicklepod (*Senna obtusifolia*) flourished. But the silver wattle, the first sign of resurrection in a time of despair, has been celebrated in Hiroshima ever since. Every year for the last three decades, the Hiroshima Acacia Appreciation Society has sent 1000 yellow ribbons to the Australian National Botanic Gardens. With each ribbon is the message: When the wattle starts to bloom, make a wish and your wish will come true.

While the tree's sense of survival may seem miraculous in the right context, it is a tenacity that, for many regions, has come at a cost. The trees have thrived in areas with Mediterranean climates, countries such as Spain and Portugal, South Africa, Chile and Argentina. In South Africa, black wattles and silver wattles, which have been planted for their tannins and timber since the mid-nineteenth century, ran wild across the Natal and ambushed the foothills of the Drakensberg. Blackwoods (*Acacia melanoxylon*), brought in for their timber, also spread fast, suckering opportunistically across areas of disturbed land and taking over the edges and rivers around the Knysna forest. The Sydney golden wattle, introduced to the Cape Province as far back as 1827, was valued for the way it stabilised sand dunes along the coast, but it soon spread to the surrounding heathland, as did the orange wattle (*Acacia saligna*). Buoyed by the jingoism of the apartheid era, people called the trees 'aliens' and 'green cancers', decrying them for their impurity and their threat to native vegetation. Experiments of biological control were used on some species, notably the gall wasp (*Trichilogaster acaciaelongifoliae*) and the seed-eating Melanterius beetle (*Melanterius ventralis*).

On 8 September 1908, Archibald James Campbell made a historic speech to members of the Photographic Club of Melbourne Technical College, addressing the crowd by saying: 'We stand on the threshold of another Australian spring – a particular time when the whole land is in beauty, arrayed with wattles all abloom in the most exquisite tints and tones of yellow, and therefrom is ascending like a continual oblation, an invisible cloud, the soft, sweet perfume of pure wattle incense.'

Campbell's agenda was for Australia to embrace a new national emblem, the golden wattle (*Acacia pycnantha*), and for the beauty of the genus to be celebrated on 1 September every year. 'What shall we say of the most excellent beauty of wattle flowers?' he said, proceeding with Woolfian verbosity. 'Curves and circles in art and nature are synonymous with grace and continuity of form; and what of their matchless yellow, before which the colour of the pure Gold of Ophir pales!' For Campbell, there was something joyfully effeminate about wattle bloom, as glorious a symbol of femininity as the laurel was a symbol of victory for the ancient Greeks or the olive a symbol of peace. '"Yellow-haired September", with her plaits of gold,' he continued, 'is suggestive of the female gender … the beau ideal.' And no species celebrated 'yellow-haired September' more than the coastal wattle, with its plenitude of 'rich lemon-yellow flowers'.

As he spoke, his words were illustrated by photographs projected by a magic lantern, an early precursor to today's modern slide projector. In one photo, a girl in a white dress with an expression not unlike that of a pre-Raphaelite muse looks down at the lavish yellow flowers of the Cootamundra wattle (*Acacia baileyana*). The photo could be a painting by Edward Burne-Jones or John Everett Millais. She looks pensive, lost in her thoughts. The flowers almost engulf her. The photo of the coastal wattle is equally as camp. The model appears Joséphine-esque in her sense of mystery but, as the shoot has elapsed, her shoulders have slumped and her inscrutable expression has given way to one of boredom.

The day after presenting to the photographic club, Campbell attended a meeting of the Royal Horticultural Society of Victoria and gave the same euphuistic speech, this time with the Governor of Victoria, Sir Thomas Carmichael, in attendance. The campaigning carried momentum. On 1 September 1910, Sydney, Melbourne and Adelaide celebrated their first Wattle Day. Two years later, the flowers and leaves of *Acacia pycnantha* formed a backdrop to the official coat of arms. 'It expresses all moods …' said one early champion. 'The happy may rejoice in its effulgent splendour and the bereaved find solace in its tender grace.'

Like the models in Campbell's artfully staged photos, one can get engrossed by the beau ideal and the yellow-haired allure. But while the wattle is indeed a beautiful tree, the radiant flowers and tassel-like leaves of showstoppers such as the Cootamundra wattle do not tell the whole story. Were you to walk every inch of the continent, the acacias you are most likely to see forgo prettiness for the sake of practicality. If eucalypts are coastal, wrote naturalist George Seddon, then acacias are the trees of the inland. Perhaps this disjunction, the disparity between the carefree coastal wattles and the hardened acacias of the bush, may be a more appropriate national symbol than the pretty but otherwise unexceptional golden wattle. Acacias dominate the arid centre. Regions are named after these trees; the trees themselves are named after Indigenous words, like the myall (*Acacia pendula*) of New South Wales, the gidgee (*Acacia cambagei*) of the centre and the brigalow (*Acacia harpophylla*) of central Queensland. They are the trees of the bush, conveying 'a picture of illimitable distances, of far horizons, of dusty cattle and of drovers estimating the distance of one waterhole from another', to use the words of Charles Laseron. It is rare for a single genus to dominate a continent's various deserts, but this is the triumph of the inland acacia.

When I first arrived in Australia, I remember reading in the Rough Guide or Lonely Planet that about 20 per cent of the continent is covered by open woodlands of mulga (*Acacia aneura*). I expected to see it everywhere, looking out for it on hikes and assuming every care-worn tree by the roadside was invariably a mulga. It would take time before I realised that mulga occupies the fifth of the country's land most residents will never see: the red soils of the centre, the Australia of sweltering temperatures and unsealed roads. I have seen mulga growing naturally on two occasions: at the base of Uluru, and on a trip to Karijini in Western Australia. Everything about the tree's appearance is testament to the conditions in which it grows. The mulga may be long-lived for an acacia, growing for over a hundred years in some cases, but it rarely reaches 10 metres in height. It adapts to its surroundings, taking the form of a dense bush on the top of Uluru or a Christmas tree in the Great Victoria Desert. The phyllodes can vary in appearance depending on location, but they are always long and thin, preventing the sun's rays from penetrating too great an area and evaporating the water. They point upwards, as if in supplication to the clouds, an adaptation that allows the tree to capture rain as it falls, like an inflowing champagne tower or an inverted umbrella channelling water to its roots. During times of drought, the phyllodes stop growing. Kill the tree and the surrounding vegetation suffers as the mulga, like other acacias, hosts symbiotic bacteria (*Rhizobium spp.*) in its roots. These bacteria absorb and process atmospheric nitrogen, releasing it into the soil and fertilising the surrounding land. Mulga is thought to be the greatest fodder tree in Australia, and researcher Roger Oxley writes of gangs of men getting together during times of drought to harvest mulga branches to keep their sheep from starving. But it has also given the traditional inhabitants food, medicine and the means to make weapons. The wood has been used to carve spearthrowers, spearheads, boomerangs and shields. The white resin, which appears as powder on the phyllodes and branches, can be scraped off and used as glue. Headaches can be cured by heating the young phyllodes over hot ashes before placing them on the head; colds can be treated by boiling the oil-rich leaves in hot water and drinking the brew. The seeds are often eaten as a paste, and the red, gelatinous exudate, released by wounding the trunk, can be sucked from the tree or dissolved in water overnight.

The acacias of the inland have generally fared well over the past 200 years, but where they've overlapped with farmland, their numbers have diminished. Farms need fences, and the upright trunks of trees like the mulga and yarran (*Acacia melvillei*) make excellent fence posts. The jam wattle (*Acacia acuminata*) in the western Australian wheat belt, so named because the bark releases a smell of raspberry jam when wounded, has been relentlessly removed for fencing. When forester Roger Underwood tried to calculate the extent of this clearing, he guessed about 25,000 trees were cleared for each farm, several million for the area. Gidgee and brigalow have also been hacked, stripped and used for fencing. Brigalow was once such a common tree, Charles Laseron said it was 'as well known in the north as the mallee in the south'. Ludwig Leichhardt, in his journal of the Port Essington expedition, describes the tree a number of times, suggesting the brigalow gives a 'peculiar character to the forest'. Where Leichhardt observed it growing north of Roche Creek in November 1844 and in the Arcadia Valley, south of the Expedition Range, these heretofore thickets of scrub are now a patchwork of open fields.

Only 10 per cent of Queensland's brigalow belt remains, and most of those 800,000 hectares are isolated patches, strips of roadside vegetation, areas of regrowth or patches of occasional trees, victims of the fertile clay soils on which they grow. But despite these grim exceptions, the inland acacia scrublands are, by virtue of their isolation, some of the areas least affected by European intrusion. Only around 3 per cent has been cleared, an inversion of the usual narrative where sometimes less than 1 per cent remains. The view of mulga scrub from Central Mount Stuart today would not be unlike the view enjoyed by John McDouall Stuart in 1860 as he looked down upon the same trees which, only the day before, had torn through his party's saddlebags and clothes. Charles Sturt's 'entrance into hell', the ceaseless sand dunes on the edge of the Simpson Desert bordered by dark masses of gidgee, would be, if one were to inhabit Sturt's mindset, as hellish today as it was in 1845. A changing climate may mean longer droughts and harsher fires but, for species such as the mulga, hardened and prepared, the outlook may be more promising than it is for those more temperature-sensitive species on the coast. So, while the aureate display of our coastal wattles gives a symbolic sense of optimism, the true sense of hope, at least for our landscape, rests in the bottlebrush flowers of the mulga. Should you find yourself walking through the gidgee scrublands of the Simpson Desert or viewing a wide-angled photo of Uluru and its surrounds, remind yourself you are viewing a landscape undisturbed by European ideas.

Sidmouth Valley

Lachlan Macquarie visited Sidmouth Valley on two occasions: in 1815 and in 1821. In the six years between these two trips, his fortunes had shifted remarkably. His health had deteriorated, and his wife, Elizabeth, once so assiduous, was now withdrawn, evincing the mental scars of both dysentery and nervous shock. The second trip to Bathurst was one of the last Lachlan would make in New South Wales, and he was doing it without Elizabeth and their son, both of whom stayed behind in Paramatta. It was December. Lachlan had served his last official duty as governor, and an enquiry had begun, led by the lawyer Sir John Bigge, that would eventually denounce many of his policies, labelling his program of infrastructure as wasteful and his rule autocratic.

While the majority of the trip passed quietly, the journey to Fish River was not without event. One of the baggage carts lost control on the hilly terrain and, as recorded in his diary, Lachlan's 'pretty little Table with the Tea and Sugar Cannisters' slipped and shattered into pieces. The following morning, the party arrived at Sidmouth Valley, where breakfast was taken by the creek. As Lachlan sat eating his food, he had a madeleine moment, one he describes with a rare affection in his diary. The tree beneath which he sat was 'the same Tree that stood immediately in front of our Sleeping Tent when my dearest Elizabeth was with me here in May 1815'. It is the only time I have seen the madeleine-like power of trees in the historical record. 'Happiness' is not a word Lachlan uses readily, and yet he deploys it here to describe the felicity of the coincidence.

When I visited Sidmouth Valley in August, it was coated with snow. I parked the car by the bridge that runs over the creek and wandered around for little more than an hour in the cold. I tried to summon an impression of the tree Lachlan described sitting beneath, but it has almost certainly died and we can only speculate what the species could have been. The thin canopies of Blakely's red gums do not provide large amounts of shade. They are similar, in trunk at least, to the forest red gums (*Eucalyptus tereticornis*) that grow around Sydney, and if Lachlan were sitting in its shade, one would imagine him referring to it as a eucalypt rather than simply a tree. Today there are manna gums (*Eucalyptus viminalis*) growing along the side of the road, and, further east, broad-leaved peppermints (*Eucalyptus dives*). The trunk of a large apple box (*Eucalyptus bridgesiana*) has fallen to the ground and new shoots, with spirals of heart-shaped leaves like those in native floral displays, extend from the roughened bark. It is likely all four trees grew in the area in 1815, and any one of them could be the species to which Lachlan referred.

I was alone in the landscape. The only sounds were the soft howling of the wind and the distant mewing of sheep. Were it not for the haggard eucalypts, their leaves whitened by snow, I could have been overlooking the Campbell's Appin residence in the Scottish Highlands or Lochbuie on the Isle of Mull. The effect was disarming. It is strange how anxiety can advance from a natural calm. The feeling of serenity is readily overtaken by unease, as if our natural state is one of sombre vigilance, a sense of apprehension at the magnitude of life. Lachlan described this feeling in a government report that was later published in the *Sydney Gazette*. Remembering the awe with which he first viewed the Bathurst Plains, he writes: 'It is impossible to behold this grand scene without a feeling of admiration and surprise, whilst the silence and solitude … create a degree of melancholy in the mind which may be more easily imagined than described.'

The trees by the roadside evince the melancholia of Lachlan's words. They stand forlorn, ghostly palimpsests of an age when roads could exist without safety barriers and land without fencing. Darkened strips of bark hang from the manna gums, their crowns thin and apologetic. The Blakely's red gums lean with an aloof poise. The apple box recoils. These are the 'ruins grey' of John Sherer's outback. Yet in the same way it is possible, with a little imagination, to reconstruct a castle from a turret or a temple from a frieze, one can redraw from these visuals the landscape of 1815 in all its magnificence and fragility, the Arcadian scene that greeted Lachlan and Elizabeth. 'The most romantic Country I had ever seen,' records Lachlan's chief confidant, Henry Antill, in his diary.

The first trip to Bathurst, on which Antill was present, was an optimistic affair. The seemingly insurmountable barrier of the Blue Mountains had been broken and a land of boundless opportunity stretched to the west. When Governor Macquarie first viewed the grassy plains beyond the mountains, he wryly named them West-More-Land. For the past two years, the settlement at Sydney Cove had feared starvation. Drought had beset the land and caterpillar plagues ravaged the crops. The grain situation had appeared perilous at times. But now, with the promise of almost endless pasture, they could relinquish those fears. It had only taken six months for William Cox and his gang of more than fifty men to build a road. A builder by trade, Cox supervised the thoroughfare that, in historian Geoffrey Blainey's words, was 'the longest and soon the most important road in the continent'. Stretching from Emu Ford to Bathurst, more than 160 kilometres, it was the conduit between a small, struggling colony and the unexplored promise of Australia.

Elizabeth had been delighted by the novelty of Australia. A ledge had been carved into sandstone overlooking Sydney Harbour, and she would sit there for hours, contemplating the passage of time. She had an interest in both horticulture and design. At Airds, the Campbell family home in Scotland, she designed a winding path that guided people to the loch. In Sydney, she would design the eponymous road that takes visitors through the Domain to the carved ledge known as Mrs Macquarie's Chair.[16] Elizabeth's passion and fortitude were a result of a tragic life. After the misfortune of several miscarriages and the death of her daughter, Jane, she would finally experience joy with the birth of a son in 1814. Lachlan, who was fond of bestowing his first and last names on streets and rivers, wasted no opportunity in naming the child after himself. When Governor Macquarie and Elizabeth travelled across the Blue Mountains in 1815, the one-year-old Lachlan stayed behind in the care of a friend.

In addition to cattle, horses, two small boats and several baggage carts, there were seventy people on that trip, including Antill, Surveyor-General John Oxley, and George Evans, the man who, through his expedition across the mountains in 1813, was responsible for the route of Cox's Road. A stately bonhomie suffused the journey. The seventy would divide into smaller groups in the evening, congregating around separate fires to relax and play cards. Despite the stresses of travel and the forced intimacy of the camps, optimism prevailed. 'Not a word of ill humour passed the whole time,' records Antill, 'on the contrary, every one appeared to use his endeavours to make the time pass as pleasantly as possible.' For Elizabeth, it was a chance to admire the natural world; she accompanied the naturalist and illustrator John Lewin as he sketched the surrounding country-side. For Lachlan, the trip represented the symbolic conquest of the land. No more would the settlement be constrained by its geography. 'Rarely has such a low barrier, its highest point little more than 3,000 feet, so defied the efforts of the explorer,' describes Charles Laseron in his book *The Face of Australia* (1953). The secret was to follow the ridges, not the valleys. An almost continuous ridge took one from Emu Ford to Cox's River.

When Lachlan arrived in Sydney in 1809, the settlement was confined to an area bordered by the Hawkesbury River, the Blue Mountains, the Cowpastures and the ocean. Roads were narrow and littered with tree stumps. Houses were makeshift and dishevelled. Sydney, under Lachlan's governorship, would double in population and mature from a ramshackle hovel into a town of ordered streets and great sandstone buildings. But his legacy was more than revitalising a township. It was the promise of travelling west, the liberation of crossing the Great Dividing Range and finding the grass not only greener but seemingly never-ending.

It would take time for European eyes to adjust to the soporific haze of the Blue Mountains. The hills were clothed in a 'sea of harsh trees', said Barron Field, 'thrown together in a monotonous manner'. But, for minds longing for the verdurous meadows of England, the land beyond was immediately agreeable. Lush kangaroo grass (*Themeda triandra*) and wattle mat-rush (*Lomandra filiformis*) covered

153

the granite plains. 'Within a distance of ten miles from the site of Bathurst,' wrote Lachlan, 'there is not less than 50,000 acres of land clear of timber, and fully one half of that may be considered excellent soil, well calculated for cultivation.'

Lachlan was an ambitious, industrious man, gruff and formidable at times, but not without sensitivity. When his first wife, Jane, died from tuberculosis, he wore a black armband for four years. Elizabeth Campbell was the daughter of his second cousin. Lachlan had fallen in love with her after seeing her at her sister's estate in Lochbuie. In manner, she was a Jane Austen character. Her superficial plainness masked a delicate allure. Lachlan's biographer, Malcolm Ellis, describes her face as friendly and dignified, the traces of 'youthful sprightliness and humour' still evident despite her almost thirty years. The courting couple went fishing together, where Elizabeth impressed him with her tenacity and skill. They travelled to Loch Lomond, where she proved, according to Lachlan, to be 'a most excellent traveller, ready to put up with any fare and fatigue'. The letters he sent to his first wife reveal a profound affection seldom present in his letters to Elizabeth, but perhaps that is a reflection more of age than sentiment. Lachlan cherished Elizabeth for the stability she brought to his life. 'Of all women living, I love her the most,' he relates in a letter to Elizabeth's cousin, 'and, in fact I consider myself … as much her husband as if I were ten thousand times married to her.' For Elizabeth, Lachlan's company was a source of peace and reassurance. They got married in 1807 and travelled to Sydney less than two years later. There is a poignant entry in Elizabeth's journal on 13 October 1809, where she reveals the happiness of that voyage from England: 'I have spent my time in the manner which entirely suits my inclination, having the great comfort of my Husbands [sic] company uninterrupted all the morning when we read or write in a social manner, which I shall never enjoy on shore, as when he has it in his power he shuts himself up alone all the morning to business.'

For three and a half weeks in 1815, as they travelled to Bathurst and back, Elizabeth and Lachlan could enjoy each other's company from the moment they woke up. Mrs M, he calls her in his journal. His words may be formal, almost impersonal, but there are intimations of fondness. He notes with an almost paternalistic pleasure the occasions when Mrs M joins them on their explorations to the Bathurst region, and he writes with pride, albeit condescendingly, that Elizabeth, whose health wavers during her time in Australia, was able to bear the fatiguing journey 'wonderfully well indeed'.

When they arrived at Sidmouth Valley, they had been travelling for seven days. The valley, a relatively level patch of land a few kilometres beyond the Fish River crossing, was the first chance for the cattle and horses to rest after the arduous, undulating terrain west of Cox's River. 'I never saw finer grass,' reported Cox as he viewed the valley for the first time. Today, one can follow their route and pass where they would have camped. Close to where the Carlwood Road crosses Sidmouth Valley Creek, there is a rusted purple sign saying '1815 Route of Cox's Road'. Somewhere around there, the tents were set up.

We have a rich impression of the valley's appearance thanks to a John Lewin watercolour, which depicts two emus in front of a quaint scene. There are eucalypts clothing the hilly rise to the north, but the creek itself is treeless. The grass is beautifully maintained, as if someone has recently prepared it with a mower. Two ducks sit calmly on the water. Perhaps one is the duck who, in Antill's words, 'appeared so tame as almost to be taken with the hand'.

This 'beautiful little valley', the phrase Lachlan uses in a letter to Lord Bathurst, had changed somewhat by the time I visited in 2019. The blanket calm has been disturbed by chevroned road signs and post-and-wire fencing. Willows (*Salix spp.*) clogged the creek, and an orderly line of Lombardy poplars (*Populus nigra 'Italica'*) had been planted as a windbreak. The trees in the far distance were still there, but it was hard to tell, without traipsing on private property, whether the species had changed over time. Eucalypts grew in a cluster in the distance, northeast of the sign, but their location was different from that of Lewin's painting. An interesting feature of Lewin's depiction is the orderliness with which the trees form a natural boundary. The eucalypts on the other side of the bank, bar a couple of outliers, appeared to be reined in by an invisible fence line. The transition between the trees and the grass was immediate.

On their final day in Bathurst, Lachlan describes being visited by three Wiradjuri men, 'handsome good looking young men', whom he supplies with gifts: tomahawks, clothes and yellow cloth. They return that afternoon for another amiable exchange, this time accompanied by two other men and nine boys. In less than a decade, martial law would be declared by Sir Thomas Brisbane and around half of the Bathurst clan of the Wiradjuri would be killed, writhing in agony after eating poisoned damper, herded off cliffs or shot with breach-loading rifles. Lachlan was not innocent of the bloodletting. Less than a year after he returned from the Blue Mountains, men, women and children of the Dharawal and Gandangara were marched off the cliff edge at Brougham Pass upon his orders. 'In the event of the Natives making the smallest show of resistance … the officers Commanding the Military Parties,' Lachlan instructed, 'have been authorized to fire on them to compel them to surrender;

hanging up on Trees the Bodies of such Natives as may be killed on such occasions, in order to strike the greatest terror into the Survivors.'

There are few references to the Wiradjuri in the 1815 journals of both Lachlan and Antill. Near the Macquarie River, they encounter a group of men and boys clothed in possum skins. A few days later, Lachlan describes a woman with a damaged left eye and no teeth. There is no mention of smoke or fire, usually a common observation in explorers' journals. George Evans, when he surveyed the road two years earlier, found the absence of First Australians unsettling. 'I think they are watching us,' he records in one journal entry, 'but are afraid and keep at some distance.'

While they were not obvious to a nineteenth-century mind, there were clues in most of the locations they passed through, signs that this land was quite clearly inhabited. When we look at Lewin's paintings today, we see in them a landscape culturally nurtured. In his depiction of the first camp at Springwood,[17] the horse and carts are shown negotiating the narrow passageways between mountain blue gums (*Eucalyptus deanei*). Were one to take these carts through a similar landscape today, at somewhere like Deanei Reserve, where a patch of remnant blue gums remains, progress would be almost impossible. The pathways are obstructed by fallen logs and messy clumps of cheesewood (*Pittosporum undulatum*). The lack of understorey in Lewin's painting is not natural; it is the effect of cyclic fires.

At the Campbells River crossing, Lewin paints a similar scene,[18] tall manna gums and apple boxes spaced evenly with nothing in between except grass, another park-like idyll fashioned by fire. The scene at Sidmouth Valley is similar. The abrupt tree line in Lewin's painting shows fire was used to re-shape the landscape. Bridging the forest mosaic with the naturally treeless fringe of the creek is a grassy buffer, the grass uncommonly short, the land exquisitely maintained.

The First Australians have been written out of the Blue Mountains story. For many years, even through to the mid-twentieth century, settlers and historians assumed that First Nations peoples could not have lived here, the geography too inhospitable. But the conquest of the mountains was also the conquest of Dharawal, Wiradjuri and Gandangara land. Only in recent decades have we discovered that their range was as extensive, if not more extensive, than the townships we visit today. The ridgeline from Emu Ford to Cox's River was not a secret. Rock engravings and arrangements of stone have been found between Linden and Faulconbridge, indicating it was an important meeting ground between the three Aboriginal nations of that area. 'Blaxland, Lawson and Wentworth ... are depicted as being intrepid explorers who found their way across the Blue Mountains into the greater expanse of Australia,' write Indigenous Elders Bruce McGuinness and Dennis Walker. 'Of course this isn't true. Aboriginal people showed them the way.'

Gregory Blaxland eschewed assistance from First Australians, disenchanted with the help he had received on an earlier trip to the Nepean River. The lithograph by M. Emile Ulm entitled *The Blue Mountain Pioneers* (1880), in which Blaxland, Wentworth, Lawson and two servants reflect on the magnitude of the scenery and their achievement, disseminates a lie, for there was no Aboriginal guide minding the horses. But there is an intriguing footnote, which has only recently been unearthed. The 'dauntless three' explorers, a term created by the bush poet Henry Kendall, were accompanied by four men. Three were convicts, their details not recorded for posterity, and the other was a man named James Byrne (or Burns). He was a forester, an early colonial term for someone who hunted kangaroos and learnt bushcraft from the local custodians. He guided the dauntless three to Mount Blaxland in 1813, following the ancient pathways he had been shown, doing the same for George Evans later that year as the surveyor mapped out the route for Cox's Road. The roles of the Dharawal, Wiradjuri and Gandangara have faded over time, these peoples appearing only as background cameos in this story of European triumph.

It is said the primitive nature of the road and its steepness in sections were deliberate attempts by Lachlan to impede the foreseeable, uncontrolled exodus to the west. But if that was his intention, it did not work. The crossing of the Blue Mountains opened up the continent. Great clouds of dust soared through the sky as cattle and sheep marched towards the Bathurst Plains. Explorers came and went. Oxley passed by a number of times on his quest for the inland sea. James Ainslie went through on his journey to Canberra. When Charles Darwin travelled the road in 1836, he remarked upon 'the extreme uniformity of the vegetation', the scantiness of the foliage and the open, shadowless nature of the woods. When Edward Hargreaves followed in 1851, on his legendary quest to find gold, it is said his horse bucked and jolted the whole way. This was the beginning of modern Australia: the ascendancy of wool, which supported the fledgling colony, and the excavation of raw materials that has propelled the economy ever since. With the chaos of migration beyond the reins of government control, conflict intensified. No more could one retreat to the naïve optimism of the early years. Bullets were exchanged instead of gifts. William Cox, the roadbuilder and erstwhile hero, was paid to lead killing expeditions along the Nepean–Hawkesbury River.

As I sit writing at my desk, or as I absentmindedly negotiate my daily duties, I often think of that trip to Sidmouth Valley. Of all the places I've explored, it may well be one of my favourite locations, my Tintern Abbey, one of the memories that, to quote Wordsworth:

> *But oft, in lonely rooms, and 'mid the din*
> *Of towns and cities, I have owed to them,*
> *In hours of weariness, sensations sweet.*

For some reason, staring at the almost puckish contortions of the manna gums, I attained a clarity of thought, a clearness of mind I have not experienced elsewhere. In Proust's *In Search of Lost Time*, the narrator views paintings of Balbec, on the Normandy coast, and falls in love with the ruggedness of the scene, the sinister buildings and precipitous cliffs, only to find, when he visits the place for real, Balbec is a banal seaside resort. In Sidmouth Valley, my experience was the opposite. The photos I amassed during my research barely piqued my attention, but when I arrived and found a landscape coated with snow, the trees unsparingly graphic, I was smitten. Perhaps it was the synchronicity of the snow-ridden journey and the audiobook I was listening to, a Murakami novel where the protagonist traipses through the snowy hills of Hokkaido. Or perhaps it was the intimacy of the scene, for I knew its history and I could view the landscape almost as a theatre set, the actors entering and exiting the stage, swapping dialogue, the trees shifting back and forth at the behest of a mercurial director. It can be hard to know what propels us forward, the spaghetti-like threads of curiosity and passion, ambition and hoped-for achievement. But every now and then, as with Sidmouth Valley, one discovers, in one's mood and emotional lucidity, something akin to purity. If we lay down roots at all, we do so not so much with the places themselves but with their associative thoughts. Perhaps it is the signals that transmit through these roots, each signal passing surreptitiously from memory to memory, that enable us, unconsciously at least, to make sense of our life's story.

I tend to imagine the tree Lachlan sat beneath was an apple box. There is no pressing conviction for this claim, just an inclination. Col Bower, who has conducted extensive research on the area's vegetation, suggests the most common trees in the area were manna gums and apple box. The trees on the right of Lewin's painting appear to be apple box, perhaps with some Blakely's red gums interspersed, and those on the left have the posture of scrappy mannas. For Lachlan, choosing where to have breakfast at eight o'clock in the morning (a time he records quite precisely), it makes sense he would find a spot by the creek's banks. The only shade offered there would have come from the tall, billowy apple box trees.

But in a way it does not matter how we imagine the Macquarie tree. Whether it has the messy form of a manna gum or the disjointed lean of an apple box, we can still observe in its branches and in the wilt of its leaves the frailty of time, the remorse we all share for decisions that can never be undone. 'The roots of the trees here run deep,' reflects the writer Stan Grant as he takes his son to visit massacre sites on Wiradjuri land, 'far deeper than the footprints of the white settlers who claimed this land nearly 200 years ago.' For Lachlan, sitting beneath the shade of this since-forgotten tree, indulging in memories of a more agreeable time, he could not have known he would be dead in less than two and a half years. Nor could he have known, as he sat with his back to the Sydney colony, that the boundless plains would be bloodied by an ignoble war.

It is tempting to accept that our past, like the road across the mountains, can only be navigated via the one preordained route. Counterfactual histories trail off from every unfulfilled decision; alternative realities abound in which hopes are reallocated, fears are rephrased. This simple moment in time – a man taking breakfast beneath a tree – symbolises, at least for me, the tipping point between the naivety of early European settlement and the behemoth of uncontrolled expanse. For others, that moment happened long before, perhaps with the flag raising at Sydney Cove or the musket fire at Botany Bay. At a time when many want history's lessons read as monochromatic slogans, it seems especially important to revivify these episodes of our past. Time ventures quickly. Landscapes fade and memories disappear. But we should never lose our connection with everything that has come before.

162

Enchanting Edens

In *The Bush* (2014), Don Watson describes with sadness how the farms of Gippsland, once spectacular forests of messmate (*Eucalyptus obliqua*), eurabbie (*Eucalyptus globulus ssp. bicostata*) and mountain ash (*Eucalyptus regnans*), are today being subdivided into lifestyle blocks and sold to hobby farmers. 'It might turn out that the forests of Gippsland were cleared for the benefit of no more than a couple of generations,' he writes.

It was rare for me to find myself travelling through this part of Victoria so, when the occasion finally occurred, I could not resist searching for the site of the world's tallest tree. Knowing only that it was located on the McDonalds Track, near Thorpdale, I drove for more than an hour, accessing the road too far north and accepting defeat by the time I reached Narracan. On my second attempt, I came from Melbourne, turning off the freeway at Trafalgar and heading south. Two hundred years ago, the freeway would have been a creek lined with swamp paperbark (*Melaleuca ericifolia*) and woolly tea-tree (*Leptospermum lanigerum*), but today it is a four-lane thoroughfare sandwiched between houses and a railway track. Utes outnumber sedans. Electronic message boards warn of roadworks. The route up to Thorpdale is hilly and there are a few messmates, which would have grown here in abundance before settlement. They have been eclipsed by the showy pink and white blossoms of the cherry plum (*Prunus cerasifera*).

The hills roll upon the horizon, their verges endowed with little more than sheep and endless grass. It could be Wales or Ireland. But there is an unusual element to the view. The green is interrupted by occasional bursts of reddish-brown. The soils here, which grow some of the finest potatoes in Australia, have high levels of iron oxide and so a strong russet colour. Ploughed fields appear like umber contusions, and the sheep display an orange discoloration to their wool.

Thorpdale is a pleasant place, the park well maintained, with a large, contemporary playground at its heart. There are the obligatory features of a country town – a bakery, a war memorial and a CFA station – and there is even an attractive art-deco pub serving the self-proclaimed 'best cold beer in the valley'. When I drive through on a Sunday, things are quiet. The swings in the playground are empty. A father and his child are the only people I see.

Past the township there is a sign: 'Site of World's Tallest Tree, one kilometre'. It directs me to turn left onto McDonalds Track, where the road weaves between treeless fenced farmland, not even bushes or shrubby understorey in evidence. The grass, after a heightened spell of rain, displays a lushness I have not seen for many months. Eventually, in the distance, a row of Monterey cypresses (*Hesperocyparis macrocarpa*) comes into view. These are the typical windbreaks of the Victorian countryside, large Californian trees that spread their crowns with a sense of entitlement. An obtrusive, craggy eucalypt grows on one side of the road. It is a eurabbie, a subspecies related to the more famous southern blue gum (*Eucalyptus globulus*). Its bark evinces an orange-grey sheen, and its warty fruit are arranged in groups of three, in contrast to the singular fruits of the latter. As I continue to drive, more eurabbies come into view, each of them radial and wide, their branches coiling and spreading low across the terrain.

It is then I notice the memorial, a thin pole that rises about 20–30 metres into the air. On top are the words 'The World's Tallest Tree'. 'This mountain ash,' reads the plaque to its side, 'grew about one hundred and sixty metres south from here on Mr Bill Cornthwaite's property. Felled by him in 1884 and officially measured by his brother George.'

It does not seem right that Cornthwaite should be honoured in this manner if the legend is true: that he and his brother George, a government surveyor, chopped it down simply to measure its height. At 114.5 metres, it was indeed the largest tree recorded at the time.[19] Science today suggests it is unlikely trees will ever grow beyond 120 metres, this being the point where the energy required for transpiration exceeds the energy gained by new growth. At the time of writing, there is only one tree living that is taller than the Thorpdale tree: the Hyperion, a coast redwood (*Sequoia sempervirens*) that grows along the northern coast of California.

The reason trees grow to such heights is from an intense competition for light, which means, across these almost treeless green fields around Thorpdale, where sheep now graze and magpies peck worms from the ground, there was once a substantial forest of mountain ash, giving way to patches of messmate, blue gum and mountain grey gum (*Eucalyptus cypellocarpa*). More than forty years after chopping the tree down, George Cornthwaite sent a letter to *The Gum Tree*, a journal devoted to the conservation, propagation and utilisation of Australian trees. In this letter, he reveals that he first noticed the tree when visiting his brother during the Christmas holidays of 1884. There were three trees growing on the edge of a clearing that he describes as 'freaks', 20 to 30 metres taller than the others. He records them as blackbutts, a term used for *Eucalyptus regnans* at the turn of the twentieth century. Measuring the biggest with a theodolite, a surveyor's instrument that uses angles to estimate height, he believed it to be 370 feet tall. When George returned in winter the following year, the largest of the freaks had been chopped down,[20] not for curiosity but for fence palings, an equally abject end for the world's tallest tree. Measuring the tree on the ground gave a different reading: 375 feet, or 114.4 metres. Cornthwaite suggested the extra height was a result of the upper branches spreading out on the ground. He also measured the other two trees. At 95 and 102 metres, they were, even by today's measurements, of exceptional size. These outliers were remnants of a time centuries ago, when the forest was dense and competition for light induced a surge-like ascendance towards the sky. It is unlikely the local Gunaikurnai burnt these forests; they did not offer exceptional rewards for food and shelter, and the regular, cool fires were inappropriate for mountain ash, a tree that requires severe burning every few hundred years. When the Europeans arrived with their axes, an age of permanence was felled in an instant. The eurabbies that grow today, trees no more than sixty or seventy years old, have from a young age grown with an absolute freedom of form, spreading outwards rather than upwards, oblivious to the demands imposed by aggressive neighbours.

We can only speculate on the age of the Thorpdale tree, but it is thought mountain ash may live for around 400 years, possibly longer. Their seeds, unlike other eucalypts, require intense heat to germinate and often the parents do not survive the blaze, their last gesture being to release the seeds from their woody capsules. It is the ultimate sacrifice. Walk through a forest of mountain ash and one can approximate, from the thickness of the trunks and a knowledge of the area's history, when each tree may have been born. They are arranged in chapters dictated by fire, a whole forest contained within six or seven cohorts of age.

In Victoria, there is a geospatial tool available from the Department of Environment, Land, Water and Planning that allows you to view how the landscape has changed since 1750. By selecting a map that extends from Hazelwood in the east to Poowong in the west, and from Ellinbank in the north to Leongatha in the south, one sees in 1750 an almost unbroken shading of green, hectare upon hectare of wet and damp forest, messmates, mountain ash, blue gums and eurabbie. Change the layer to show today's remnant vegetation, and the green of the forest is now speckled upon a pale background, occasional dots on an almost unbroken field of white. The white indicates disturbed land: urban settlements, roads or farms. Only a few areas of forest remain in places like Tarra-Bulga and Mount Worth. One can do similar around Hopetoun, where grain has replaced the mallee eucalypts (*Eucalyptus dumosa, Eucalyptus behriana*), or along the Murray and Goulburn rivers, where river red gums (*Eucalyptus camaldulensis*) were cleared for railway sleepers and to fuel the fires of paddlesteamers. The green shading around Horsham and Lubeck, once open woodland, is now a blotchy white, the yellow gums (*Eucalyptus leucoxylon*), yellow box (*Eucalyptus melliodora*) and grey box (*Eucalyptus microcarpa*) replaced by wheat fields and grazing sheep. Regimental forests of trees have been colonised and vanquished. 'Ninety per cent of vegetation cut down in Australia,' writes Don Watson, 'was cut down to make way for livestock'.

It can be hard to comprehend the scale of this destruction. The effort involved in felling one tree is not easy: in the first five to ten years on the land, one selector recalled nine-tenths of the labour being devoted to felling trees. Small trees were hacked and undergrowth slashed. Larger trees were ringbarked or in some cases felled, taking out smaller trees as they crashed to the ground. When the weather became hot and dry enough, the annual burn would begin. As historian Tom Griffiths describes in *Forests of Ash* (2001), the community gathered around to watch 'the giant burns that, they hoped, would turn last year's fallen and ringbarked forest into this year's clearing'. At a given signal, the fire starters, spaced evenly across a large area, would light torches made from strips of bark. The torches were thrown to the ground, igniting the fire, but not before spiders scuttled for safety up people's arms, awakened from their timber retreats.

The book *The Land of the Lyre Bird* (1920) anthologises the memories and recollections of those first Gippsland pioneers. For many, there was a utilitarian satisfaction in taming the forest, but for others, there was a tinge of regret amid the colonial pride in destroying this 'enchanting Eden'. Inconvenient it may have been, and disorientating at times, the so-called scrub was also magnificent. One could admire the open country, the rolling hills shaded by the afternoon sun, while simultaneously mourning the dead trees that, like 'silent witnesses', rose ghostlike from the land, 'appealing as it were to heaven against their destruction by the hand of man'.

Mr W. Johnstone, who settled in the region in 1879, wrote a poem to describe this conflict:

Never more shall I see the green forest again
Wave free in the sunshine, droop sullen in the rain ...

170

But away with these fancies. 'Tis better today
Where the forest encumbered, the children now play.

There is a magic to mountain ash forests that makes you feel, spiritually at least, like you have left reality behind and are in some form of interstitial state, perhaps on your way to Hades, as the Styx Valley in Tasmania would suggest, but more likely towards a strange and aberrant world. The air seems unnaturally cold, the trees and their crowns almost endless. Griffiths describes the trunks as 'cathedral-like pillars', as if they might support a person's ascension to the heavens. Ribbons of bark hang menacingly from these pillars. Lyrebirds babble and rave. The effect is mesmeric.

It is possible to get a sense of the Thorpdale tree's height without going too far from the centre of Melbourne. Dominating the sky-line at the Carlton end of Swanston Street is a building called the Swanston Square Apartment Tower. When viewed from the north, it is a patchwork of luminescent colour. When viewed from the south, the careful arrangement of white balconies and black windows creates an image, the face of William Barak, the King of the Yarra. Barak was a Wurundjeri leader who, in 1863, took about forty of his people across the mountain ash forests known today as the Black Spur, towards the 'promised land' between the Yarra River and Badger Creek. They built a community there called Coranderrk, a self-sufficient enclave that combined European farming with traditions of Wurundjeri culture. Barak, a storyteller who could keep an audience enthralled with his slow and hesitant delivery, was also a man of exceptional talent and agility. A French visitor to Melbourne, Oscar Comettant, recalls Barak climbing a tree. 'He began by making an incision at head height,' he says, 'then embracing the tree he climbed up it until he was able to get his left toe in the little hole.' Barak supported himself in this position with his left arm while making another incision further up, lodging his right foot in this toe hold and repeating the process several times until he had climbed the tall eucalypt. The Swanston Square Apartment Tower, which many call the William Barak building, presides over Swanston Street and dwarfs the meagre plane trees below. At thirty-three storeys and 115 metres, it is the height of the Thorpdale tree. Skyscrapers may now be our closest link to the heavens, but for thousands of years these trees were the tallest structures on the continent.

In Richard Flanagan's 2007 article on the Tasmanian timber industry, 'Out of Control', he describes the process by which some of the last unprotected stands of old-growth *Eucalyptus regnans* are being reduced to piles of ash: 'Clearfelling, as the name suggests, first involves the complete felling of a forest by chainsaws and skidders. Then, the whole area is torched, the firing started by helicopters dropping incendiary devices made of jellied petroleum, commonly known as napalm. The resultant fire is of such ferocity it produces mushroom clouds visible from considerable distances.'

These magnificent trees are reduced to paper, sold to Japan for as low a price as $200 worth of pulp, their heavyset trunks scrunched up and thrown into the bins of Japanese offices thousands of times over. It does not seem just that some of the finest trees in Australia, the tallest flowering plants in the world, could be misused for such ephemeral commodity, sold to a country that has already obliterated its own old-growth forest and replaced it with plantations of Japanese cypress (*Chamaecyparis obtusa*) and red cedar (*Cryptomeria japonica*). Individual mountain ash trees can provide food and shelter to a range of birds, mammals, reptiles and invertebrates, species like the powerful owl or the endangered Leadbeater's possum. Mountain ash forests are some of the greatest carbon sinks in the world, and Melbourne's water supply depends on the evapotranspiration of these trees. It is thought that less than 15 per cent of the original old-growth mountain ash forests of Tasmania remains. In the Central Highlands of Victoria, the figure is close to 1 per cent, and there are recommendations to classify the forest as critically endangered. At the end of *City of Trees* (2019), a book that details the catastrophic impact of the Anthropocene epoch, author Sophie Cunningham writes, 'There is much that broke my heart when researching the essays in this book. But it is this, our wanton destruction of the mountain ash and those that live in them, that has brought me closest to giving up hope.'

At a talk given by Bob Brown at Melbourne Town Hall, a teacher in the audience stood up and asked the former Greens leader how we can inspire the next generation to care about nature. Take them to the mountain ash forests of Victoria and Tasmania, he said. Let them see the majesty of nature up close and be overpowered by its beauty. I have experienced this euphoria among the karris (*Eucalyptus diversicolor*) of Pemberton, the brown barrels (*Eucalyptus fastigata*) of the Blue Mountains, the mountain white gums (*Eucalyptus dalrympleana*) of the Strathbogie Ranges, and the red and yellow tingles (*Eucalyptus jacksonii, Eucalyptus guilfoylei*) of the Valley of the Giants, the vast, buttressed, Tolkienesque eucalypts of southwestern Australia. 'To stand in a tingle forest in even a moderate breeze is to experience a force no research can prepare you for,' writes Tim Winton in his book *Island Home* (2014). 'With their giant, fire-hollowed buttresses and restless crowns, these trees creak with enough pent-up energy to make your flesh crawl.'

We now know, due to a study undertaken at the University of California, that being in the presence of large eucalypts may affect our behaviour, at least in the short-term, compelling us to acts of

173

kindness we may not otherwise have considered. Conducted within a grove of towering blue gums at the university's Berkeley campus, along Strawberry Creek, the study measured the power of awe and its associative effects. Experimenters contrived a scenario in which, pretending to conduct a questionnaire, they dropped a box of pens on the ground. Participants who were given a minute to view the trees beforehand were more likely to retrieve the fallen pens. Those in the control group, who had instead spent their allocated time in the presence of tall buildings, were less likely to assist.

Awe is a complicated sentiment. It encompasses fear and sub-servience, transcendence and blissful surprise, and it recalibrates us, expelling our tendencies for solipsism and narrow-mindedness. When astronauts look back on the Earth and experience the overview effect, it is a response to the world's enormity and an awareness of their diminished size within it. It is this awareness that has the power to make us more social as human beings, more generous and ethically minded. Cathedrals can have the same effect, but, as the experiment suggests, it is not simply the building's size that creates the sentiment. Awe is underscored by the sense that concealed within those arches is the potential for empyreal contact and that somewhere, if one were able to judge the location correctly, it may be possible for those twin worlds of reality and heaven to be simultaneously exposed.

As with cathedrals, it is not the size or the age of trees that sparks this sense of the sublime. There is something more powerful. And while we cannot describe the effect, we can certainly sense it. I felt it among the tingles of the Valley of Giants. Rosalind experienced it famously in Shakespeare's *As You Like It* (1623), as she reflected, with sharpened focus, on the practicalities of love while exiled within the Forest of Arden.

Emanating from those aloof trunks is something we might describe as a recondite presence. A tree's consciousness is so far from ours, it may be impossible for us to ever conceptualise of an equivalence. They cannot rhapsodise about beauty or feel the prickles of awe, but they can, as we are discovering only now, show an instinctual predisposition for generosity. Above ground, the trees compete in an endless struggle for light. But below the surface, the root systems share nutrients and information. Chemical signals and electrical impulses, warning neighbours of imminent attack, are sent from tree to tree via hyphae. Nutrients are passed along these fungal pathways, travelling from healthy trees to those that are suffering, not just between trees of the same species but also between different species. Trees exist in a community, an enclave of shared responsibility, each member aware, at a primal level, that its survival depends not just on its own health but on that of the entire ecosystem.

It is perhaps this benevolence we feel as we traipse through forests of mountain ash or stand within a grove of planted blue gums. Some may say it is a similar affinity we intuit in the presence of dolphins and cockatoos, penguins and chimpanzees. Humans view cooperation and the idea of the Hobbesian social contract as perhaps the most important stage in our triumph as a species. But while the ideas of the social contract were tested at the point of first contact, often with death and hostility as the unintended results, unknown to those first colonists the trees around them were existing in a far superior concept of community, one free from the shackles of law, religion and property.

The next time I was in the area, I was with Pip. As we negotiated the long driveway into the Valley of Giants, we wound down our windows, and it was possible to hear the trees as they rustled and sighed, as they murmured, that strange pulsing hiss seeming to derive from a collective, almost synchronised exhalation. Walking along the boardwalk, 40 metres in the air, we could both sense these gargantuan eucalypts, red and yellow tingles, exuding their calm forbearance, and we had that rare moment couples may experience only a handful of times in their lives. We realised, without the need to confirm with words, that our thoughts were aligned; our emotions, as difficult as they may have been to describe, had coalesced for a brief moment. Among these munificent trees, it is not just awe one can feel, but devotion, empathy – and even love.

A Tasmanian Romance

It was hard to miss the office of the Wilderness Society, its red brick façade and cream balustrades a distinct contrast to the neighbouring houses of grey and whitewashed sandstone. However, I was looking for something else in the vicinity: a large tree on the corner of Davey and Molle streets. The photo suggested it was somewhere near the southwestern corner of the park, but there was nothing there, just a hummock of asphalt and a low timber wall. I was searching for Bob Brown's favourite tree, the one he selects for Peter Solness's book *Tree Stories* (1999): a giant blue gum (*Eucalyptus globulus*) which, for decades, greeted him on his commute to the Wilderness Society's office.

Most likely the tree was a nineteenth-century planting, perhaps one of the earliest plantings of blue gums around Hobart, but one could be mistaken for thinking it was a remnant. When those first colonists were building the storehouses and homes of Hobart Town, the foreshore would have been littered with blue gums. And yet today, while occasional blue gums pepper the streets of South Hobart and Sandy Bay, the city centre does not reveal a single remnant eucalypt. 'Trees like this add greatly to the beauty and relaxation of a city,' says

Brown in the book, 'and yet the vast majority of people passing here are rushing by enclosed in motor vehicles with the windows up and the radio on.' It has not taken long for the blue gum to be forgotten in its homeland. 'It's a wonder it's still here,' opines Brown of the Davey Street tree. 'It's a wonder somebody in an office somewhere hasn't driven past one day and said, "I think that tree should go," having had no relationship with it, no romance with it, and no empathy for it.'

His words were farsighted. The tree was deemed unsafe and removed by the local council in March 2017, a year and a half before my visit.

As Brown suggests, it is possible to have a romance and relationship with any tree. The strength of that passion lies in the memories and associations we create with it, the way a tree, like the St Helena mimosa or Daylesford's Cootamundra wattle, can become imprinted within the abridged narratives we create for our lives. Bob Brown has spent much of his life surrounded by natural beauty. Campaigning for the Franklin River during the 1970s, the cause that propelled him into federal politics, he was in the presence of Huon pines (*Lagarostrobos franklinii*), their trunks as old as ancient Greece and their root systems dating back to the Bronze Age. Immersed within the Tarkine, the setting for decades of environmental protest, he has viewed some of Australia's most baroque and uncompromising myrtle beeches (*Nothofagus cunninghamii*). And sheltered in the Daintree rainforest, where he planned to recuperate after the success of the Franklin campaign only to become embroiled in a ten-month blockade, he would have walked past spectacular king ferns (*Angiopteris evecta*), some more than 7 metres high; strangler figs (*Ficus spp.*), their roots draped towards the ground like arboreal harps; and the huge trunks of white booyongs (*Argyrodendron trifoliolatum*) and stonewoods (*Backhousia hughesii*), their bark camouflaged by epiphytic ferns, hoya and native monstera. So, it is instructive to read that his favourite tree is not a rare or unusual species but a blue gum, a rather louche and dishevelled tree with oversized leaves and bark hanging off in long, tawdry strips.

It was Christmas when we drove along Davey Street. Pip and I were on our honeymoon and, bathed in the afterglow of the wedding, we ambled dreamily around the city without want of purpose. The rasps of the goldfinches and swallows were transformed into jaunty melodies, and the southwesterlies soothed rather than lacerated our faces. We drank wine and ate oysters by the dozen, and frolicked on the beach at Sandy Bay as if it was the coast of Bora Bora.

Southern blue gums grow in the wild close to our hometown of Melbourne, and we sometimes see them on hikes around Wilsons Prom or when we find ourselves driving through the Otway Ranges. However, it seemed appropriate to be looking for the species in Tasmania, not only for the extremities of form displayed on this island (from the 90-metre giant called Neeminah Loggorale Meena to the dwarfish castaways on the Freycinet coast), but because it was here that the type specimen was collected in 1792. Jacques-Julien Houtou de Labillardière, an old and caustic-lipped naturalist who was in charge of the botanical team on the Bruni d'Entrecasteaux voyage, gathered flowers and leaves from a tree at Recherche Bay. 'We were filled with admiration at the sight of these ancient forests, in which the sound of the axe had never been heard,' relates Labillardière in his journal. 'The eye was astonished in contemplating the prodigious size of these trees.' Labillardière realised the potential of the blue gum early on, foreseeing its value as a shipbuilding material. The carpenters on the ship agreed, and they used the timber planks to raise the gunwales on the expedition's rowing boats.

Labillardière would no doubt have been pleased to discover the tree's fate as one of Australia's most well-travelled trees. *Globulus*, the species name, translates as 'globe', another example of Linnaean serendipity. Most likely the term relates to the spherical shape of the fruit. By 1905, 4 million feet of blue gum timber supported the wharves of British ports. Today, there are around 20 million hectares of blue gum plantations around the world, and the tree has spread to unusual locations. It grows alongside date palms (*Phoenix dactylifera*) near the pyramids of Egypt, and in the Chilean Andes, where it stabilises the slopes. In other countries it has become semi-naturalised, so much so that it is called the Canton blue gum in China and the California blue gum across San Francisco Bay.

An indication of the tree's commercial value can be adduced from its prominence at the 1851 Great Exhibition in London where, surrounded by opulence and innovation, it was one of the more salient pieces of the Australian collection. More than 100,000 objects were on display: tractors and locomotives, textiles and jewellery, the world's first single-barrelled weapon, and a machine that could roll 100 cigarettes in a minute. The 191-carat Koh-i-Noor diamond was close by, laid out on a velvet cushion and housed behind bars.

The Australian section, tucked away in the western part of the building, favoured practicality over indulgence. 'There is nothing picturesque in a sack of wheat,' describes the exhibition's chronicler, John Tallis, 'nothing interesting in a tin of preserved Australian beef.' Not far from the samples of gold, malachite and copper, there were logs of blackwood (*Acacia melanoxylon*), around 20 feet long and 1 foot wide, southern sassafras (*Atherosperma moschatum*) and myrtle beech. But the most impressive timber was the Tasmanian blue gum. 'Equal to oak as a ship-building timber,' described the official catalogue. Its height and consistent girth were represented by the two columnar display logs, cut from different ends of the same tree roughly 40 metres apart. The timber was, by virtue of its resistance to naval shipworm, ideal for use in shipbuilding and wharfs. 'Unparalleled forestral importance' is how Ferdinand von Mueller described the species, his promotion of the tree so rhapsodic that he was awarded the title Baron Blue Gum.

In the article 'A Global History of Australian Trees' (2011), Brett Bennett asks why native trees planted so widely abroad were not planted equally as widely at home. Plantations in Australia tend to be foreign pines such as Monterey (*Pinus radiata*), slash pine (*Pinus elliottii*) or maritime pine (*Pinus pinaster*), while plantations of native trees tended to be hoop pines (*Araucaria cunninghamii*) or bunya pines (*Araucaria bidwillii*). There was a trend in the late 1990s for small blue gum plantations. It was due to the *Managed Investments Act 1998*, a Howard government initiative to triple native plantations by using tax incentives as an enticement. But by the time 2007 came around and the first blue gums were earmarked for removal, the global financial crisis had hit and Japan's demand for paper had receded. The venture was a failure, and the blue haze of unfelled trees can still be observed across the country, particularly on the pastoral slopes of Western Australia.

Where eucalypts are logged today, they are often from old-growth forest and natural stands. During our holiday to Tasmania, I visited an area of Bruny Island named Inala Nature Reserve, which is surrounded by coupes that are regularly logged. Pip booked me in for a one-on-one tour with the reserve's manager, Tonia Cochran. Tonia pointed out flame robins and olive whistlers, and many of the Tasmanian endemics, such as dusky robins, green rosellas and the resolute honeyeaters – which, as is traditional with the *Meliphagidae* family, have been given double-barrelled epithets such as strong-billed, black-headed and yellow-throated. For most visitors, the highlight is climbing the stairs of a 4-metre-high timber platform where one can watch forty-spotted pardalotes, a rare and rather delicate bird, skipping along the branches of the surrounding manna gums (*Eucalyptus viminalis*). However, my highlight was elsewhere. Looking through Tonia's scope, I viewed a swift parrot emerging from the hollow of a particularly large blue gum. At the time, there were about 2000 swift parrots left in the world. This may have since dropped to around 750, and if rates continue, little more than a dozen pairs of swifties may remain by 2040. The endangered birds feed on the flowers of messmates (*Eucalyptus obliqua*), but they nest in the hollows of blue gums. Inala has both, and it is one of only two places in Tasmania, Maria Island being the other, where the birds are free from their main predator: the somewhat insidious sugar glider.

Earlier that year Tonia had appeared on *ABC News*, appealing for a halt to Forestry Tasmania's plans to log a coupe adjacent to the reserve, recalling a fight almost ten years earlier to save the blue gums of Wielangta in Tasmania's southeast. Tonia's campaign was successful, largely because a groundswell of international tourists, many of whom were on Inala's mailing list, wrote vehemently to state and federal politicians, pleading for the logging to stop. But while Inala's victory was a bloodless one, other campaigns have attracted worldwide attention for the intensity of the protestors' methods. At the beginning of Anna Krien's book *Into the Woods* (2012), she describes a video taken during the mid-2000s campaign to halt logging in the Upper Florentine. The person filming appears to be hiding in the crown of a tree, a tangle of branches framing most of the shot. They are capturing a car that is blocking one of the access ways into the forest, its wheels removed and its undercarriage cemented to the ground. Two protestors are huddled inside, under a blanket, their arms fastened to pipes that secure them to the vehicle. Through the gaps in foliage, one can see a man approach the back of the car, where he pulverises the window with a sledgehammer, shouting obscenities as he carries out the attack. Another man shatters the passenger-side windows with his foot. The primordial roar of one of the attackers, clearly pushed to the outer limits of desperation, makes the video rather harrowing.

'In 1988, the famous violinist Yehudi Menuhin came out,' recalls environmentalist Geoff Law, reflecting on the campaign to save the Trident tree, a 70-metre-tall messmate near Wylds Craig, 'and said that destroying the tall forests of Tasmania to make waste paper was akin to gassing the Jewish people and boiling them down for soap.' It is a confronting association, and one that assumes logging is the primary cause of old-growth destruction whereas, in truth, around 90 per cent of tree removal in Australia clears a path for livestock to graze. But logging, through its brutal juxtaposition of raw material and output, exposes the ruthlessness of our values. Trees, some many hundreds of years old, are pulped and transformed into toilet paper and tissue wrapping, most of the profits going overseas, the trees replaced by saplings that may never reach the same heights as their predecessors.

My wife was sitting on the beach when I returned from Inala. We went for a swim in the Tasman Sea and then walked north along the beach to a place known as Two Tree Point. Pied oystercatchers flew past and hooded plovers trundled along the line of high tide. In 1792, George Tobin, accompanying Captain Bligh on the journey made famous for its mutiny, painted a watercolour of this view.[21] Unlike most of coastal Australia, the landscape around Adventure Bay has barely changed in the last 200 years, and some of the messmates and blue gums are old enough to have observed Cook's landing during his second expedition. There are two blue gums prominent in the painting, and they are the trees that give the point its name. They appear to be the same trees as today, almost identical in appearance despite the passing of 200 years. Tobin's respect for the trees is evident. He paints the leaves not as the large, clumsy fingers so characteristic of the blue gum but as small feathery strands. Similarly, the bark is smooth. The trunks are neither garnished with messy shades nor festooned with the ribbons of dead bark. These are eucalypts viewed through the eyes of someone who appreciates their elegance, the beauty of their candelabra-like form.

In the time that has elapsed since Tobin's painting, Tasmania has changed irrevocably. Until the arrival of Europeans, the Palawa had enjoyed almost 8000 years of solitude and isolation, cut off from the mainland by the Bass Strait. And then, within a generation, they were, as historian Lyndall Ryan writes, 'nearly wiped off the face of the earth'. Mangerner, the father of Truganini, was there when Captain Cook visited Adventure Bay in 1777. He presided over amicable relations, despite the affront his people must have endured as trees, some many centuries old, were razed by European axes. Even when a musket was fired by Omai, Cook's Tahitian interpreter, the hospitality of the Nuenonne did not falter. By the time of Nicolas Baudin's visit in 1802, the Nuenonne were rightfully wary of white strangers, the enforced vigilance precipitated by the actions of sealers, 'brutal men, capable of extreme, wide-ranging violence', to use the words of historian James Boyce. Truganini, at an age when she could barely utter words, witnessed sealers murdering her mother. Around a decade later, two of her sisters would be captured in a similar raid, taken off as sex slaves.

The South Island of Bruny, a patchwork of forests, heathland and coastal scrub, was not settled until 1825. The open grasslands of central and eastern Tasmania, meanwhile, were a veritable Eden, and land grabs proceeded with an alacrity and violence not seen before in the colony. In his book *Van Diemen's Land* (2008), Boyce cites the proliferation of the hunting dog as one of the main reasons for Tasmania's vicious frontier, for these dogs hunted kangaroos and wallabies at such a rate that a food shortage arose within two years of settlement. The Tasmanian emu, which was once widespread across the island, was quickly driven to extinction. So, too, the Tasmanian tiger. Deprived of their traditional food sources, the Palawa retaliated, hunting sheep with their spears and setting fire to buildings and crops.

'I am on the island of last things,' Anna Krien writes towards the end of *Into the Woods*. For Bob Brown, the island's history still breathes amid the chatter and exhaust fumes of modernity. When he talks of the survival of the Davey Street blue gum, the last of four that were planted in the same area, he is conscious of the unavoidable sadness of those last individuals that have, over the years, been given the bathetic names 'terminarchs' and 'endlings'. The blue gum was more than just a motivating presence on his daily commute; it was an embodiment of Tasmania's annihilated past. Krien cites biologist Edward O. Wilson's prediction of an Age of Loneliness, a future in which the world's latest mass extinction is not signalled by the trumpeting of an apocalypse or riven by collective hysteria, but finds expression in a sadness that seems to permeate the entire world.

When I was searching through the catalogues from the 1851 Great Exhibition, I noticed one of the objects exhibited was a knitted artwork of a blue gum in flower, its branches decorated with little birds perched on the twigs: a fairy wren and a pardalote, a honeyeater and a robin. The artist was Mrs Burgess of Davey Street in Hobart Town. For a moment, I realised there is a possibility, slim albeit real, that the blue gum she drew inspiration from was the same tree that stood on Davey and Molle streets, the tree deemed too dangerous to retain. 'The ghosts of these absences linger,' writes Krien. 'If ever there was a canary at the bottom of the world, it is Tasmania, and Wilson's warning about the Age of Loneliness is never far from my mind.'

The Pilliga Forest

There is one tree that, for me at least, symbolises freedom, not for any great libertarian streak it appears to display, but due to a coincidence of geography. Its emergence along the roadside marks the beginning of our holiday, a symbol of welcome for the two destinations my wife and I visit on an almost annual basis. Heading towards Brunswick Heads, I notice them as we leave the highway behind and turn the car onto Tweed Street. The coast cypress-pines (*Callitris columellaris*) emerge surreptitiously among the pink bloodwoods (*Corymbia intermedia*) and forest reds (*Eucalyptus tereticornis*). They hide in plain sight, trees that vanish with a conjurer's assurance so that, even for someone like me, eagerly awaiting their silhouette, it can take three or four individuals before their presence is fully recognised. Approaching Beechworth, the effect is the same. After leaving the Hume and driving along the Beechworth–Wangaratta Road, I start to notice them slowly, one by one. The cypress-pines begin to sharpen as the other trees, mostly eucalypts, recede. They are signifiers of calm, the liminal boundary between work, with all its grievances and stress, and the unfettered hopes of vacation. When I finally become aware of their presence, my mind settles to an orderly pace.

Cypress-pines are deceptive trees. Until someone points out their existence, they are, like damselflies or wattlebirds, brush boxes or currawongs, largely inconspicuous, but once you are aware of them, you realise how common they are. One might compare them with actors who appear in many films, but only in minor roles, and thus remain nameless to the majority. But for those who do know their name, a selective bond arises. 'This tree has not had any particular influence on our national psyche – but I think it ought to,' says writer Eric Rolls of the old greys, the white cypress-pines (*Callitris glaucophylla*) of the Pilliga. 'Only a handful of people would even know what it was, or even realise the significance of it when it was explained to them.' To be part of that handful is exalting: to see trees growing along a road verge and understand, in a driver's momentary assent, the role they have played in the narrative of this country.

I used to get asked why I discovered nature at such a late age, why, for someone who had only sought out the concreted landscapes of England, I found it necessary, as a resident of Australia, to learn the scientific names of trees or to identify species when for most people the genus would suffice. It was because I was an outsider trying to fit in. I could never scrutinise the country's politics with the eye of someone who had lived through the Whitlam or Howard eras; I did not have access to the same trove of cultural references and ideas. In Moranbah, like Bruce Chatwin in Alice Springs, I was able to enjoy drinks with the locals. But when the buff, murky dust of the central coalfields settled, I was just 'an effete Pommy with baby-blue eyes, a plummy voice and a fancy notebook', to quote Richard Cooke's description of Chatwin. Learning about trees gave me a connection to the land, an investment in the country's future; at the same time, it provided me with a purpose, an esoteric pursuit.

Perhaps my familiarity with Europe helped fashion my regard for *Callitris*. It is not inconceivable to view the forest of black cypress-pine (*Callitris endlicheri*) on the slopes of the Pilliga Nature Reserve and recall, by squinting your eyes, the paintings of Van Gogh. The trees are elegant, courtly and composed, and yet they shimmer with a blazing intensity. Study them closely and they reveal a cypress-like foliage. Like their northern hemisphere cousins, they have decorative, almost Gorgonian branchlets. The coast cypress-pine is more dream-like and cartoonish than the black cypress-pine. It associates less with the expressionism of Van Gogh and more with the naïve art of Henri Rousseau. 'An architect's dream-tree,' says P.J. Hurley in his book *In Search of Australia* (1943): 'tall, columnar, compact and billowy'. The tree's altocumulus crown forms a backdrop to my every memory of Brunswick Heads, the bark grey and angelic like that of the Aleppo pine (*Pinus halepensis*), the foliage dark, green and brooding, similar to the Monterey cypress (*Hesperocyparis macrocarpa*). It can be a joyous feeling to walk amid eucalypt leaves and to be startled, momentarily, by the hazy, impressionist fog of *Callitris*.

Driving along the roads of southern New South Wales in December, I have seen fairy lights draped over white cypresses. Perhaps their beauty derives from this childlike association. They are pyramidal, like a spruce, although their foliage is softer, more diaphanous. They are similar in appearance to the pencil pines (*Athrotaxis cupressoides*) of the alpine lakes of Tasmania, but while pencil pines can live for up to 2000 years, most *Callitris* species would be lucky to reach 200. The name of the genus comes from the Greek words *kallos*, meaning beautiful, and *treis*, meaning three. But the beauty does not refer to its delicate form. It refers to the leaves which, in whorls of three, interlink to create the characteristic branchlets.

In my time researching for this book, I have come across few Australian genera with a more capricious taxonomy than *Callitris*. It can be confusing at first. The Rottnest Island pine (*Callitris preissii*) and southern cypress-pine (*Callitris gracilis*, *Callitris robusta*) were once separate species, but now they are consolidated within the former. The white cypress-pine reads like a litany of indecision. Where once you read the names *Callitris huegelii* and *Callitris glauca*, you now read only the one name: *Callitris glaucophylla*. Many botanists insist the white cypress of the Pilliga (*Callitris glaucophylla*), the aromatherapy tree of the north (*Callitris intratropica*), and the architect's dream tree of Brunswick Heads (*Callitris columellaris*) are the one species, the differences between them are so slight. But in 1998, Ken Hill disentangled the three once again based upon their range: *intratropica*, the tree Leichhardt would describe as 'of a most striking character', is found along the northern coast of Australia; *glaucophylla* spreads out from east to west below the Tropic of Capricorn, and *columellaris* grows along the northern New South Wales and south Queensland coast. 'Species names have changed so often I am uneasy about giving them,' jokes Eric Rolls in his essay 'Perfumed Pines'. To confuse things further, many still refer to *glaucophylla* and *intratropica* as the one species: *columellaris*.

No person has championed the tree more than Rolls, a farmer who lived near Baradine on the western edge of the Pilliga. *Callitris glaucophylla* was his favourite – the 'old greys' as the sawmillers called them, trees that ensconced the surrounding forest. 'I love cypress pine because it lives life passionately,' he wrote in 2001. Once a year, around September, when the flowers are brown and weighed down with pollen, the reproductive season is announced with what sounds like gunshot. The branches recoil and the tree shivers as a brown cloud of pollen is released into the air. 'The spring of 1973 amazed men who had seen eighty years of pine flowering,' he writes in *A Million Wild Acres* (1981). 'In the early morning thousands of trees exploded together. Dense clouds rolled up from the forest. So much pollen drifted into a shearing-shed on the edge of the forest the shearers found it almost too dark to shear by early afternoon.'

A Million Wild Acres is Rolls' masterpiece. It was one of the first books to be written on Australia's environmental history, an ambitious work punched out in between ploughing and crop spraying. A book that was meant to take seven months to write took five years, the author in a constant battle between writing and tending to the land. For long periods, he would immerse himself in the books of the Mitchell Library. At home, he worked in a feverish trance, ignoring the calls of his wife, Joan, as she summoned him for dinner. His study was chaotic. A pile of handwritten notes and eleven dictionaries sat on his desk. On the floor lay over thirty piles of notes on one side, maps on the other, each pile devoted to the life history of an early squatter, their movements played out across several maps. Reading the resultant chapters can be laborious at times, the wandering and workload of squatters and selectors recalled in excruciating detail. But even the dullest prose can be absorbing. The metronomic rhythm lulls you into a dream, the behavioural details of termites, birds, butterflies and wasps immerse you within the forest.

'It is as long as the good road between Narrabri and Coonabarabran,' begins *A Million Wild Acres*. 'It is busy with trees, with animals and with men. It is lonely and beautiful. It is a million wild acres. And there is no other forest like it.' Tom Griffiths, in an essay on the book, recalls driving through the Pilliga as a child. 'I could remember the vast tracts of the Pilliga Scrub rolling endlessly past the car window.

It had not seemed extraordinary, magical and especially dynamic then.' He was, as the English gold-seeker John Sherer was, unimpressed by the 'dully-dead' landscape, his 'imagination at a standstill'. But through Rolls' book, Griffiths would be awakened to the magic of the forest. The cypress-pine, although it is mentioned on fewer than a dozen of the 400 or so pages, is the hero of *A Million Wild Acres*, important not only for what it tells us about the Pilliga but for what it says about the country's inconstant landscape. For many years, it was valid to imagine the European settlers as wistful naïfs, so uncomprehending of the Australian scenery that those first painters transformed what they observed into picturesque English parks, their vision filtered to turn forest into meadow, Sydney Cove into St James's Park. And yet those park-like scenes were real. Large trees were spaced so far apart they could fall and not brush the leaves of another tree. Walking between them, one could skip through a grassy understorey, at times knee-length, at other times short. It was as if George III, in advance of the First Fleet, had sent out his finest groundsmen to prepare the land for the convicts' arrival.

John Oxley's exploring party, the first Europeans to visit the Pilliga, had not intended to pass that way but were diverted by the summer floods. Oxley's intention had been to head west in the hope of finding the mythical inland sea but rain saturated the soil and the ensuing mud weakened the horses' legs. The party stopped at the Macquarie marshes and, unable to traverse the boggy mire, returned southwards to Mount Harris. For the next fortnight, they trekked towards the Warrumbungles, the mountain range that heralded the southwestern edge of the Pilliga. It was from this vantage point, as they left Mount Harris and headed east, that second-in-command George Evans took out his pencil and made a sketch.[22] The Warrumbungles appear as a jagged, unbroken formation on the horizon, a picturesque succession of craggy peaks and wavelike canyons. Roger Deakin compared them to 'Hokusai waves in a choppy sea'. But like Hokusai's thirty-six views of Mount Fuji, it is the foreground that commands the attention. Beyond two weeping gum trees, there is an exquisite parkland of white cypress-pine, the trees scattered as if planted, their form bushy and pompous like the yew trees of Hampton Court. To the right, almost pushed off the paper, is a dense forest, a cypress thicket, what appears to be a plantation on the outskirts of a beautiful park. The two are unnatural companions. One is reminded of Charles Griffith's comments when faced with the pre-European plains west of Melbourne: 'It is difficult … not to fancy that the hand of man had been engaged in combing and arranging the elements of natural beauty.' Griffiths was correct. Large parts of the continent had been combed by humans. The concatenated façade of copse and open forest was a fabrication, a scorched mosaic of two contrasting canopies. The land would be burnt every few years, a process that killed the saplings of cypress-pine and ironbark while nurturing the grass. The dense thicket was an unburnt remnant. Marsupials, lured by the succulent grass, would take refuge in the safety of the forest only to be speared as they ventured out into the pregnable expanse.

When Europeans came, the landscape changed. Not used to the cloven hooves of sheep and cattle, the soft soils hardened. Rainwater, rather than soaking through the ground, ran off into streams and creeks. Windmill grass (*Chloris spp.*) took over from *Themeda*, barley grass (*Hordeum leporinum*) from *Paspalidium*. And then in 1879, a miracle happened. Floods came through the valleys, revivifying the landscape, the muddled plains changing from green to glaucous blue. Cypress-pine and ironbark (*Eucalyptus crebra*) flourished in plague-like proportions, and a parkland of grasses and large, colossal trees became a chaos of saplings, weeds and wilful survivors. Rolls talked to a stockowner who could remember shepherding 1000 sheep through the forest before the floods. 'I could stand in one place and watch the whole flock,' recalled the farmer. 'Now if I walked in there twenty yards and didn't watch where I was going I'd bloody get lost.'

This transformation would happen elsewhere in the country, and it would happen again in the Pilliga with the fires of 1951. Trees would begin life in an open grassland and they would die in heavy forest. 'What happened in the Pilliga forest happened on a lesser scale in most of Australia's forests,' says Rolls at the beginning of the last chapter. 'It was only by concentrating on one that I could bring the men and animals to life.' According to Rolls, even the densely wooded slopes of the Great Dividing Range was an open landscape before Europeans came, kept in check by cultural burning for thousands of years. Were one to fly over the Australian continent in the mid-eighteenth century, Rolls suggests, the only consistent patches of dark green would be the jarrah and karri forests of the southwest, and the rainforests around Brisbane and the Gold Coast hinterland. 'Despite the burning of rainforest and cedar brush and the years of ringbarking,' Rolls writes in the concluding chapter, 'just as there are now more kangaroos in Australia than at the time of settlement, there are more trees.'

How many more is an open question. We may never know. Eric Rolls would make the controversial claim in *A Million Wild Acres* that only four trees grew per hectare at the time of Oxley's visit to the Pilliga, but this figure changed to six trees in his interview for *Tree Stories*, to four older trees and a dozen younger ones when he wrote an article for *The Sydney Morning Herald* in 1991, and to four large trees and twenty-five striplings in his essay 'The End, or New Beginning?' The principle was always the same: to picture the pre-European landscape one should imagine a football field in which only a few large, mature trees prevailed. There would not be many English parks with a canopy cover as low as this. John Benson and Phil Redpath, in a famous essay entitled 'The Nature of Pre-European Vegetation in South-Eastern Australia', disputed Rolls' hypothesis, citing the explorer-cum-artist George Evans who, after crossing the Blue Mountains in 1815, counted the trees along the Bathurst plain and estimated twenty-five per hectare. In 1827, Peter Cunningham did the same while visiting farms in the upper Hunter Valley and got a similar result. It is not in Rolls' favour that he relies solely on the calculations of James Ward, the first ranger of the Pilliga, whose assessment was made in 1877, fifty-nine years after Oxley's visit. Rolls also cites the words of explorers to back up his ideas, but as Benson and Redpath contend, there may be reasons for why grassy woodland features more prominently in their journals. It was easier for explorers to pass through, and it was also the land they were seeking: fresh pasture for sheep and cattle to exploit. Delve deeper into the journals and one would find references to dense scrub and forest. Even Oxley's 1818 journal, the same text Rolls uses to support his parkland thesis, describes ridges and summits thick with cypress brush west of the Warrumbungles, and a forest of small ironbarks, so thick as to be impenetrable, close to today's township of Coonabarabran.

It is in the Benson and Redpath essay that we are introduced to idea of First Australians burning opportunistically, 'in a mosaic fashion for "green pick" to attract game'. Benson and Redpath suggest mosaics were the result of unplanned, indiscriminate fires, but the term seems misplaced in this context. One can think of nothing more contrived or beautifully arranged than the intricate mosaics of the Roman or Byzantium empires. The term would find its rightful place fourteen years later in *The Biggest Estate on Earth* (2011). Instead of using the term to lessen the extent of Indigenous land management, historian Bill Gammage employs it to illustrate the process's complexity. Patches of vegetation were burnt at regular intervals as if a written schedule determined their timing. An aerial in 1750 would have shown a patchwork of different canopies, a mosaic of tiles and distinct vegetation, grassland alongside forest, open woodland fringing scrub, the borders between them as angular and precise as those of farm lots or parks. The effect was widespread rather than local. Each tribe managed its own template of mosaics, the series of templates creating a reciprocated whole. We will never know for sure how much was open grassland and how much was forest. One statistic goes to the other extreme, suggesting only 7 per cent was grassland and over three-quarters forest and scrub. But one thing we do know is areas like Wadjemup, which are now treeless, were once forests, and areas that were once parklike, like the Pilliga, are now covered in invasive trees.

Eric Rolls passed away in 2007. His coffin was assembled by a local carpenter and fashioned from white cypress-pine harvested from the local forest. 'At night fires glow in the round rough high-walled corrugated-iron sawdust pits,' wrote Rolls of Baradine, where he lived for forty-five years. 'Day and night the aromatic smell of burning resin drifts about.' This was a similar smell to that which Willem de Vlamingh reported on Wadjemup in 1696, the smell of the perfumed pine. The tree may have failed to capture the national psyche but it continues to haunt our landscape. The spirits of the fallen marro, the ghostly souls of these beautiful trees, have left Wadjemup and floated across the continent. They have settled in the dry forest of the Pilliga, transmorphing into a glaucous variant, a symbol of defiance, strength and resurrection.

Any trip to Baradine should feature a visit to the Local Aboriginal Land Council on Wellington Street. Behind a glass cabinet lies the dead trunk of a white cypress-pine. The tree, which has moved between Sydney and Melbourne since it was cut down in 1918, was beautifully inscribed to commemorate the burial of five Gamilaroi men. The patterned lines curve with serpentine swirls. At a time when Aboriginal artworks hang in the offices of Tokyo and the galleries of New York, dendroglyphs are little known even within Australia. Around sixty engraved trees still stand at Collymongle, two hours north of Baradine, but hundreds have been lost forever. These axe-incised trees once grew as far north as the Tweed, as far south as the Hawkesbury, and as far west as the Macquarie marshes. The surviving artworks may be some of the most beautiful objects to outlive the cultural tumult of twentieth-century Australia, their allure as immediate as the hand art of Carnarvon Gorge or the depictions of Wandjina in the caves of the Kimberleys. More people should realise the significance of these old greys of the Pilliga landscape. Stories prevail in even the most unassuming forests.

Witjweri

We say it's her favourite tree. Ever since she was born, we have taken her to this spot along Elwood canal. The drooping she-oak (*Allocasuarina verticillata*) provides enough cover that it is possible for us to imagine nothing exists beyond its feathery, curtain-like crown. Now, as a nine-month-old, she sits beneath the tree, bending the wiry branchlets until they snap, often waving them like a wand, as if they have the power to summon gregarious spirits. We have sat beneath this tree so many times, the picnic rug is permanently interlaced with the tree's branchlets. At home, our daughter is beholden to capricious whims and mood swings that veer between delight and agitation. But in nature, she is calm. Most trees demand her attention, the dark, filtered crown of the brush box (*Lophostemon confertus*) a repeated obsession, but there is something particularly fascinating about this drooping she-oak, especially for a child who has not accumulated the biases that, over time, tend to dictate our reactions. The tree stands alongside a yellow box (*Eucalyptus melliodora*) with only one of the three trunks alive. Birds go past and cockatoos quarrel. The teal use the canal as a flight path, travelling dangerously close to ground level as they steer towards the wetlands and Yalukit Willam Nature

Reserve. Once, we watch a baby magpie following her father around, whining as her guardian picks up earthworms and drops them into her mouth.

I am not sure why we first chose this spot, but there may be an intuitive reason. For the Wathaurung people, sitting beneath the crown of a she-oak is one of the safest places you can be, the litter of fallen branchlets providing a sanctuary from the prospect of snakes. I have read that the branchlets are eaten as a means of preventing thirst and diarrhoea, but I have not been able to observe this beneficial effect for my daughter. Whenever she puts them into her mouth, she recoils almost immediately. Nor does she enjoy touching the seed cones, which, when the valves are fully open, can feel spiky to the touch. I wonder what she is thinking when she stares at the cones, sometimes for several minutes, placing them in her hand and rotating them in her palm. They can appear, rather befittingly, like a nest of baby chicks, their bodies submerged, almost invisible, beneath a cover of open, upturned beaks.

My wife's pregnancy coincided with one of Melbourne's most intense periods of lockdown. I would drive Pip to her appointments with the obstetrician, but I would have to wait outside, in observance of the restrictions. The side road near the clinic became an avenue of husbands waiting patiently in their cars. Pleased to be out of the house, I would walk up and down the road, listening to the riotous sound of lorikeets in the trees. There was a large eucalypt on the corner of the hospital grounds, a yate (*Eucalyptus cornuta*), and I would look up into its crown, counting the number of musk lorikeets feeding on its nectar and looking out for little lorikeets, their smaller, less common cousins. Seeing a little lorikeet would be a sign of the embryo's health, I thought, my mind strangely superstitious when put under pressure like this. But while I never saw a little lorikeet, I did not need to worry about our daughter's health. 'She's gorgeous,' my wife said, immediately following the birth. 'How could she just be so gorgeous.'

One day, as we were preparing to leave her favourite tree, I held my daughter up to the branchlets so she could grab them and feel their coarse texture against her skin. Shaking them as hard as she could, mimicking the intensity of a cyclone, she laughed, blissfully entertained by the power she could wield. A lady walked past and remarked upon my daughter's joy, saying how important it was for children to be introduced to nature at an early age. She told us that many years ago she used to do the same thing with her grandchild, around 100 metres from where we were, holding him up as he grabbed the leaves of the large peppercorn tree (*Schinus molle*) on the corner of Glenhuntly Road. The peppercorn, despite being an ornate tree, has become sullied in our minds due to its status as a weed, but it has no such association for children. With its pustular bark, the tree has a fairytale quality, warmly grotesque at times, inviting at others. The drooping she-oak has a similar allure. There must be something instinctively welcoming about the branchlets, for they are not dissimilar to the beaded curtains that, for reasons unfathomable, play a welcoming role in the houses of new age aficionados. There must be something in the languidness that invites calm. When one is instructed to immerse oneself in nature, that remedy for an urban mind on the brink of nervous exhaustion, the prescription usually involves a forest or woodland, alpine scenery or coastal scrub. And yet there is one tree, the drooping she-oak, that, on its own, can offer a large measure of this analgesic power. Beneath the crown of this tree, it is possible to pretend nothing else exists. Time slows to a leisurely thrum, and the background noise of modern existence, with all its stammers and irksome jolts, recedes and dissolves.

When the Islanders took to the beaches of Mackay, sitting with their accordions as they rested from the backbreaking work of the cane farms, they were in the presence of the coastal she-oak (*Casuarina equisetifolia*). It was a tree that would have reminded them of home: the most beautiful of all she-oaks. In Mackay, the tree grows among wattles and banksias,[23] but it also grows naturally on the sands of South-East Asia, New Caledonia, Tonga, Solomon Islands and Vanuatu. The seed cones, large and heavy, ride with the ocean currents until they find sanctuary on an unsuspecting beach. In Tahiti, they call the tree *aito*, formerly *toa* or *etoa*. In Malaysia, it is the *rhu*. *Agoho* in the Philippines. *Nokonoko* in Fiji. For the Islanders, the trees were a vestige of familiarity among the lank, pungent leaves of the eucalypt and the oddly anthropomorphic cobs of the banksia. The first time they saw it might have been overwhelming, the power of that moment, its 'madeleine' arousal.

When Joseph Banks saw the tree for the first time in Queensland, he would also have found it a familiar sight. He knew the tree as *etoa* from his time in Tahiti. The Tahitians favoured the wood for its strength, using it for cooking tools, spears and other instruments. In June 1769, Banks recalls several of the trees growing near a collection of stones. The stones, some of which were almost 4 foot in height, were arranged in ascending tiers. The imposing artifice, the size of a four-storey building, was a marais, a ceremonial assemblage somewhere between a pyramid and a cairn. It was not uncommon for coastal she-oaks to be planted near these monuments as the wind sighing through their branchlets created a suitably mournful sound. Three months later, Banks observed coastal she-oaks growing on a beach in Timor. The following year, he would see the same trees fringing the coastline of Seventeen Seventy in Queensland.

In *A Million Wild Acres*, Eric Rolls describes a tribe in the southern highlands of New Guinea, near the shores of Lake Kutubu, planting thousands of coastal she-oaks in distinct arrangements. They have varied the density and the shape of the plantations to produce different notes,' Rolls describes. 'And on windy days, they dance to the singing of the trees.' The Wathaurung, from the Geelong area and Bellarine Peninsula, have a word for this sound: witjweri. It is a soft gentle whistle, the persistent soprano note often accompanied by the baritone creak of the trunk as it buckles and leans with the wind. It is not dissimilar to the sound of pine forests in Europe and North America. There is an old word for this, rarely used today: psithurism. It is the sound of wind as it whistles through the trees: the wind in the willows, the wind through the pines, or the wind against the long, drooping phylloclades of a soft, feathery she-oak. For the Wathaurung people, this sound acts as a connection with the voices of their lost ancestors. For some of the early settlers, this drone-like sound, akin to the tuning up of a string section, was comparable to the music of a harp.

'Adventure' is the association Matthew Condon, the Brisbane-based journalist, makes with the casuarina forest around Main Beach. Looking through family photographs, he often notices the blurred outline of she-oaks in the background. The tree is both mysterious and comforting. Running through the forest every afternoon as an adult, he would duck under the casuarina archway opposite Sea World and lose himself to the pulse of the forest. On the days he didn't run, he would feel unsettled. The further he entered the forest, the more he could disengage the screaming sound of the roller coasters with the psithuristic sound of the trees. As Condon recalls: 'The tops of the trees are quivering and sending out their music. It is melancholy at times. Or happy. Or eerie. Sometimes it sounds like how you feel inside. Sometimes it's the sound of memories. And other times I have no idea what the tunes mean. Whether they're coming from an unsettled present. Or whether they're songs from an unknown future.'

In his autobiography, *A Fortunate Life* (1981), Albert Facey, whose life jolts from the austerity of the western Australian wheat belt to the front line of Gallipoli, recalls a moment during his childhood when, escaping from a savage boar, he climbs up a tree to seek shelter. It was a she-oak tree, he writes, 'with a lot of small limbs attached to its trunk'. The she-oak, possibly a rock oak (*Allocasuarina huegeliana*), becomes Albert's favourite tree, a place of sanctuary amid the harshness of his childhood. It was, he says, 'the nicest tree I had known'. Albert Facey is probably not the only person to find reassurance in the tree's unassuming crown. Its feathery form is always a comforting sight when approaching an unfamiliar beachside resort, and out in the bush, the tree can have a curative effect amid the harsh, foreign scrub of chenopods, anaemic against the burgundy soil.

But for city dwellers, the tree can appear gaunt and messy when next to the upright verdure of a brush box (*Lophostemon confertus*) or the fixed poise of an English oak (*Quercus robur*). Its music may be haunting, but its appearance can be dowdy, the phylloclades pallid, and the branches arranged in loose, dishevelled sprays. It merges awkwardly with its surroundings, like a pencil sketch in a world of acrylics. Condon's and Facey's comments aside, I often wonder whether the she-oak is Australia's most unloved tree. Different species display different inadequacies. The orange-yellow flowers of a male

drooping she-oak dangle lifelessly in summer, giving the impression
the tree is dying. The stunted form of the dwarf she-oak (*Allocasuarina
humilis*) can be particularly uninspiring, littering the ground in dense,
unlovely clumps. The forest she-oak (*Allocasuarina torulosa*), meanwhile, is messy and unkempt. The tree presents itself with all the grace
and refinement of an errant schoolboy. While people may casually
extol the beauty of the wattle in bloom or, with pride, speak of the
magnificence of the eucalypt, it is rare they ever mention the luckless
she-oak. It is the ghost of the Australian landscape. A weakening
spirit. Indeed, the haunting whistle of the wind through its branchlets
may carry a message, a reminder of the speed with which we have
uprooted these trees from the landscape.

Around Brisbane airport, their drabness is a cause for celebration. The dense plantations of swamp oak (*Casuarina glauca*) were
planted deliberately to limit bird numbers at the airport. These trees
are familiar to anyone who has driven along Airport Drive from the
city. Approaching the airport, you register a Brisbane different from
the colourful city that glows with an unconstrained neon brilliance
like a Scott Redford sculpture. The radiance of the poinciana trees
(*Delonix regia*), trumpet trees (*Tabebuia pallida*, *Tabebuia palmeri*)
and golden penda (*Xanthostemon chrysanthus*) is replaced by the grey-
green, monochromatic intrusion of *Casuarina glauca*. But these trees
serve a purpose. Except for Torresian crows, which enjoy the shelter of
the canopy, or white-bellied sea eagles, which may nest in the crowns,
large birds tend to avoid these plantations. You might find a dainty
rufous whistler emitting its alarm-like call or a skittish grey fantail
attracted by the insects around the trees, but for many birds, the
austere casuarina plantations act as a vegetated moat, protecting the
castle of Brisbane airport from the advance of unwanted intruders.

For me, the dull grey monotony of the airport plantations came to define my impression of the casuarina. It was an unfortunate impulse as not all she-oaks exhibit the same lethargic obscurity. The swamp oaks that fringe Southern Cross Drive, as one drives from Sydney to its airport, are less profuse and more graceful than their Brisbane counterparts. And I recall driving in a taxi around Singapore and passing elegant and pert she-oaks, their attractiveness augmented by their relative infrequency. Ask me today for my image of a she-oak and I am as likely to picture the pre-Raphaelite swamp oaks in the Domain gardens in Sydney, the desert oaks (*Allocasuarina decaisneana*) used to frame photos of Uluru, or the exquisite river she-oak (*Casuarina cunninghamiana*) ornamenting the corner of Swanston and Little Collins streets in Melbourne. In the same way the tree's beauty depreciates from clustered repetition, so too does its capacity to welcome life. On its own, it repels with its dreariness. But place the tree in its natural setting, among a diversity of other trees, and its seeds will attract rainbow and musk lorikeets, galahs and gang-gang cockatoos. Kites, butcherbirds, magpie-larks and ospreys often nest in the trees, and glossy black cockatoos feed almost exclusively on casuarina seeds.

Melbourne, where I currently live, was once dominated by the drooping she-oak. Walk to the east, west or north in the early 1800s, and one would invariably notice the breadth of their distribution. They grew in an almost continuous line from today's Williamstown to Yarraville, and they prevailed along the coastlines of both the Bellarine and Mornington peninsulas. The tree has various names. The Dhauwurd Wurrung, who inhabited a large stretch of southwestern Victoria, call it gneering, whereas the Wathaurung call the tree ngarrai or narada, referring to the hair-like appearance of the branchlets.

Children would be encouraged to chew on the immature seed cones, an important source of vitamin C, and the timber, which is hard and durable, was fashioned into weapons and tools. But there is also an importance to the trees we will never understand. William Thomas, Assistant Protector for Aboriginals of the Port Phillip District, tells a story of three men waking up in a state of furious delirium. They were overcome by a condition they described as tur-run. Overnight, sorcerers had thrust thin branchlets of she-oak into their eyes. They were healed by a group of Aboriginal women rubbing hot leaves onto their breasts and stomach, 'repeating all the time strange songs and wild notes of sorrow and defiance'.

It is a measure of the casuarina's ability to evanesce that an entire species clinging to the rugged coastal sandstone of Australia's largest city was not noticed by Europeans in Australia for almost 200 years. The Nielsen Park she-oak (*Allocasuarina portuensis*) watched the First Fleet arrive at Sydney Cove. It watched the midden shells of Bennelong Point transform into the turreted edifice of Fort Macquarie and then, finally, into the white, vaulted shells of Sydney Opera House. And it was only identified in 1986 when a walking track was developed close to where the species grew. Over a short period of time, ten individual trees were located within 100 metres of each other. With only two males and eight females left, the Nielsen Park she-oaks were on the brink of extinction.

When I was last in Sydney, I braved the cloying humidity and headed on foot towards Vaucluse. The serenity of this suburb, one of Sydney's most desirable, is undercut at every turn by the noise of cement mixers and building site chatter. When I get to Nielsen Park, there is a strange stillness in the air. The park's entrance is guarded by swamp mahoganies (*Eucalyptus robusta*) and the divine, angelic calls of

211

the pied currawong. Shark Beach is almost empty when I arrive. I take a seat outside the café and breathe in my surroundings, a few people staring across the water, a few children dipping their feet into the bay. There is a sadness to this place, a deep melancholia. As I walk the narrow footpath, a child skips, a strange dreamy apparition that serves to conjure up a different century. This is a place that does not ascribe to any given age or historical foothold. It is timeless, almost unreal.

The plants along the Hermitage Foreshore Walk are not too dissimilar from the landscape Arthur Phillip and others would have seen as they sailed through the heads for the first time in January 1788: Sydney red gums (*Angophora costata*), Port Jackson figs (*Ficus rubiginosa*), cheese trees (*Glochidion ferdinandi*) and wild yellow jasmine (*Pittosporum revolutum*). Coast banksias (*Banksia integrifolia*) are common. Even non-remnant trees like the brush box (*Lophostemon confertus*) merge seamlessly into the background. The first couple of times I walk the circuit, I fail to see any Nielsen Park she-oaks. A few scrub she-oaks (*Allocasuarina distyla*), their branchlets pointing upwards, corymbose and upstanding, jut out from the almost bench-like protrusions of rock. The phylloclades are reasonably thick for a she-oak, and the longitudinal lines that run up and down the length of these branchlets are distinct and vaguely yellow. Black she-oaks (*Allocasuarina littoralis*) also grow in the area. They are gothic-looking trees, distinguishable from the other two species as their bark is noticeably fissured. When Banks and Solander surveyed Botany Bay in April 1770, the male trees may still have exuded a reddish tint, a result of the red flower spikes extending from the ends of each branchlet.

It is on my third circuit that I see the trees I have been looking for. There are a couple of brashly shaped rocks to the left of the footpath, which invite you to climb and wander off the track. The trees are hidden in this sanctuary. One grows in a pair with a coast banksia, its trunk almost 4 metres tall, its branchlets drooping haphazardly. The orange flowers dangle from the ends, giving the impression of hairy spider legs. The branchlets are thinner than those of the scrub she-oak. The leaves are not as pointed or crown-shaped, and the seed cones are darker and stockier. A second tree is leaning in the direction of the shore; another is almost horizontal. Its form is as evanescent as its future, the thin, wispy branchlets disappearing as one's view begins to change.

I have never felt a sadness in nature quite like my first view of the Nielsen Park she-oak. Trees usually appear so stern and forthright even if, underneath this veneer, they are suffering, dying of thirst or disease, or rotting and crumbling within. These she-oaks, rewilded in an attempt to prolong the species' decline, deceive in another way. The health of each individual tree may not be as terminal as the species itself, but one would think, from their meagre appearance, that they could be a mistimed flutter away from death. The similarly lacklustre tick bush (*Kunzea ambigua*) and prickly-leaved paperback (*Melaleuca nodosa*) grow in a cluster, and were it not for the golden sprays of the Sydney golden wattle (*Acacia longifolia ssp. longifolia*), the absence of colour would be palpable. Dead branches cover the outcrops of sandstone. Against this brash, darkened shelving of rock, an overt symbolism plays out. The frailty of the trees jars with the rock's apparent immutability. The more I stare at the tree, the more it shirks my gaze as if, shy and embarrassed, it rejects my attention, wishing for no one to observe its final resignation. There should be no curtain call for this species. No tear-stained farewell. The trees will simply fade away unnoticed, vanishing beneath the shadow of an overbearing cloud or against the flicker of the sun's shallow rays.

A more flamboyant species may have exacted a greater degree of attention. A tree with Mesozoic lineage or unusual flowers may have made headlines around the world. But the Nielsen Park she-oak did not excite the passions of even the most ardent nature lovers. James Woodford categorised them as 'one of nature's least charismatic critically endangered species'. Paul Ibbetson, the senior field officer with the National Parks and Wildlife Service, agreed. 'They're not a very exciting plant,' he said. 'They don't appeal to people the way the Wollemi pine does.' There is nothing distinctive about the tree. It is not glamorous or unusual. How many times did European eyes notice the Nielsen Park she-oak – and then dismiss it as just another dowdy casuarina?

A search was made of the remnant vegetation around the rest of the harbour foreshore, but, despite a concerted effort, no one could locate a second outpost for the species. Many years ago, the tree may have been common along the harbour foreshore. As with other serotinous species, the Nielsen Park she-oak relies on fire for the germination of its seeds. It prospered when members of the Gadigal took burning flower spikes of the grass-tree (*Xanthorrhoea resinosa*) and set alight the foreshore scrub around the harbour, its samaras released by the vicious heat of the fire, the ashy soil providing ideal growing conditions for the seedlings. The last of the ten original trees died in 2003. Had the trees remained undetected, this would have been the strange moment of pathos when a species, one that may have existed for millions of years, slips from the world without a valedictory flourish, never to grow again. But its departure from this Earth has been delayed because a number of seeds were collected from the female trees before they died. In the botanic gardens of Sydney, Mount Annan and Canberra, attempts were made to propagate the species, trees that now grow within Gap Bluff and Nielsen Park, the same trees I viewed on that melancholic afternoon.

Not far from the Hermitage Foreshore, the British flag may well have been hoisted on a casuarina, in this case a swamp oak (*Casuarina glauca*), as part of the militaristic revelry of 26 January 1788. Four shots were fired, toasts were raised, and the land was formally declared for the King. It is odd to think that a casuarina might have been at the centre of such a significant moment in Australia's history, and, indeed, contrary evidence exists, namely the paintings of Algernon Tarmage and Captain John Hunter, that show the flag raised on a pole, the position of the flag in line with today's Loftus Street, close to Customs House. But for others, the pole was a she-oak and the location was near the bottom of Bethel Steps on the corner of Hickson Road. One would find it hard to think of a less pompous tree for the occasion, one less befitting of a grandiose ceremony, than the ethereal swamp oak. When the historic tree was cut down in May 1832, there was outrage, according to a *Sydney Herald* article, that this tree 'considered sacred by Governor Macquarie, and the old hands of the colony' was to be removed for the purpose of road repairs. An obituary for the last of the First Fleeters, a man named John Limeburner who died in 1847, read: 'Jack remembered the British Flag being first hoisted in Sydney on a swamp-oak tree, which was placed in the spot, at the rear of Cadman's house, now occupied as the Water Police Court. The tree stood until the government of General Darling, when it was ordered to be cut down. A remnant of this tree is now in the possession of one of Australia's sons, who intends to deposit the relic in our Colonial Museum when erected.' What became of this relic is unknown.

A couple of older swamp oaks survive in the grounds of Sydney Botanic Gardens, close to the Maiden Pavilion, their branchlets pendant and immodestly long. Presumably they are descendants of the trees that graced this area when the First Fleet arrived, when the reclaimed land was still mudflats and swamp. They may even be the mature suckers of the same trees J.H. Maiden, whose name now adorns the aforesaid pavilion, records growing naturally in the same spot in 1920. The Gadigal word for the swamp oak is guman. They are a gentle reminder of times gone by when, for thousands of years, Sydney Cove was a quiet secluded beach. Maybe today, were you to filter out the sound of the ferries and the din of didgeridoos, you might hear the sound of the westerly breeze whistling through the thin pseudo-branchlets of these ghostly, secretive trees. In thousands of years, the same vista might be a seemingly endless expanse of water. In hundreds of thousands of years, it could be a desert. 'If you stand in its shadow by the light of the full moon,' W. Somerset Maugham says of the casuarina, 'you will hear, whispered mysteriously in its dark rampage, the secrets of the future.'

The Museum of Trees

In Murray Bail's novel *Eucalyptus* (1998), the main character, Holland, is so obsessed with eucalypts he creates 'an outdoor museum of trees', planting at least one of every species on his New South Wales property. Protecting the length of one side of the house is a windbreak of red ironbarks (*Eucalyptus sideroxylon*) and Steedman's gum (*Eucalyptus steedmanii*). A salmon gum (*Eucalyptus salmonophloia*) takes pride of place at the front gate. Other trees, like the Darwin woollybutt (*Eucalyptus miniata*) and silvertop stringybark (*Eucalyptus laevopinea*), grow nearby as one-off individuals. When Holland offers his daughter's hand in marriage to the first person who can identify every species, there is a flurry of contestants from all over the world. A Chinese suitor from Darwin trips up, quite literally, on a varnished gum (*Eucalyptus vernicosa*), the shrubby Tasmanian endemic that bulges like an eager succulent. A New Zealander gets beyond the halfway stage, only to be defeated by a scraggy-looking stringybark (*Eucalyptus youmanii*). And Roy Cave, a man who resembles the taut, columnar form of a mountain ash or spotted gum, powers through the first 300 or so species but struggles to separate *Eucalyptus fruticosa*, a 'maddeningly nondescript mallee', from *Eucalyptus foecunda*, the narrow-leaved red mallee of sand dunes around Perth.

A film was to be made of *Eucalyptus*, but production was aborted when, four days into the read-through, director Jocelyn Moorhouse tended her resignation. Had it progressed to the filming stage, actors Russell Crowe and Nicole Kidman may well have walked amid the myriad eucalypts of Dean Nicolle's Currency Creek arboretum in South Australia, acting out the absurdist fantasy on a 32-hectare property with views towards Hindmarsh Island. I visited the arboretum on one of the open days that Dean holds around September every year. It was 2019 and, although I did not know it at the time, it would be my last interstate trip before the pandemic curtailed travel for a couple of years. Flying from Melbourne, I anticipated receiving the honour of being the visitor who had travelled the furthest, but I was usurped by a landscape gardener who had driven from Geelong, a journey of almost 650 kilometres, his ambition to see the large-fruited mallee (*Eucalyptus youngiana*), with its ginormous, alien-eye fruit.

It is hard to imagine anyone volunteering for Holland's eccentric, patriarchal competition today. Had I signed up, I would have failed rather quickly as a suitor. Without hesitation, I identified the first tree I saw as a bushy yate (*Eucalyptus lehmannii*), a reasonably common planting in Victoria, discovering later it was the rare species *Eucalyptus mcquoidii*, distinguishable from *lehmannii* by its thinner leaves and spikier fruit. There are examples of species on the arboretum that would trouble even the most celebrated of experts. The four individuals of Molloy red box (*Eucalyptus leptophleba*), which can attain heights of 20 metres in the tropical heat of Cape York, are less than a foot high after almost twenty years of growth. The trees wither back to nothing in winter only to rejuvenate in the bright, expectant months of the spring. The broadleaf box (*Eucalyptus oligantha*) of the Kimberley is the same. Nearby grow a few candlebarks (*Eucalyptus rubida*), which are equally unidentifiable, lacking the diagnostic glaucous and orbicular juvenile foliage that can help distinguish them from manna gums (*Eucalyptus viminalis*) and mountain grey gums (*Eucalyptus dalrympleana*). Were the story of *Eucalyptus* transposed to the setting of Dean's arboretum, Ellen, Holland's daughter, would remain a bachelorette for the rest of her life.

Approximately 80 per cent of Australia's forests are dominated by eucalypts. 'No other comparable area of land in the world,' writes the historian Tom Griffiths about the Australian continent, 'is so completely characterised by a single genus of trees.' In her book *Gum* (2002), writer Ashley Hay asks us to imagine the continent as a grid, with each box defined by a single degree of longitude and latitude. In this artificial division, eucalypts grow in 93 per cent of the approximately 800 squares. And yet within the genus (or, rather, three genera, if we count *Corymbia* and *Angophora* as well), there is an extraordinary degree of variance. For P.J. Hurley, 'No other tree family in the world shows such a diversity in form, habit and colour of trunk and limb pattern', from the graceful lemon-scented gum (*Corymbia citriodora*) to the 'always delightful' Argyle apple (*Eucalyptus cinerea*), 'a grey-blue cloud in a forest of green'.

At Currency Creek, which is home to around 950 different species and subspecies of eucalypt, the full range can still be sampled in an afternoon. There is the exquisitely structured broad-leaved apple (*Angophora subvelutina*) and the glowing yellow bloodwoods (*Corymbia watsoniana, Corymbia bloxsomei*), trees that would make ideal street plantings, perfect counterpoints to the messy, sprawling form of the mottlecah (*Eucalyptus macrocarpa*), a shrub of the northern sandplains. A tree named *Eucalyptus insularis*, the seeds of which Dean had to take from North Twin Peak Island off the coast of Esperance, grows on Currency Creek's alkaline soils as a soft bush, so soft that the kangaroos sometimes use it as a cushion. It is considered the most distantly related of all eucalypt species and it looks out of place. So too does the narrow-leaved mallee (*Eucalyptus angustissima*), appearing from afar like a shrubby melaleuca, its leaves and flower arrangement becoming more acacia-like the closer you get. One need only walk for a short time to see there are few large trees on the arboretum, partly because of the age of the plantings and the alkaline soils, but also because the average eucalypt is not a towering east-coast giant but a small, mallee-like tree, unlikely to top 10 metres in its lifetime.

Indeed, walking through parts of the arboretum sometimes reminded me of the South Australian mallee, not that the visual affinity is immediate. The rolling hills of Currency Creek are unlike the flat expanse of areas like Gluepot Reserve, and the grasses are naturally more effusive than the red, laconic soils of the mallee. But in both locations, a sense of disorientation prevails. To walk through Gluepot, the largest area of intact mallee in Australia, is to pass through a wild grove of unreserved sameness. Trees grow as dispersed individuals, their trunks fountaining from the ground in aggregated clumps. 'Of all the eucalypts, the mallees leave me cold,' says the unnamed suitor in Murray Bail's novel. 'They can never make up their minds which direction to take.' It is an astute remark, for it is easy to become lost within the mallee. The view to the north is the same as the view to the west, and the views to the east and the south are no different.

Upon closer inspection, it is possible to detect up to four species of eucalypt at Gluepot Reserve: *socialis*, with its gnome-hatted buds; *oleosa*, with buds shaped like acorns; *gracilis*, with its cup-shaped fruits; and the ubiquitous *dumosa*, its gumnuts shaped like barrels. But from afar, the trees appear identical, their silhouettes all imitating the same capitulatory poise. The plantings at Currency Creek are more regimented, the trees arranged in rows of four like a polytypic planta-tion, but in other respects they are the same, as cold and inscrutable as those of the mallee. At one point, I find myself hypnotised by a row of Deua gums (*Eucalyptus wilcoxii*), experiencing the same feeling I had at Gluepot Reserve, a Hitchcockian effect of vertigo where my focus on the trees remains constant while the mallee scrub expands exponentially behind me.

According to Holland in Murray Bail's novel, Adelaide is the city of eucalypts. 'More than any other city,' adds the suitor Mr Cave, 'the things are everywhere.' Perhaps Cave and Holland are imagining the landscape before the South Australian Company lured settlers with the prospect of cheap land, high ideals and an agreeable climate. For there was indeed a time when the southern part of Adelaide was covered in grey box (*Eucalyptus microcarpa*), and when mallee box (*Eucalyptus porosa*) accented the west and the north, and blue gums (*Eucalyptus leucoxylon*) were a feature of the east. But while eucalypts may have dominated the distant past, this is not the case today. Modern Adelaide is a city of plane trees (*Platanus spp.*) and jacarandas (*Jacaranda mimosi-folia*), cotton palms (*Washingtonia filifera*) and English elms (*Ulmus procera*).

How fitting, though, for the country's largest eucalypt arboretum to be located in the state that redefined our image of the gum tree. I am thinking, in particular, of the Hans Heysen paintings *Red Gold* (1913), *Droving into the Light* (1921) and *Red Gums of the Far North* (1931), the first of which hangs today in the Art Gallery of South Australia. In this picture, two monolithic river reds (*Eucalyptus camaldulensis*) stand either side of an informal trackway as a herd of cattle passes through. The painting reveals the spirit of the trees, at once muscular and frail, the dusty scene impassioned by the rich, flame-like colours of the lower trunks. If eucalypts, up to this point, had merged into the cultural background, they were now protagonists. No longer viewed in terms of the effete, decorative swirls of a John Glover painting or the thin, submissive scrawls of Joseph Lycett and Augustus Earle, they were irrevocably redefined by Heysen, their role as richly emblematic as that of the hardworking drover's wife or the implacable pioneer. To quote Matthew Colloff, under Heysen's stewardship the trees had become 'heroic, resilient and enduring'.

Evening Shadows (1880) by Henry James Johnstone, also hanging in the Elder Wing of the gallery, was one of the main inspirations for Heysen's work. In this painting, the river reds are more dignified and sublime, and the scene they frame more tranquil, but the trees share a similar magisterial poise.

The study of eucalypts was still in its infancy at this time. Heysen, when he refers to the species at all, calls them white gums, a rather vague term that may be applied to any number of different trees. The main reference book was Ferdinand von Mueller's *Eucalyptographia* (1883), released when Heysen was a child, which established the number of eucalypt species at 100. It is a rather conservative estimate, for we now know this figure is closer to 1000, and we recognise that the eucalypts Heysen painted are not only river reds but two distinct subspecies: *camaldulensis*, the more common taxa, which grows in the Adelaide Hills and is differentiated by the beaked operculum of the gumnuts; and *minima*, the subspecies that grows in the Flinders Ranges, its bud cups elongated so they resemble, if one's eyes allow the conceit, the funnel-shaped hat of the tin man in *The Wizard of Oz*.

The last few decades have seen a vast expansion in our knowledge of eucalypts, and much useful research has emerged from Dean Nicolle's pseudo-laboratory at Currency Creek. Some species are deliberately burnt or pruned to assess how readily they can revivify from underground lignotubers. Oils are extracted for their medicinal value. DNA is removed on demand, enabling scientists to use genomic sequencing to build up our knowledge of the plant group's phylogeny and capacity to adapt to change. Nicolle is suitably fastidious, recording details such as when a tree first flowers and how much it grows every year. But it would be wrong to think this level of knowledge is unique to European science. In a time before Joseph Banks was even born, most people on this continent might be described as botanists. The average person, according to Indigenous scholar Alison Page, had an intricate knowledge of around 400 plants. He or she knew which leaves could be soaked in water and applied as a poultice to treat sores and infection, or at what time of the year a tree flowered, and what that blooming signified for the surrounding environment. This was, in Page's words, a compendium of scientific data, one not recorded in textbooks or academic journals, but rather 'downloaded ... by Aboriginal people through story'.

Songlines – a collective consciousness of stories, belief and instruction. In these stories, the trees are often personified, their attributes revealing the singer's specialised knowledge, such as which parts of the tree are poisonous or when the fruit is ripe enough to be eaten. Trees are community members, 'part of our mob', says Ngarigu academic Jakelin Troy. The trees on which the spirits of ancestors have come to rest are not just *like* those ancestors, writes researcher Diana James, they *are* those ancestors. And people treat them accordingly, caring for them and interacting with them as their own kin. There is a memorable passage in Kim Scott's *That Deadman Dance* (2010) where the settlers pass through a woodland of paperbarks and banksia, grass trees and peppermints. The merchant observes what he perceives as strange behaviour from his Nyoongar guide: 'Wooral addressed the bush as if he were walking through a crowd of diverse personalities, his tone variously playful, scolding, reverential, affectionate.' The landscape was alive. The trees, like acquaintances on the street, local characters from one's neighbourhood, demonstrate their own personalities and charm. They brim with memories and ideas, rich with desire and suggestion.

Such nuance can often be obscured by an obsession with detail. Science is as want to churn out an automaton as it is a storyteller, and it is indicative of an obsession with nomenclature and classification that physical fights were rumoured to have broken out among botanists when, in the 1990s, the *Eucalyptus* genus was subdivided into *Corymbia*, *Eucalyptus* and *Angophora*. Names are not seared into the tree's bark: a eucalypt by any other name would still smell as mentholated. 'In English, we give things very static names and then that's what something is known as, always,' says Jakelin Troy in an interview for *Wonderground* magazine. 'But from an Aboriginal point of view, trees and plants get different names at different times of year.' Why give two trees different names if they are both harvested only for their manna, the lerp secreted by leaf-sucking psyllids? And why limit a tree to one name if it provides delectable sap in spring, nectar in summer and a ready supply of bark at any other time of the year? It is a system of practicality rather than categorisation. It is also one that allows for personalisation. Older trees are given individual names and recognised for their roles within the Dreaming. One is more likely to care for a tree if it is anthropomorphised in this way, as successive environmental campaigns have demonstrated. It worked for the Ada tree near Powelltown in Victoria and the Tolkien Track through the Styx Valley in Tasmania. It also helped save the forests of Wylds Craig, for once the Trident Tree was given a name, writes Ashley Hay, it 'stopped being an anonymously shaggy messmate somewhere along an unknown track'. Instead, it became a martyr, an intimate symbol for the destruction of Tasmania's ancient forests.

We have, as an overtly rationalist society, sought to tame and demystify our environment, admiring orchards and neatly pruned gardens while being repulsed by the wildness of grasslands and railway verges. Intrigue has been surrendered for order, poetry traded for practicality. A false dichotomy has emerged, one where humans stand apart from nature. We have lost the art, writes critic and novelist John Fowles, of viewing 'nature as a mirror for philosophers, as an evoker of emotion, as a pleasure'. This may be why Bail is so obsessed with mirrors in *Eucalyptus* – why they appear as a repeated motif connecting stories about barbershops and Omeo gums, fruit stores and the narrow-leaved red mallee. The characters themselves are also reflections of this dichotomy of wildness versus control. The unnamed suitor's dreaminess is portrayed as an archaic affectation while Roy Cave, nothing more than a Linnaean machine, is admired for his bureaucratic observation.

Where *Eucalyptus* disappoints, at least for me, is its reliance on stories set in Europe. It is an understandable trope, given this is a story of European settlers attempting to conquer what is, to them, a foreign and formidable land. But this one-sided perspective detracts from the novel's potential to be *the* Australian allegory. As a reading experience, it feels closer to Italo Calvino than Peter Carey or Patrick White. Could there be a parallel novel, perhaps, where the unnamed suitor takes us through the rugged plains of Adnyamathanya country rather than the streets of Eastern Europe? For there, within the deserts of the Flinders Ranges, close to the Milyaru Wayakanha waterhole, is a river red so omnipotent that it has the power to alter the weather. When people hit its trunk with branches and large stones, the spirits listen, suppressing the heat and accelerating the cool change. Is that not a more powerful story than a tale of stamps set in Switzerland and Spain? Perhaps he could venture a little further south, to the Yankaninna homestead, where two river reds have been bisected by a road. These trees, referred to as wida adrupa by the Adnyamathanya people, were once husband and wife, but they have been separated by the intrusion of the road. Their divorce, a product of circumstance, stands as a warning: stare at them for long enough and your marriage may endure a similar fate.

Imagine this scene, says the unnamed narrator as he sits in the shade of a particularly insouciant river red: a husband, wife and son drive their car into Adnyamathanya country. They travel through the rusted pathways of the Flinders Ranges and stop by a large tree, its base hollowed out and its roots exposed by the crumbling bank on which it stands. As the wind rustles the leaves, the man feels what he describes as the tree's living element pass through his body. It is an understanding that transcends words. When his son dies a few years later on the battlefields of Tobruk, one of the photos the man took that day is found on the dead son's body.

Another photo taken that day is sent to the London Salon of Photography, where it is exhibited with the title *A Giant of the Arid North* (1937). Another version is shown later and given the name *Spirit of Endurance* (1937). Not only would Harold Cazneaux's photo become one of the most iconic shots ever taken of the Australian landscape, the tree would also become a tourist attraction, and for decades after, people would make the five-hour pilgrimage from Adelaide to stand in its presence. When Paul West, in the 2022 ABC program *Australia's Favourite Tree*, says of the river red, 'You can come to know each tree, they're so unique in their character and their personality,' his sense of familiarity has been primed by photos like Cazneaux's and paintings like Heysen's.

Trees can help us reflect. Through their ridges and patterned crowns, they can push the limits of our visual acuity. The roots of the Cazneaux tree, exposed, almost skeletal, their nakedness the result of erosive floods, utter cries like a visceral hymn. And that gutted trunk, 'scarred and marked by the elements', to use Cazneaux's words, conveys the central contradiction in all of us. In its trauma, we feel our own frailty, our own vulnerability to outside forces. In its resistance, we see our own pure bloody-mindedness. Trees are poetic. They help us 'see into the life of things', to borrow a phrase from William Wordsworth. They stand in nature as crooked, uneven mirrors, and as we walk through their corridors and galleries, we would do well to stop and observe these living, breathing exhibits.

New Dreamings

On most Saturdays between 1885 and 1888, the painters Tom Roberts, Frederick McCubbin and Louis Abrahams alighted from the train at Box Hill Station and walked south. They headed towards their friend David Houston's farm, following the line of Station Street before turning west towards the creek. This was many decades before the front yards and California bungalows of Box Hill South would be built. They would walk past the future site of Roberts McCubbin Primary School, which would be named in their honour. The painters were in one of the last remnant patches of bush within a train ride from Melbourne.

Roberts, in a letter to McCubbin after the war, remembers the camp fondly, the last light of the sun ghosting the trees as the artists were comforted by the sound of the southern boobook owl. There were no footprints of other humans, no anthrophonic sounds to dispel their sense of peace.

One of the paintings from that time is Roberts' *The Artists' Camp* (1886). McCubbin is seated, drinking from a tapered cup, while Abrahams is by the fire, cooking some meat. The painting captures the serenity of the bush – one can almost hear a chorus of bellbirds

– but there is already the hint that as the light fades, it will be accompanied by foreboding. Not far from this spot, McCubbin painted *Lost* (1886). Here, the trees lean with an ominous disregard. Off-centre is a young girl, maybe eleven or twelve years old, in a blue dress and white apron. She is clutching something in her right hand, possibly a sprig of mistletoe, and is dwarfed by the trees around her, as if on the verge of being swallowed by the bush. Her left hand covers her eyes: is she crying? 'It frightened me,' writes author Hannah Kent of the first time she saw the painting as a child. 'I knew how thirsty you could become when the shadows lay thin on the ground, and how the scrub could rise around you – grey, scorched and watching – until you were afraid you would never get out.'

We are a country of lost children, wrote Peter Pierce in 1999, taking his lead from an unexplored, almost throwaway line in Bruce Chatwin's *Songlines*. 'The lost child is the symbol of essential if never fully resolved anxieties within the white settler communities of this country,' he continued. The child in McCubbin's painting is a metaphor for the European distrust of a landscape populated not by oaks, elms and birch but by eucalypts and acacias. It was an environment they would never understand with the same lucidity as the First Australians, a land of arcane secrets and endless space. Children wandered into the bush, lured by the promise of discovery, never to be seen again. 'We are all that McCubbin child,' playwright Tom Wright has said, 'and our great anxiety and our great fear is that we won't just be overwhelmed by the landscape, but that we will actually be genuinely wiped out.'

McCubbin based the painting on a story he heard a year before. Twelve-year-old Clara Crosbie disappeared in the bush and was found alive in the hollow of a peppermint tree[24] twenty-one days later, her apron hanging outside in a vain attempt to suppress the wind.

She had survived on creek water, her hunger reaching such a point she sampled the bark from a tree only to spit it out in disgust. When she was discovered, her two saviours fed her toast and wrapped her emaciated body in blankets. A few months later, she was up on stage recounting the experience at the behest of her father.

Clara's journey was unusual in that she had a destination: the house where her mother was staying, a few kilometres to the north. The Duffs of the Wimmera were searching the mallee for broombush (*Melaleuca uncinata*), the branches of which were used for fencing, when they wandered too far afield. McCubbin's child appeared to be looking for mistletoe.

For three lost children of Daylesford, it was the allure of wild goats. One can follow the route William, Thomas and Alfred took in 1867, beginning at the Daylesford mill markets on the outskirts of town and following the blue signs to Wombat State Forest. The trio curled up together in the hollow of an old eucalypt, sheltering from the frost. They died overnight, and yet their bodies were not discovered for another eleven weeks.

I was not quite prepared for the shrine at the end of Wheelers Hill Road, a cairn around 4 feet tall, surrounded by a small garden planted with decorative species such as hairpin banksia (*Banksia spinulosa*) and rosemary grevillea (*Grevillea rosmarinifolia*). There was a toy train set and a couple of teddy bears, and signs alerting visitors to the presence of wombat holes. Wheelers Hill Road is now a series of open fields with Montpellier broom (*Genista monspessulana*) and blackberry (*Rubus fruticosus*) growing alongside. There was no trace of the overbearing forest that would have dominated this area 150 years ago. Only a few medium-sized blackwoods (*Acacia melanoxylon*) grow around the cairn, one of which had become a message tree, laminated messages pinned to its trunk. It was possible to guess the age of the message by the rustiness of the pin. 'The bush has secrets,' said one that looked several decades old. 'The trees, they are all quiet. Sometimes though, you hear a sound. Small voices break the silence.'

On another tree was a picture of the eucalypt in which the children sought shelter. The photo, taken around 1930, shows the tree shortly before it died. It stands alone, the forest of which it was part having been cleared many years before. Only a few branches cling to the waning trunk. It would remain standing, a posthumous figure of defiance, for almost twenty years before it was uprooted in a storm. Jan Smith from the Daylesford & District Historical Society was kind enough to send me a photo, taken in September 1950, showing two ladies in winter jackets and chequered skirts with the trunk behind them, lying insentient on the ground. Like the statue of Ozymandias, the fallen trunk conveys only a glimpse of the tree's erstwhile majesty: a 'colossal wreck, boundless and bare'. How this contrasts with the oldest record we have, a photo taken in 1867 as part of a re-enactment of the boys' discovery, where the tree exhibits an almost almighty presence. It is blacker and thicker than the surrounding trees, a regent among subjects, a lord revered by his liege. It is hard to determine the species from the photo, but it may well be a messmate (*Eucalyptus obliqua*), with its roughened trunk and buttressed roots. There are about a dozen trees in the background, their upright trunks spaced evenly apart but close enough so that the secondary trees on the horizon form an almost unbroken blur. It is not easy, when looking at the photo, to imagine the whole area as a forest, the nearest dwelling an afternoon's horse ride away.

A strange meeting occurred around 2 pm on the day the children went missing. The three children, William, Thomas and Alfred, ran into the local storekeeper close to where Ridge Road meets the Daylesford–Ballan Road. The storekeeper walked with them for about a quarter of a mile, explaining they just needed to follow the new telegraph line to get back to town. The eldest boy was William Graham, a freckly seven-year-old, wearing a black cap and a tartan cravat. 'Wires,' he said, almost hypnotically. 'Wires …' There was no reason now for getting lost, yet at some point the boys lost sight of the wires and strayed eastwards to Specimen Hill goldmine. On any other day there would have been around fifty people digging for gold, but it was a Sunday and the place was empty. Later, as dusk was falling, they encountered John Quin, a local boy working on a farm. John, who was only ten years old, picked William up and turned him around, explaining, by way of the gesture, that Connell's Gully was in the opposite direction. But it was as though the boys were being pulled by a force beyond their control.

When the children disappeared, Melbourne was almost thirty-two years old and Daylesford was barely five. It is easy to imagine, as I first did, that the children had to navigate through impenetrable forest, but it was not so. Following close to Sailors Creek, one walks today through the relatively dense stands of manna gums (*Eucalyptus viminalis*) and narrow-leaved peppermints (*Eucalyptus radiata*) of the Hepburn Regional Park. Back then, the land was characterised by open woodland, with giant trees roughly 10 to 20 metres apart. 'The boys would have little real hindrance as they wandered forward through the open forest grassland country,' writes historian John Menadue. This was land that was managed for centuries by the burning regimes of the Dja Dja Wurrung. Any younger trees would have been chopped down and burnt by the gold diggers for warmth: Specimen Hill goldmine would have appeared like the surface of the moon.

It would only be as the children entered what was then the Bullarook Forest, east of today's Specimen Hill Road, that the trees would have begun to enclose them. One gets a sense of their final moments by walking the Lost Children route through the quiet tracks of the Wombat State Forest. It is a mournful place. The trees tower, messmates and candlebarks (*Eucalyptus rubida*), manna gums and broad-leaved peppermints (*Eucalyptus dives*). The understorey shimmers with a ghostly, evanescent haze. There are roads and open fields less than a kilometre away but it feels like the forest could go on forever. One need only venture off the path for 20 to 30 metres to get a sense of the boys' likely disorientation. As they approached Wombat Creek, they descended into the valley, and any thought of finding home must have disappeared in this moment. As fear and tiredness took over, their ears would have been alive to the creaking of trees and the crack of branches underfoot. They may have heard the incessant taunting of the spotted pardalote or the mewling screams of the yellow-tailed black cockatoos.

The sad thought is the boys were not far from help. Beyond this patch of forest, there was a small field cleared to grow potatoes and oats. The Carmichaels' house was nearby. The McKays' house was even closer.

After visiting the Wheelers Hill Road memorial, I travelled home via the Calder Freeway, driving through what was once the notorious Black Forest. In the days of the gold rush, this was the quickest route to the goldfields of Bendigo and Mount Alexander. People vanished here routinely, many of them callously murdered and their bodies left to rot. This was a forest where travellers were robbed by bushrangers; where people stumbled across broken carts with human bones strewn across the ground; where a group of mounted troops discovered a body in a tree hollow, its face pulverised, its hands and feet tied together, the victim's pockets turned inside out. Reading the literature of the time, one gains the impression that few traversed the area without incident – an exaggeration, perhaps, but an indication of the fear with which the area was regarded.

The Black Forest, a name few Melburnians would be familiar with today, grew in a dense, auriform clump between Gisborne and Woodend, 'so thickly set,' wrote English author Ellen Clacy, 'that the rear-guard of the escort cannot see the advance-guard in the march.' The entrance to the forest, as if imagined by Jim Henson or the Brothers Grimm, required travellers to pass underneath the overhanging branch of a large tree. The road veered along verges and gullies, over morasses and holes, the soil turning into a quagmire with just the slightest hint of rain. For some, the large black stump halfway through brought a sense of relief; for others, it was a sign they were as deep as they could be.

Today, the forest is virtually no more. Around Gisborne, a group of cattle loaf about on a large, graceless field. Golden cypresses (*Hesperocyparis macrocarpa 'aurea'*) and poplars (*Populus spp.*) dot the landscape. There is a forest in the distance, dark and brooding, but it is a plantation, row upon row of Monterey pine (*Pinus radiata*) fringed at the roadside by messmates and candlebarks. A small area of the forest still stands along Black Forest Drive. The black gums (*Eucalyptus aggregata*) said to give the forest its name are now an endangered species in Victoria.[25] What was once the most feared part of the colony has barely left a trace. Landscapes can change in a generation or two; vast stands of eucalypts were cleared to fuel the fires of those chasing gold.

A few weeks after my trip to Daylesford, I got in the car and headed towards Ararat. I was looking for the type specimen of *Eucalyptus aromaphloia*, the scentbark of northwestern Victoria, a 200-year-old tree that still lives today by the side of the Western Highway. It is part of a strip of trees between the highway and the main road in Buangor. J.H. Willis, a naturalist who was rumoured to differentiate eucalypt species by the taste of their leaves, realised in 1954, along with botanist Lindsay Pryor, that the scentbark was its own species despite its tendency to hybridise with *Eucalyptus viminalis*.

It took me a while to find the tree. I took a wrong turn, parking on a gravel road alongside what appeared to be a village green, and traipsed across an area of old river red gums (*Eucalyptus camaldulensis*) while a black-shouldered kite, perched in the crown of a particularly menacing tree, kept watch. After almost an hour, I realised I was lost. My hands shaking from the cold, I returned to my car and made my way along Main Street back towards the highway. Luckily, the scentbark is quite evident once you glimpse it. Its branches fork out at sharp angles in contrast to the younger trees, and the dark, aggressive tint of its trunk stands out against the fulgent green leaves of a nearby golden wattle (*Acacia pycnantha*).

Driving a little further towards Ararat, I saw a camp by the roadside. At first it looked like a small outdoor market place, but on closer inspection, I saw signs and banners among the tents. One of the signs said 'No Trees, No Treaty'. Another said 'The World is Watching' and a third, the letters a mix of black, yellow and red, 'Indigenous Land Theft 1788 to 2018?' I would later find out that this was the Djabwurrung Embassy, a name deliberately chosen to symbolise its sovereignty from the Australian nation. The three camps positioned along the highway had, over time, become the symbolic heart of a battle between heritage and progress. For the protestors who stayed there during the winter months, it was not an easy venture. Fires were lit and tea consumed regularly. People swapped stories and others kicked a football around.

The protestors were fighting to save a number of trees due to be removed as part of the planned duplication of the highway. A video on the VicRoads website showed the trees that would be bulldozed to make way for the asphalt. The 3D visual glided down the proposed highway, highlighting the ill-fated trees as orange, ghostly appari-tions. They were mainly river red gums, but there were a few yellow gums (*Eucalyptus leucoxylon*) and yellow boxes (*Eucalyptus melliodora*) along the way. The problem with the video was that it was hard to distinguish between sapling and venerable giant. Some of the trees marked for destruction might have been twenty years old. Others may have germinated in the thirteenth century.[26]

It is unimaginable that the larger trees, with their bases hollowed out, do not have special significance for the Djabwurrung people, as sanctuaries for shelter and cooking, places for women to give birth, marker trees whose existence is embodied in songlines. One of these birthing trees is located to the south of Langi Ghiran State Park. It is actually two trees deliberately intertwined, conjoined when the trunks were young and malleable. Once a certain girth was reached, the tree was carefully burnt to create an entrance. It is known as a grandmother tree and, according to a 2017 report, is 'one of the finest examples still in existence of a culturally modified habitation tree which is still living'. Nearby is another river red which, because it leans towards the grandmother, is referred to as the grandfather tree. Ancestors shelter in these trees, protecting the Djabwurrung from evil spirits.

Across the road, a large yellow box called a directions tree grows beside a plantation of blue gums (*Eucalyptus globulus*). The patterns of the bark, which curve back and forth like the waves of the sea, were carved into the trunk when the tree was still young. Placentas were buried beneath this tree, and when those babies grew up and needed

239

help, they would return to the tree and seek guidance. These trees carry their DNA, say the Djabwurrung. The directions tree is said to have grown from the seeds and placenta of their ancestors many centuries ago. But bureaucratic judgements do not give weight to powers of belief. There are no photographs showing the birthing tree illuminated by a small fire as a mother prepares to give birth. Nor is there a journal entry from a man reflecting upon his future as he seeks guidance from his directions tree. There is only a collective spirit of knowledge passed from one generation to the next.

A few months later, after finding a couple of reports online and cross-referencing the data, I drove again to the Langi Ghiran area. Nestled in the central console of my car was a sheet of paper on which I had drawn a mud map, showing what I believed were relatively accurate locations for the grandparent trees and the directions tree. I also had crosses marked for another two grandparents less than 10 kilometres to the north. According to the news that week, the likelihood of saving the trees was looking slim. For the last few days, I had allowed the anticipation of this trip to build to something of a crescendo, much as a birdwatcher might nervously visit a location where a rare bird has been sighted, knowing this may be the only opportunity to savour such a glimpse.

Just before Langi Ghiran State Park, I pulled off onto an access road. Maybe I have remembered this falsely, because almost certainly the piping calls of magpies filled the air, but my recollection is of a morose, intermittent silence, readily punctuated by the drone of cars as they rocketed past. I began walking towards where I believed the birthing tree was located, only to stop almost immediately. My heart was pounding. I tried again, but the same thing happened. I could feel the weight, the crushing boorishness of my steps. Where others before me had tiptoed through this landscape, awake to the promise of what they might find, I felt myself once again to be the heavy-footed tourist who, oblivious to anything but the present, ascended the sacred pathway of Uluru.

It was at this moment I had an epiphany, a temporal reset that shifted my mind from the past to the present. The language used in the media and filtered through the many reports, the word 'heritage' repeated incessantly, relegates these trees to the past, as if they were artefacts, relics, an outdoor museum of trees. And yet the trees are alive, undeniably so, as alive as the culture that celebrates their presence. 'Western views of heritage are about static objects from the past,' writes academic Libby Porter, but '… this view fails to honour the substance and spirit of living cultures.'

When the politician Lidia Thorpe visited one of the birthing trees, she said, 'I sat in that tree with my youngest daughter and just closed my eyes and felt the presence of my ancestors.' Through this tree, she was connected to her culture. As I tried to imagine what it would be like to stand in front of these great survivors, I realised my engagement could only ever be facile by comparison. Uluru had shown me the carelessness of my curiosity. These trees were sacred to the Djabwurrung people, narrative signposts that were on the brink of elimination. I stood motionless for five, maybe ten minutes, gripped by my desire to see these trees but overcome by a deep humility. Eventually, I headed back to the car.

Aboriginal beliefs are about 'continuity, constancy, balance, symmetry, regularity', says anthropologist Bill Stanner. One takes from nature only enough to preserve its bounty, and one's grandchildren should enjoy the same level of comfort as one's ancestors. It is an inversion of the Bible's instruction to have dominion, as God says to Adam and Eve, over everything that creeps upon the earth. To walk

241

between the grandparent and the birthing trees at Langi Ghiran is to hear the sounds of people laughing, babies crying. 'To sit in a tree that saw your people birthed, your people massacred, and now your people's resistance is a feeling that the English language will never be able to capture,' writes Nayuka Gorrie, one of the leading campaigners against the trees' removal. Through the trees, she understands her purpose. The land is story; story is the land. One is born from the folds of the land and when one dies, one returns there. The feelings, motives and desires that propel one through life are bound to the trunks of these trees, revealed in their hollows. 'A forest is language,' writes Murray Bail at the end of *Eucalyptus*. 'Accumulated years.'

In Rolf de Heer's film *Ten Canoes*, the Ramingining of east Arnhem Land tell stories to themselves as they craft canoes from Darwin stringybark (*Eucalyptus tetrodonta*). The film premiered at the Cannes Film Festival, winning the Special Jury Award. De Heer tells a heartening story about the excursion to Cannes. It was the first time many of the crew had travelled outside Australia and, while the beauty of the French Riviera was beguiling, the flashing cameras were too much for actors Richard Birrinbirrin and Peter Djigirr. De Heer took them to a nearby island, Sainte-Marguerite, where alongside Aleppo pines (*Pinus halepensis*) there were plantations of blue gums. The gum trees soothed their souls. Djigirr went up to one of the trees and hugged it. 'He was at peace with the world again,' writes de Heer. 'He addressed every other gum tree he saw, saying, "Tell your cousins over there I'll be home on Thursday!"'

Djigirr's yearning is similar to the soldiers returning home from World War I, relishing the smell of eucalyptus floating across the sea. Many Australians would have felt a similar pang of pleasure in seeing a river red while on holiday in Italy or a blue gum while driving

242

through California. Those of us who are not First Nations may never experience the same spiritual immersion as Nayuka Gorrie, but we can, through walking the forests of this continent, leave the volatility of modern life and observe a time when constancy prevailed.

A day may come, not too far in the future, when Australia is viewed as a pioneering country: the first modern state to redefine progress as the maintenance of stability. The lively chatter of children as they gather mud crabs and oysters, or the sound of stone axes hammering footholds into mighty trees, may become as ingrained in the Australian narrative, as vivid in our national imagination, as the booming commands of Governor Phillip or the shellfire of Anzac Cove. Humility and stewardship could be cultural traits. The practices and patience of cultures that have existed for thousands of years can benefit not just the landscape, but our economy and our politics. Alas, we are some way from this ideal.

'We need to discover new dreamings,' writes researcher Matthew Colloff, 'new stories of our country, new reasons to celebrate the nature of our land and its waters that all of us can connect with.' This imagined future, with its fresh discourse of balanced progressivism, could well be our new dreaming. But for the moment, we have reached an impasse. White Australia fears engagement with the past for what it reveals about ourselves, in the same way those first settlers once dreaded the bush. And yet we fail to appreciate that the world's oldest continuing cultures, which have survived previous environmental unrest, have a roadmap for the country's future. The wisdom is there; it is whether we are capable, as Pitjantjatjara Elder Tony Tjamiwa says, of clear listening, starting with the ears, then moving to the mind and ultimately settling in the heart as knowledge.

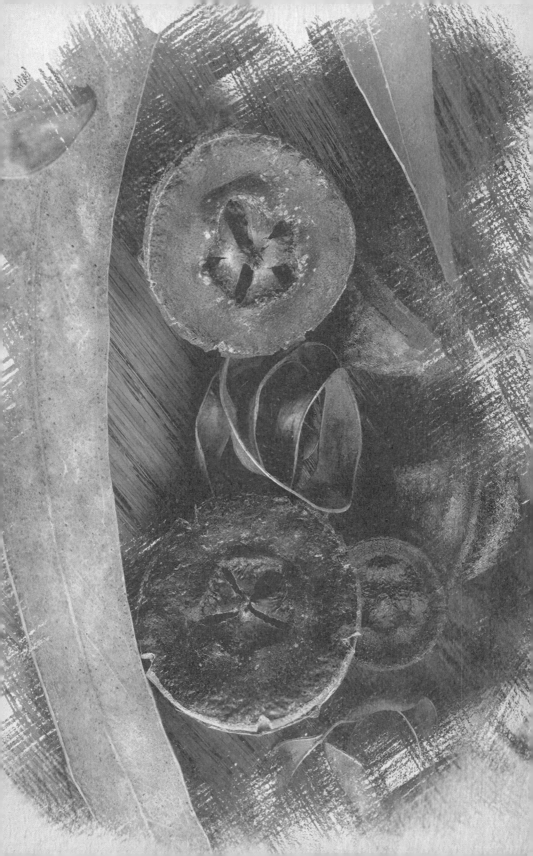

Epilogue:
Saint-Hilaire Trees

We arrived at our accommodation in a rental car. It was our first trip as a family of three. The flat was located in the northern Sydney suburb of Wollstonecraft, not far from Smoothey Park. As I lifted our four-month-old daughter from the child seat, I glanced at the street trees and recognised them immediately. They were brush box. Queensland box trees. Lopcons. To visualise them, imagine the smooth trunk of a Sydney red gum roughened with patches of loose-hanging bark, the leaves like those of a fig tree or a red flowering gum. The trunks were upright in some; in others, they were tumescent, a ring of burls circling the tree like an ungainly necklace. They were jungle trees taking over the suburbs. In her book *Understory* (2017), writer Inga Simpson says brush box were the first trees she learnt to identify on her Queensland property. 'Of all Australian trees, brush box remind me the most of J. R. R. Tolkien's ents – the trees who can move, talk and sing songs.' If one can ever glimpse the enchantment of fairytales in an urban street, one might do so through a Queensland box.

Our daughter knows these trees well, for there are a small number of brush box trees at the end of our road. We pass them every day.

When we used to push her in the bassinet, the sunlight would filter through the gaps between the leaves, and she would smile, entranced by the dappled patterning of the light. My wife also knows these trees well. We have traipsed through their habitat many times on our way back from Cape Byron Lighthouse. In Lamington National Park, there are brush box trees more than 1500 years old, making them the oldest carbon-dated trees on the Australian mainland. And although we have not visited these survivors, we have stood beneath towering lopcons near Minyon Falls: giant, merlinesque individuals that have lived for centuries, their anxieties and stresses visible within the overblown burls of the trunks.

I am not sure anyone has a favourite tree species any more than they have, when asked, a favourite colour or a favourite film. Birdwatchers are the same. Consumed by their knowledge of several hundred birds, they are often loath to promote one species above all others. But I believe people do have certain trees that offer solace, as if their leaves, like vivid talismans, are paragons of fellowship and dispensers of calm. For Tim Winton out at sea, it is the welcome silhouette of the Norfolk Island pine. For Albert Facey and Matthew Condon, it is the humbleness of the she-oak. And for Richard Birrinbirrin and Peter Djigirr from *Ten Canoes*, it is the eucalypt, the Saint-Marguerite blue gums inspiring in them a reverie akin to healing. Personally, I feel safe, composed, in the presence of a Queensland box, as if the trees are looking out for me. Madeleine trees would be the wrong term for these palliative species. But perhaps, if we are to continue the Proustian references, we might call them Saint-Hilaire trees, their presence as omniscient and consoling as the steeple of Saint-Hilaire, the landmark that gives Combray, to quote Proust's narrator, 'all the occupations, all the hours, all the viewpoints of the town their shape, their crown, their consecration'.

I found a study, admittedly fifteen years old, that revealed the Queensland box as Melbourne's most commonly planted tree. It is ubiquitous, and yet it is almost entirely unnoticed by anyone other than arborists and landscape architects. Somehow, and I am not sure how, these trees perform a trick: discreet enough to evade notice, but once you do become attuned to their presence, you realise how striking they are, the luscious green of the rainforest suspended on bold, eucalyptus-like trunks.

I became aware of them one morning as I drove through Altona, smoke rising in the distance from the refineries. I had been in Melbourne for a month, arriving in the city with a job and a partner of twelve years and managing to lose both in the space of seven days. My mind in disarray, I was unsure whether to pack up and journey back to England, or to stay and reassemble my life. I did not know it then, but the job interview I was attending would reset my trajectory: with the decision I made that day, I would instigate an abscission of my previous life and a leafing of new ideas. As I turned onto Civic Parade, I passed an avenue of unusual trees, the smoother trunks bold like Hellenic statues, a fire of valiant green rising from their muscular arms. Everything about them was exaggerated. The exclamatory nature of the leaves. The clusters of fruit, bunching in almost endless arrays. The trunks, so smooth in parts and so scabrous in others. Never, I thought at the time, had I observed such extraordinary trees – although I had, many times. On my very first day in Australia, I had walked past them on the way to Kings Park. And on those first few trips to Sydney, exploring the streets of Ultimo, I had seen them every day, the streets lined with a mix of brush box and broad-leaved paperbark (*Melaleuca quinquenervia*).

When I consider the parent alighting at Wollstonecraft and compare him to the young naïf walking the streets of Ultimo, I see two different people, the separation of years creating an almost discontinuous series of thoughts. But both minds, distanced in time, viewed those trees in a similar way. As diverse as humans can be, in thrall to an infinitude of thought, the constancy with which trees are often envisaged and admired is perhaps surprising. In this way, they are great facilitators of empathy. The Nyoongar Elder imprisoned on Wadjemup, remembered largely as a statistic before now, is brought to life when one imagines him passing, for the very first time, the trees on which his ancestors fell. The indentured labourers, working the cane fields of Mackay, are similarly revived when we view them boarding the ship, the sight of the Leichhardt tree bringing back memories of their arrival thirty-nine moons before.

Early for my job interview, I tapped some words into a search engine – dark green leaves, red-brown trunk – and there, within a blog revealing the most common trees in Melbourne, I discovered its name: *Lophostemon confertus*. Family: *Myrtaceae*. A tree of wet schlerophyll forest. The beginnings of the global environmental protest movement. Terania Creek. The rainforest war. Blockades of bulldozers. The felling of brush box several hundred years old. And a victory for the protesters, the first of its kind – ever. The same protesters travelling a few years later to the Franklin and Gordon rivers. Trees have so many stories to tell; too many for one book.

As I was reading through a text on Sydney's remnant vegetation, I found a counterpoint to John Sherer's quote about the 'ruins grey' of fine old fortresses. These words, quoted in *Taken for Granted* (1990), are copied from a nineteenth-century guidebook for Sydney: 'Tis true we have no mouldering monasteries, time-honoured cathedrals, or moss and ivy-clad dilapidated castles ... but we have a fauna extensive and unique, a brilliant sunshine, a clear blue sky, gorgeous flowering shrubs and plants; vast wooded ranges, deep solemn glens and mountain gorges, which … are amply sufficient for poetical inspiration.'

When prompted to visualise the Australian landscape, many of us have an unfortunate reflex: rather than picturing the rainforests of Far North Queensland or the old-growth forests of Tasmania, we summon to our mind a land of ancient geology, poor soils and disfigured trees. And yet there is a poetry to the flourishes and swirls of brush box trees and eucalypts, a transcendence of life appreciable in the eccentricities and unworldliness of the banksia. I have been to every continent in the world except Antarctica and still not found anywhere as pictorial or allusive as the mountain ash forests of the Great Dividing Range or as majestic as the Valley of Giants in southwestern Australia. 'There is,' wrote Sherer as he walked through the forests of central Victoria, 'no association of the past.' But how facile is that remark. Because stories hang from every branch, much as European dreams were said to hang from the branches of Norfolk Island pines. And whether we are walking along our local streets or through the trackways of national parks, the stories are there, waiting to be disclosed. On every route, new scenes and new characters may be awakened, every journey an exercise in psychogeography. 'The land is alive,' says Nyikina Warrwa academic Anna Poelina, 'the rivers are alive, the Country is alive, because it holds memory.' We are, as historian Simon Schama says, inheritors of these memories, protectors of their testimony, emissaries of their unique revelation.

Acknowledgements

The reason why this manuscript is in bookshops rather than languishing on my desk is the faith of one person: my publisher and editor, Julia Carlomagno. I am also grateful to Helen Koehne and Kate Morgan for their work on the manuscript, and to Sarah Cannon for her efforts in promoting the book. Thank you, too, to Peter Long for ensuring this is a special product for those who judge books by their covers.

The path to publication began when I won the Rosina Joy Buckman Award in The Nature Conservancy Nature Writing Prize in 2021. It is tremendous to have such a high-profile organisation promoting Australian nature writing. Special thanks to the The Nature Conservancy's Ally Catterick and to Kinchem Hegedus from Life at Springfield for sponsoring the award.

Writing can be a lonely pursuit and I am grateful to the following authors for their advice along the way: Jen Hutchinson from Journeys to Words; Antoinette Holm for her publishing suggestions; and Robert Hillman, whose early advice pushed me over that initial barrier of self-doubt.

I would also like to thank the following people who helped with specific elements of my research: Irene Champion and Grant Paterson from North Queensland Plants (Mackay); ethno-ecologist Fiona Walsh; Michael Cawthorn at Charles Darwin University; John Leslie Dowe, Frank Zich and John Elliott for their comments on the foxtail palm; eucalypt expert Dean Nicolle; Donal McCracken at the University of KwaZulu-Natal; Adam Sizeland at the Museum of St Helena; David Goldney from Greening Bathurst; Erica Boyne, curator at the Western Australian Museum; Seanna McCune at the National Herbarium of New South Wales; Jan Smith at Daylesford & District Historical Society; Paul Boon at Victoria University; Chris Lill at Gluepot Reserve; and Louise Griffiths for sending me a copy of *Dhuway*.

Lastly, a special mention to Tanvi Patel, who became my impromptu research assistant for a few months in 2020. She wandered the libraries of Sydney to check references for me when Melbourne was in the midst of its second lockdown.

References

Introduction: Ruins Green

There can be no walk, no journey of any kind ... John Sherer, cited in Robert Hughes, *The Fatal Shore*, Harvill, 1986 (first published 1986), p. 599.

Keneally likened the way the settlers bastardised the land ... Thomas Keneally, *Napoleon's Last Island*, Random House, Sydney, 2015, p. 415.

Bill Gammage describes a manna gum... Bill Gammage, *The Biggest Estate on Earth*, Allen & Unwin, Sydney, 2011, pp. 23–4.

'When anyone asks me about the Irish character ...' Edna O'Brien, cited in Brooke Allen, 'Thrilling Description', *The Atlantic*, March 2002.

George Worgan, surgeon and passenger of the First Fleet ... George Worgan, cited in Robert Hughes, op. cit., p. 92.

The Norfolk Island pines ... Robert Hughes, op. cit., p. 101.

One settler referred to eucalypts ... Godfrey Mundy, cited in Rod Ritchie, *Seeing the Rainforests in 19th-Century Australia*, Rainforest Publishing, Sydney, 1989, p. 15.

'There was something about its tangle ...' Kate Grenville, *The Secret River*, Text Publishing, Melbourne, 2005, p. 88.

Where some hear only a drone of endless green ... Tim Flannery, cited in 'Let Nature Be Your Teacher', *Big Ideas*, ABC Radio National, 5 January 2017.

In the first episode of the BBC series **Civilisations** ... Simon Schama, 'Episode One: The Second Moment of Creation', *Civilisations*, BBC Two, March 2018.

In the hypnotic film **Ten Canoes** ... Rolf de Heer and Peter Djigirr, *Ten Canoes*, Palace Films, Melbourne, 2006.

Wadjemup

'*She knew every rock hole …*'Marie Taylor, cited in Gina Pickering (ed.), *Fanny Balbuk Yooreel: Realising a Perth Resistance Fighter*, National Trust of Western Australia, Perth, 2017, p. 3.

Perth, before Europeans arrived, was an open forest of jarrah … Information on Perth's pre-European vegetation comes from George Seddon and David Ravine, *A City and its Setting: Images of Perth, Western Australia*, Fremantle Arts Centre Press, Fremantle, 1986, p. 81.

'*When a house was built in the way …*'Daisy Bates, *The Passing of the Aborigines: A Lifetime Spent Among the Natives of Australia*, G. P. Putnam's Sons, New York, 1939, p. 70.

Jarrah timber was cut and put on ships bound for England … Jonathan Drori, *Around the World in 80 Trees*, Laurence King, London, 2018, pp. 148–9.

Before the island was separated, the vegetation was similar … Information on Wadjemup's pre-European vegetation comes from L.J. Pen and John William Green, 'Botanical Exploration and Vegetational Changes on Rottnest Island', *Journal of the Royal Society of Western Australia*, vol. 66, 1983, pp. 21–4.

'*The finest wood in the world …*'Willem de Vlamingh, cited in *Rottnest Island Cultural Landscape Management Plan 2014–2019*, Rottnest Island Authority, Fremantle, 2015, p. 15.

When botanist and explorer Allan Cunningham visited in 1822 … L.J. Pen and John William Green, op. cit., pp. 21–2.

The decline of the marro was rapid … ibid., pp. 22–3.

The first prisoners arrived on Wadjemup in August 1838 … Information on these first prisoners comes from Glen Stasiuk, *Wadjemup: Rottnest Island as Black Prison and White Playground*, PhD Exegesis, Murdoch University, Perth, 2015; Kevin Moran, *Rottnest Volume One: Ghosts of Wadjemup*, Horizon Syndicate, Perth, 2001; and E.J. Watson, *Rottnest: Its Tragedy and Its Glory*, D.L. Watson, location unknown, 1998.

According to a letter Robert Thomson wrote to the Colonial Secretary … Robert Thomson, cited in Glen Stasiuk, op. cit., p. 100.

Welch's diary entries … Constable Welch, cited in Glen Stasiuk, op. cit., p. 103.

David Mitchell … recalls feeling the heaviness of a presence … David Mitchell, presentation for the Wheeler Centre, The Edge, Melbourne, 19 May 2015.

For a friend of journalist Kirsti Melville … Kirsti Melville, 'Rottnest Island: Black Prison to White Playground', *Earshot*, ABC Radio National, 2016.

The prisoners were sometimes chained together at night … Descriptions of prison conditions are taken from Glen Stasiuk, op. cit.

It would be nearly thirty years before a ground-penetrating radar … Lily Hibberd and Glen Stasiuk, 'Rottnest or Wadjemup: Tourism and the Forgetting of Aboriginal Incarceration and the Pre-colonial History of Rottnest Island' in *The Palgrave Handbook of Prison Tourism*, Palgrave Macmillan, London, 2017.

'It's worra,' said his Nyoongar grandmother … Glen Stasiuk's grandmother, cited in Kirsti Melville, op. cit.

Gods of the High North

Mark McKenna has compared the isolated grandeur of Uluru … Mark McKenna, *Return to Uluru*, Black Inc., Melbourne, 2021, p. 21.

'Like an ant at the door of a cathedral' … Arthur Groom, cited in Mark McKenna, op. cit., p. 21.

Thirty-seven people died in the space of sixty-nine years … 'Closing the Uluru Climb', Ayers Rock Resort, ayersrockresort.com.au/stories/closing-the-uluru-climb

'Ahead of us was the winding Todd River …' Doris Blackwell, cited in Peter Solness, *Tree Stories*, Chapter & Verse, Sydney, 1999, p. 29.

'It is as if you were stepping back about 50,000 years …' Penny van Oosterzee (photography by Reg Morrison), *The Centre: The Natural History of Australia's Desert Regions*, Reed Books, Melbourne, 1991, p. 56.

The river is vivified with the green shoots of spikerush … Two people assisted me with information on the flora: ethno-ecologist Dr Fiona Walsh and Michael Cawthorn, consultant anthropologist at Charles Darwin University.

'If the rock could be wrung out …' Penny van Oosterzee, op. cit., p. 58.

'Botanic remnants from millions of years ago …' 'Finke Gorge National Park', Northern Territory Tourism, northernterritory.com/alice-springs-and-surrounds/destinations/finke-gorge-national-park

'Marvel at ancient Palm Trees …' '1 Day Palm Valley 4WD Tour', Emu Run Experience, emurun.com.au/tours/1-day-palm-valley-4wd-tour

It was in Strehlow's first report of Hermannsburg … Carl Strehlow, cited in David Bowman, Jason Gibson and Toshiaki Kondo, 'Aboriginal Myth Meets DNA Analysis', *Nature*, vol. 520, no. 33, 2013, p. 33. Most of the information in the next two paragraphs comes from this article.

'According to the old heathen beliefs …' Carl Strehlow, cited in Anna Kenny, *The Aranda's Pepa*, Australian National University Press, Canberra, 2013, p. 89.

David Bowman, part of a Japanese Australian team ... David Bowman, Jason Gibson and Toshiaki Kondo, op. cit., p. 33.

There is a Creation story that offers us a clue ... Peter Solness, op. cit., p. 172.

'Gigantic mop ...'A.G. Hamilton, 'Concerning Palm-Trees', in Alec Chisholm, *Land of Wonder: The Best Australian Nature Writing*, Angus & Robertson, Sydney, 1964, p. 69.

'The trees were not very large and stood separate ...'Joseph Banks, *The Endeavour Journal of Sir Joseph Banks, 1768–71*, available on Project Gutenberg, gutenberg.net. au/ebooks05/0501141h.html, diary entry for 27 April 1770.

The Eora used Livistona fronds as boughs ... Val Attenbrow, 'Appendix S – Precolonial Aboriginal land and resource use' in *Centennial, Moore and Queens Parks – assessment of historical and archaeological evidence for Centennial Parklands Conservation Management Plan*, Australian Museum, Sydney, 2002, p. 4, and Philip A. Clarke, *Aboriginal Plant Collectors: Botanists and Australian Aboriginal People in the Nineteenth Century*, Rosenberg Publishing, Kenthurst, 2008, p. 32.

'All were cut down within a year ...'Robert Hughes, op. cit., p. 90.

'Extraordinary blindness ...' Ashley Hay, 'Gums: Eucalypts and their Champions', *Saturday Extra*, ABC Radio National, 4 December 2021.

'As the woods were opened ...' Watkin Tench, cited in Grace Karskens, *The Colony: A History of Early Sydney*, Allen & Unwin, Sydney, 2009, p. 67.

'The absence of these trees has taken away ...'Barron Field, cited in Rod Ritchie, op. cit., p. 92.

'The overall impression is ... a haphazard plantation ...' Ian Hoskins, *Coast: A History of the New South Wales Edge*, NewSouth Publishing, Sydney, 2013, p. 39.

'Clear listening ...' Tony Tjamiwa, cited in *Seeing the Park Through Anangu Eyes, Interpretation Strategy 2020–2030*, Australian Government, Canberra, 2020, p. 8.

Monarchs of the Woods

It was remarkably buoyant ... James Jervis, 'Cedar and the Cedar Getters', *Royal Australian Historical Society* (journal), vol. 25, part 2, 1939, p. 144.

The first sign of trouble ... Most of the information on the castaways comes from Chris Pearce, *Through the Eyes of Thomas Pamphlett: Convict and Castaway*, and Jim Lergessner, *White Specks on a Dark Shore*, both Boolarong Press, Brisbane, 1993.

Perhaps Matthew Flinders had observed the mouth of this river ... Clem Lack, 'In the Footsteps of Flinders: Memorial to Great Navigator Unveiled', *Journal of the Royal Historical Society of Queensland*, vol. 7, issue 1, 1963, p. 41.

A kindness and generosity ... Chris Pearce, op. cit., p. 125.

Describing the event years later ... as recorded in Jim Lergessner, op. cit., p. 43.

As Elder Paddy Jerome described in an address ... Paddy Jerome, 'Boobarran Ngummin: The Bunya Mountains', *Queensland Review*, vol. 9, issue 2, 2002.

'If you grew up in Brisbane ...'David Malouf, cited in Peter Solness, op. cit., p. 139.

It was passing under the span of Story Bridge ... Most of the information on Oxley's exploration comes from J.G. Steele, *The Explorers of the Moreton Bay District, 1770–1830*, University of Queensland Press, Brisbane, 1983.

Oxley appears to inspect the hoop pine up close ... John Oxley, cited in J.G. Steele, op. cit., p. 113.

'Brisbane owes its foundation to Oxley's enthusiasm ...'J.G. Steele, op. cit., p. 90.

Cunningham was aware of the hoop pine from his 1819 exploration ... David Mabberley, *Botanical Revelation*, NewSouth Publishing, Sydney, 2019, p. 175.

'Hitherto in our examination of this River ...'Allan Cunningham, cited in J.G. Steele, op. cit., p. 165.

'It was totally impossible not to halt a few moments ...' Allan Cunningham, cited in J. G. Steele, op. cit., p. 165.

Although named Araucaria brisbanii *at first* ... According to J.G. Steele, op. cit., p. 91. Cunningham wrote *'Araucaria brisbanii'* in the margin alongside a sketch he made of the Brisbane River.

Governor Brisbane ... impressed by the hoop pines ... J.G. Steele, op. cit., p. 91.

The following year, 1825, Edmund Lockyer ... Edmund Lockyer, cited in J.G. Steele, op. cit., p. 165.

Forester Peter Holzworth described the hoop pine as one of the finest timbers ... Peter Holzworth, *Monarchs of the Woods*, Queensland Department of Primary Industries, Brisbane, 1999, p. 5.

Almost 50 hectares of bunya and hoop pine plantations ... John Huth and Peter Holzworth, 'Araucariaceae in Queensland', Australia and New Zealand Forest Histories, Australian Forest History Society, Canberra, Occasional Publication 2, 2005.

Roughly ten Aboriginal lives taken for every European life ... Raymond Evans, 'Against the Grain: Colonialism and the Demise of the Bunya Gatherings, 1839–1939', *Queensland Review*, vol. 9, issue 2, 2002, pp. 50–1.

In Queensland alone, up to 50,000 First Australians were murdered ... Timothy Bottoms, *Conspiracy of Silence*, Allen & Unwin, Sydney, 2013, p. 181.

Marianne North visited the Bunya Mountains in 1880 ... Most of this paragraph references Raymond Evans, op. cit., p. 54.

Trees that had served families ... John Huth, 'Introducing the Bunya Pine – a Noble Denizen of the Scrub', *Queensland Review*, vol. 9, issue 2, 2002, p. 17.

Under the Norfolk Pines

'Under the Norfolk pines gulls bickered on the grass ...' Tim Winton, *Cloudstreet*, Penguin Books, Melbourne, 2007 (first published 1991), p. 7.

'A stand of these soughing giants ...' Tim Winton, cited in Peter Solness, op. cit., p. 125.

'I was now almost tired of a Coast ...' James Cook, cited in Vanessa Collingridge, *Captain Cook: Obsession and Betrayal in the New World*, Globe Pequot, Connecticut, 2003 (first published 2002), p. 303.

Elsewhere, the place was a jungle ... Information on Norfolk Island's pre-European vegetation comes from Kevin Mills, *Allan Cunningham: Journal of a Botanist in Norfolk Island in 1830*, Coachwood Publishing, Curramore, 2012; Peter Coyne, *Norfolk Island's Fascinating Flora*, Petaurus Press, Belconnen, 2011.

'The worst place in the English-speaking world ...' Robert Hughes, op. cit., p. 99.

European dreams once hung from its symmetrical branches ... George Seddon, *The Old Country: Australian Landscapes, Plants and People*, Cambridge University Press, Port Melbourne, 2005, p. xv.

'Might it not be ...' Alan Frost, *Botany Bay: The Real Story*, Black Inc., Melbourne, 2011, p. 10.

'Britain's military strength and an increasing part of her commerce ...' Geoffrey Blainey, *The Tyranny of Distance*, Macmillan, Melbourne, 1982 (first published 1966), pp. 29–30.

'Key to the plan to send convicts to Australia ...' Geoffrey Blainey, op. cit., p. 33.

'It snapped like a carrot ...' Robert Hughes, op. cit., p. 101.

European dreams once hung from its symmetrical branches ... George Seddon, *The Old Country: Australian Landscapes, Plants and People*, Cambridge University Press, Port Melbourne, 2005, p. xv.

Of thirty-four trees to be chopped down ... J.C.H. Gill, 'Norfolk Island – the First Phase', *Journal of the Royal Historical Society of Queensland*, vol. 10, no. 1, 1975, p. 147.

The trees were deceptive ... Robert Hughes, op. cit., p. 101.

The navy was forced to look elsewhere ... Information on the navy's quest for suitable timber comes from P.K. Crimmin, 'Searching for British Naval Stores: Sources and Strategy c. 1802–1860', *The Great Circle Journal*, vol. 18, no. 2, 1996. Further information on red pine is from *The Nautical Magazine: A Magazine for Those Interested in Ships and the Sea*, January 1833, Simpkin, Marshall and Co., London, p. 24. Further information on poon is from William L. Crothers, *The Masting of American Merchant Sail in the 1850s: An Illustrated Study*, McFarland & Company, Jefferson, 2014, p. 33.

'I've been damn grateful ...' Tim Winton, cited in Peter Solness, op. cit., p. 125.

The Wollemi Paradox

When journalist James Woodford was helicoptered in ... James Woodford, 'The Jurassic Tree and the Lost Valley', *The Sydney Morning Herald*, 6 July 1997.

Air tankers flew across the surrounds ... Most of this information comes from Greg Bearup, 'The Last Stand', *Weekend Australian Magazine*, 21 February 2020.

Steve's first task was ... Greg Bearup, op. cit., p. 20.

'Even the best walkers who have hiked with Noble ...' James Woodford, *The Wollemi Pine*, Text Publishing, Melbourne, 2005 (first published 2000), p. 11. Most of the information on Noble's discovery comes from this book.

'Considering the detailed understanding ...' James Woodford, 2005, op. cit., p. 54.

John Benson, one of the first people ... James Woodford, 2005, op. cit., p. 55.

'Only a few times this century ...' James Woodford, 'Found: Tree from the Dinosaur Age, and It's Alive', *The Sydney Morning Herald*, 14 December 1994.

'It's the son – or seedling of the Jurassic Bark ...' No author, 'Scientists Cultivate Jurassic Tree Seedling', *The Japan Times*, December 1994, available on the Wollemi pine website, wollemipine.com/news/japan-times.php

In order not to damage the few remaining trees in the wild ... James Woodford, 2005, op. cit., p. 128.

'One of the most conservative organisms ...' James Woodford, 2005, op. cit., p. 171.

Using the latest techniques in DNA sampling ... Marcus Strom, 'Genetic Diversity Found in Wollemi Pine Gives Hope of Survival for Australia's Dinosaur Trees', *The Sydney Morning Herald*, 5 January 2017.

'It is hard, after this week ...' James Woodford, 'Wollemi Pines' Survival Shows what Humans Can Do When Determined', *The Guardian*, 17 January 2020.

'Only one or two seedlings out of every hundred need to make it to maturity ...' James Woodford, 1997, op. cit.

Wodyeti

'This is the story of its discovery ...' story posted by Dave Butler, International Palm Society, palmtalk.org/forum/topic/657-wodyetia-bifurcata

'Wodyeti ... clearly intended for Johnny Flinders ...' the original citation comes from Anthony Irvine, 'Wodyetia, a New Arecoid Genus from Australia', *Principes*, vol. 27, no. 4, 1983, p. 158.

The first time Peter Sutton met Johnny ... Catherine Ford, 'The Aurukun Blues of Peter Sutton', *The Monthly*, May 2013.

'Puzzled, amused or made hostile at my interest ...' Peter Sutton, '"BIILT" Research in Far North Queensland in the 1970s', in Tom Dutton, Malcolm Ross and Darrell Tyron (eds), *The Language Game: Papers in Memory of Donald C. Laycock*, Department of Linguistics, Research School of Pacific Studies, Australian National University, 1992, p. 454.

'Many of these languages were almost extinct then ...' ibid., p. 453.

'An extremely lively man ...' ibid., p. 456.

Johnny knew his Country as Yiirrku ... Johnny Flinders and Peter Sutton, 'Land Rights: Flinders Island Story', in Luise Hercus and Peter Sutton (eds), *This is What Happened: Historical Narratives by Aborigines*, Australian Institute of Aboriginal Studies, Canberra, 1986, p. 327.

To walk with him through the landscape was to be awakened ... Information on the vegetation around Cape Melville comes from: the Queensland Globe online mapping and data resource, qldglobe.information.qld.gov.au, and Athol Chase and Peter Sutton, 'Hunter-Gatherers in a Rich Environment: Aboriginal Coastal Exploitation in Cape York Peninsula', in Allen Keast (ed.), *Ecological Biogeography of Australia*, W. Junk, Boston, 1981, p. 1842.

'Pincerlike pressure ...' Athol Chase and Peter Sutton, op. cit., p. 1824.

'Gradually died out or moved away ...' Johnny Flinders and Peter Sutton, op. cit., p. 327.

'I'm happy to go back and see my mother's land ...' Bob Flinders, cited in Lew Griffiths, *Dhuway*, Oziris Productions, Manuka, 1996.

'Have you got another book yet ...' Peter Sutton, cited in *Dhuway*, op. cit.

His words arpeggiate ... Johnny Flinders, cited in *Dhuway*, op. cit.

'They may be deceased over there to you people ...' Bonnie Walker, cited in *Dhuway*, op. cit.

'Botanical Shangri-La ...' Murray Hogarth, 'Foxtail Smugglers', *Four Corners*, ABC-TV, 11 April 1994.

Smugglers strapped handsaws to long poles ... Most of this information comes from Murray Hogarth, op. cit., and Gavin Ricketts, 'From the Vault – Operation "Foxtail Palm",' Queensland Police Museum website, mypolice.qld. gov.au/museum/2014/08/12/vault-operation-foxtail-palm

Another was Pat Shears ... a Rambo ranger ... Greg Wellard, cited in 'A Report of an Investigation into the Cape Melville Incident', Criminal Justice Commission, Toowong, 1994, p. 50, available at ccc.qld.gov.au/publications/ report-investigation-cape-melville-incident

A real-life Crocodile Dundee ... Murray Hogarth, op. cit.

'I think I remember saying ...'Pat Shears, cited in Murray Hogarth, op. cit.

The six travellers, estranged from their car ... Information on the incident comes from 'A Report of an Investigation into the Cape Melville Incident', op. cit.

'Entirely without foundation ...''A Report of an Investigation into the Cape Melville Incident', op. cit., p. 33.

According to Joan Sheldon, the deputy leader of the Opposition... Joan Sheldon, cited in Hansard, 13 April 1994, p. 7507, available on documents.parliament. qld.gov.au/events/han/1994/940413ha.pdf

'Entirely without foundation ...''A Report of an Investigation into the Cape Melville Incident', op. cit., p. 33.

'We are frightened for our lives up here ...'Pat Shears, cited in 'A Report of an Investigation into the Cape Melville Incident', op. cit., p. 129.

'There's nobody there to meet me ...'Tony Flinders, cited in *Dhuway*, op. cit.

'Aampa aaku-l-wa aathi-y-ntu utakala ...'Johnny Flinders, cited in Johnny Flinders and Peter Sutton, op. cit., pp. 329–30.

The Leichhardt Tree

When the great cyclone of 1918 came through ... Information on the tree comes from Mackay Regional Council, *Local Heritage Register: The Leichhardt Tree*, Mackay Regional Council, Mackay, 2017.

John Spiller, a gruff man ... The description of Spiller is based on E.W. Docker, *The Blackbirders, the Recruiting of South Seas Labour for Queensland, 1863–1907*, Angus & Robertson, Sydney, 1970, pp. 95–6.

Spiller eyed up his target ... This story is recounted in Henry Ling Roth, *The Discovery and Settlement of Port Mackay*, F. King & Sons, Halifax, 1908, p. 86.

Labourers would need to wake at dawn and finish with the dusk... The main texts I relied on for understanding the history of blackbirding were: Kay Saunders, *Workers in Bondage*, University of Queensland Press, Brisbane, 1982 (first published 1981); Clive Moore, *The Forgotten People: A History of the Australian South Sea Island Community*, ABC-TV, 1979; and Tracey Banivanua-Mar, *Violence and Colonial Dialogue: the Australian–Pacific Indentured Labor Trade*, University of Hawai'i Press, Honolulu, 2007 (first published 2006). Good articles include B.H. Molesworth, 'Kanaka Labour in Queensland', *Journal of the Royal Historical Society of Queensland*, vol. 1, no. 3, 1917, pp. 140–54.

More sensationalist accounts were written at the time, and these have been read with a degree of caution: Hector Holthouse, *Cannibal Cargoes*, Rigby, Adelaide, 1969; George Palmer, *Kidnapping in the South Seas*, Penguin Books, Melbourne, 1973 (first published 1871); Thomas Dunbabin, *Slavers of the South Seas*, Angus & Robertson, Sydney, 1935; and E. W. Docker, op. cit.

'Fraught with the highest importance ...' Mackay Mercury, cited in Clive Moore, *Kanaka: A History of Melanesian Mackay*, Institute of Papua New Guinea Studies and University of Papua New Guinea Press, Port Moresby, 1985, p. 124.

We must remember, when imagining the scene ... Information on Mackay's pre-European vegetation comes from Tim Low, 'Investigations into a Blady Past', *Wildlife Australia*, Autumn 1990, pp. 18–20; Queensland Globe online, op. cit., and correspondence with the Mackay branch of Native Plants Queensland.

'Quite picturesque with clumps of palms' ... Andrew Murray, cited in K.H. Kennedy, *Mackay Revisited*, Mackay City Council, Mackay, 2002, p. 12.

Perhaps 1000 or 2000 people lived in the Pioneer Valley ... Clive Moore, 'Blackgin's Leap: A Window into Aboriginal–European Relations in the Pioneer Valley, Queensland in the 1860s', *Aboriginal History*, vol. 14, 1990, pp. 74, 77.

The wrinkled, lychee-like spheres ... astringent but not unpalatable ... Rainforest Australia, rainforest-australia.com/Leichardt.html, and Some Magnetic Island Plants, somemagneticislandplants.com.au/leichhardt-tree

'Gazing round, I saw on a plot ...' John Mackay, cited in No author, 'A John Mackay Monument', *Daily Mercury*, 14 December 1928.

A town of 500 non-Indigenous residents ... J.A. Nilsson, 'Mackay in the Nineteenth Century: How a New Frontier was Opened', *Journal of the Royal Historical Society of Queensland*, vol. 7, issue 2, 1964, pp. 358, 362.

A quarter of the Yuwibara died ... Clive Moore, interviewed for 'Australia's "Sugar Slaves" Remembered', *RN Breakfast*, ABC Radio National, 14 August 2013.

The last two Indigenous Australians ... Clive Moore, 1990, op. cit., p. 77.

Roughly three Islander males for every white male ... According to the 1881 census, cited in Tracey Banivanua-Mar, op. cit., p. 86.

The etymology of the term 'blackbirding' has been obscured ... The term 'blackbird-hunting' is used in Reid Mortensen, 'Slaving in Australian Courts: Blackbirding Cases 1869–1871', *Journal of South Pacific Law*, vol. 4, 2004, pp. 7–37. There appears to be no reliable explanation for the etymology of the term 'blackbirding'. World Wide Words and Wikipedia suggest the connection with hunting blackbirds, but offer no evidence to support this claim.

Historian Noel Fatnowna ... says sugar became a synonym for hard work ... Noel Fatnowna, cited in Clive Moore, 1979, op. cit., p. 52.

There is a moving scene in the documentary **Sugar Slaves** ... taken from the film Trevor Graham, *Sugar Slaves*, Annamax Media, Coogee, 1995.

'Even from the 1860s, there were people going backwards and forwards ...' Clive Moore, cited in Alex McKinnon, 'Blackbirds: Australia's Hidden Slave Trade History', *The Monthly*, July 2019.

His companion, Christie Fatnowna, pointed out ... Christie Fatnowna, cited in Clive Moore, 1979, op. cit., p. 54.

She recalls the story of Ueuega ... Tracey Banivanua-Mar, op. cit., p. 52.

'Straight and strong in your youth you stood ...' Dorothy Moffatt's poem 'To the Old Leichhardt Tree' is reproduced in Lesley Williams, *If the Leichhardt Tree Could Talk: An Account of the Establishment of the Williams Family in Mackay, Queensland*, L. M. Williams, Mackay, 1987, p. ii.

'Small ragged pine tree ...' Major Athelstan Markham Martyn, cited in David W. Cameron, *The Battle for Lone Pine: Four Days of Hell at the Heart of Gallipoli*, Viking, Melbourne, 2012, p. 46.

'In death they didn't even want us ...' Noel Fatnowna, cited in Clive Moore, 1979, op. cit., p. 52.

Starrett Vea Vea ... a symbol of hope ... Starrett Vea Vea, cited in Reuben Wylie, 'New Storyboards at Bluewater Quay', *Daily Mercury*, 21 April 2018.

People don't want to talk about it ... Starrett Vea Vea, cited in Lucy Smith, 'Filmmaker Draws on Family History in Her Documentary', *Daily Mercury*, 6 June 2015.

A Mangrove Story

Sitting beneath it, the artist describes ... Louise Martin-Chew, *Fiona Foley Artwork for Mackay Bluewater Trail*, Artspace Mackay, artspacemackay.com. au/__data/assets/pdf_file/0018/108360/FionaFoley_text.pdf

During the late 1990s ... Information on the mangrove dieback in Mackay comes from A. Kirkwood and R. Dowling, *Investigation of Mangrove Dieback in the Pioneer River Estuary*, Queensland Government, Brisbane, 2002; Norm Duke, *Serious Dieback of Mangroves Around Mackay*, University of Queensland, Brisbane, 2003, and Norm Duke et al., 'Mackay Mangrove Dieback: Investigations in 2002 with Recommendations for Further Research, Monitoring and Management: Report to Queensland Department of Primary Industries Northern Fisheries Centre, and the Community of Mackay', Centre for Marine Studies, Brisbane, 2003.

Only woody species, more than 1.5 metres tall ... This definition comes from Norm Duke, *Australia's Mangroves*, University of Queensland, Brisbane, 2006, p. 12.

'Ugly ducklings ...' Norm Duke, cited in Kate Wild, 'Shocking Images Reveal Death of 10,000 Hectares of Mangroves Across Northern Australia', *ABC News*, ABC-TV, 10 July 2016.

When the museum's Department of Conservation and Scientific Research ... Val Attenbrow and Caroline Cartwright, 'An Aboriginal Shield Collected in 1770 at Kamay Botany Bay: An Indicator of Pre-Colonial Exchange Systems in South-Eastern Australia', *Antiquity*, vol. 88, 2014, pp. 883–95.

'The most iconic moment in our history ...' Peter FitzSimons, 'Who was Captain Cook?', *Saturday Extra*, ABC Radio National, 23 November 2019.

Ray Ingrey ... says the phrase has another meaning ... Ray Ingrey cited in Ray Ingrey, Shane Ingrey, Paul Irish, Kodie Mason and Sophie Youngberry, 'Telling Our Stories Our Way', National Museum of Australia, Canberra, 2022, nma.gov. au/exhibitions/endeavour-voyage/kamay-botany-bay/telling-our-stories-our-way

Attempts at communication were unsuccessful ... For a description of this incident, I turned to the primary sources: Captain Cook, *Captain Cook's Journal During his First Voyage Around the World Made in H. M. Bark 'Endeavour',* 1768–71, available on Project Gutenberg, gutenberg.org/files/8106/8106-h/8106-h.htm; Joseph Banks, *The Endeavour Journal of Joseph Banks*, 1768–71, available on Project Gutenberg, gutenberg.net.au/ebooks05/0501141h.html; Sydney Parkinson, *Voyage to the South Seas*, 1773, available on National Library of Australia, catalogue.nla.gov.au/catalog/87364; and the 'official' account of the voyage: John Hawkesworth, *Account of the Voyages Undertaken by the Order of His Present Majesty for Making Discoveries in the Southern Hemisphere*, W. Strahan and T. Cadell, London, 1773, available on Trove, trove.nla. gov.au/work/21118962?l-decade=192&l-decade=191&l-decade=198&l-geocoverage=Australia&l-geocoverage=Antarctica&l-year=1833&l-year=1812

The shield is ... one of the most potent objects ... Neil MacGregor, *A History of the World in 100 Objects*, Viking, Melbourne, 2010, p. 581.

'Cook was a remarkable navigator ...' Jonathan Green, @GreenJ, post on Twitter, 29 April 2020.

Nicholas Thomas, an anthropologist and historian ... Nicholas Thomas, 'A Case of Identity: The Artefacts of the 1770 Kamay (Botany Bay) Encounter, *Australian Historical Studies*, vol. 49, no. 1, 2018, pp. 28–43.

Mangroves skirt almost one-fifth of the country's coastline ... Norm Duke, 2006, op. cit., p. 10.

'Has something ancient, something other ...' Jeremy Stafford-Deitsch, *Mangroves: The Forgotten Habitat*, Immel, London, 1996, p. 15.

'The tree cares for me, it gives me this food ...' Bob Randall, 'Indigenous Storyteller Bob Randall', *Conversations with Richard Fidler*, ABC Radio National, 20 November 2015.

Ford was at Bathurst Island to run a photography workshop ... Maggie Finch, *Sue Ford*, National Gallery of Victoria, Melbourne, 2014, p. 123.

'Miserable land ...' Ludwig Leichhardt, *Journal of an Overland Expedition in Australia*, entry 17 July 1845, available on Project Gutenberg, gutenberg.net. au/ebooks/e00030.html

Leichhardt describes in his journal ... Ludwig Leichhardt, op. cit., entry 13 July 1845.

'The world narrows in these conditions ...' Alan Moorehead, *Cooper's Creek: The Story of Burke & Wills*, Nelson, South Melbourne, 1985, p. 71.

John Lort Stokes had remarked upon the monotony ... Michael Cannon, *The Exploration of Australia*, Reader's Digest, Sydney, 1987, p. 118.

Leichhardt, walking across the Gulf from Maramie to Borroloola ... Ludwig Leichhardt, op. cit., entries 9, 14, 18, 19, 24 and 28 July; 19, 22 and 25 August; 2 and 5 September 1845.

It is hard to move beyond the caricature of Burke ... Information on Burke comes mainly from: Alan Moorehead, op. cit.; Frank Clune, *Dig: The Tragic Story of the Burke and Wills Expedition*, Angus & Robertson, Sydney, 1976 (first published 1937); Tim Bonyhady, *Burke & Wills: From Melbourne to Myth*, David Ell Press, Sydney, 1991; and E. Joyce and D. McCann (eds), *Burke & Wills: The Scientific Legacy of the Victorian Expedition*, CSIRO Publishing, Collingwood, 2011, Chapter 9.

'I cannot keep any record in a systematic manner ...' Tim Bonyhady, op. cit., p. 42.

'Cordial demeanour, urbane and frank manner ... sterling qualities ...' Tim Bonyhady, op. cit., p. 41.

An observant eye, one that could unlock secrets … Henry Turnbull, cited in Colin Roderick, *Leichhardt, the Dauntless Explorer*, Angus & Robertson, Sydney, 1988 (first published 1985), p. 234.

'He was rather given to melancholy …' Patrick White, *Voss*, Penguin Books, Melbourne, 2012 (first published 1957), p. 7.

'The first sight of the salt water …' Ludwig Leichhardt, op. cit., entry 5 July 1845.

'About five miles from the camp …' Ludwig Leichhardt, op. cit., entry 18 July 1845.

A bird English writer Alan Moorehead described as … Alan Moorehead, op. cit., p. 78.

'Stout hearty man …' Thomas Dick, cited in Alan Moorehead, op. cit., p. 70.

'There is something you must do for me …' Graeme Clifford, *Burke & Wills*, Hoyt's Edgley, Sydney, 1985.

'Mangrove swamps blocked the way …' Alan Moorehead, op. cit., p. 80.

'Burke's hopes of reaching the sea were dashed …' Tom Bergin, *In the Steps of Burke and Wills*, ABC Books, Sydney, 1981, p. 122.

'Fantastic tangle of branches …' Michael Cathcart, *Starvation in the Land of Plenty*, National Library of Australia, Canberra, 2013, p. 86.

The mangroves were 'impenetrable' … Jessica Campion, 'Burke and Wills: Botany's Untold Success Story', *Australian Geographic*, 27 July 2011.

'Unable to penetrate the tangle of trees …' Annabel Venning, 'The World's Worst Explorer', *Daily Mail*, 9 March 2010.

McKinlay and his men arrived at a fine mangrove creek … Information on McKinlay's expedition is taken from Kim Lockwood, *Big John: The Extraordinary Adventures of John McKinlay 1819–1872*, State Library of Victoria, Melbourne, 1995.

David Hillan, a retired surveyor … Information on David Hillan's expedition comes from Anthony Hoy, 'Burke and Wills to the Gulf', *The Bulletin*, 8 February 2000.

It is one of vast tidal salt flats … Information on the vegetation comes from Queensland Globe online, op. cit., and my own observations around Karumba.

When Dave Phoenix, president of the Burke and Wills Historical Society … Dave Phoenix, *Following Burke and Wills across Australia: A Touring Guide*, CSIRO Publishing, Collingwood, 2015.

'It is not the mangroves ahead that trap and block them …' Peter FitzSimons, Burke & Wills, Hachette, Sydney, 2017, p. 313.

Today, mangroves are in the news for a different reason … The main references for the mangrove dieback in the Gulf are Norm Duke and Penny van Oosterzee, 'Extreme Weather Likely Behind Worst Recorded Mangrove Dieback in Northern Australia', *The Conversation*, 14 March 2017; Norm Duke et al., 'Large-scale Dieback of Mangroves in Australia's Gulf of Carpentaria: A Severe Ecosystem Response, Coincidental with an Unusually Extreme Weather Event', *Marine and Freshwater Research*, vol. 68, no. 10, 2017, pp. 1816–29.

The worst incidence of climate-related mass tree dieback … 'Gulf Mangrove Dieback Discovery' (media release), James Cook University, Brisbane, 28 July 2022.

Trees scream when they are desperate for water … Peter Wohlleben, *The Hidden Life of Trees*, Black Inc., Melbourne, 2016, p. 48.

Hidetoshi Kudo, known to his friends as Mikey … Information on the Haines mangrove discovery comes from two articles by Hidetoshi Kudo: 'Mangrove Discoveries in FNQ', Cairns and Far North Environment Centre, no date, cafnec.org.au/wildlife-issues/mangroves-wetlands/mangrove-discoveries-in-fnq, and 'Southerly Extension of the Known Range of the Mangrove *Bruguiera cylindrica*', *North Queensland Naturalist*, vol. 46, 2016, pp. 11–15.

'For water such as you would not even taste …' William Wills, cited in Andrew Jackon, *Robert O'Hara Burke and the Australian Exploring Expedition of 1860*, Smith, Elder and Co., London, 1862, p. 33.

Survivors

The tree has lived for around 300 years … Information on the tree comes from the National Trust of Australia's 'Trust Trees' website, trusttrees.org.au/tree/VIC/Beechworth/Cnr_Tanswell_Street_And_Dowling_Court

Around 250 years ago, this Queensland blue gum … Information on the tree comes from the National Trust of Australia's 'Trust Trees' website, trusttrees.org.au/tree/QLD/Brisbane/Brisbane_City_Botanic_Gardens_147 According to Queensland Globe online, the vegetation along this part of the river was complex notophyll to microphyll vine forest (regional ecosystem 12.3.16), op. cit.

It has survived the threat of removal … Information on the tree comes from Peter Solness, op. cit., p. 85.

For a tree that is around 170 years old … Information on this tree comes from the City of Sydney's 'Significant Trees' page, trees.cityofsydney.nsw.gov.au/map

When it was young, the tree blew over in a storm … Information on the tree blowing over comes from an article found online called 'The Old Gum Tree' by local historian Dieuwke Jessop: history.sa.gov.au/chu/programs/history_conference/

DieuwkeJessopPaper-%20GumTree.pdf. Its death was reported in 'The Old Gum Tree', *Observer*, 23 February 1907.

You may be able to picture the streets of North Adelaide ... Information on Adelaide's pre-European vegetation comes from R.T. Lange, 'Vegetation' in C.R. Twidale, M.J. Tyler and B.P. Webb (eds), *Natural History of the Adelaide Region*, Royal Society of South Australia, Adelaide, 1976, Chapter 7; Phil Bagust and Lynda Tout-Smith, *The Native Plants of Adelaide*, Wakefield Press, Adelaide, 2010, p. 44; and M. Long, *A Biodiversity Survey of the Adelaide Park Lands South Australia in 2003*, Department for Environment and Heritage, Adelaide, 2003.

For thousands of years, this area was an important meeting place ... 'A Heritage Tour of Ainslie', National Trust of Australia, Canberra, 2009.

Songlines are information pathways ... The term 'maelstroms of knowledge' comes from Alison Page, 'Songlines: The Foundational Australian Story', *Big Ideas*, ABC Radio National, 24 January 2018.

***'Just as we see stars when we gaze at the night sky* ...'** Marcia Langton, *Welcome to Country*, Hardie Grant, Melbourne, 2020 (first published 2018), p. 34.

***'Most important historic trees* ...'** Bob Beale, *If Trees Could Speak*, Allen & Unwin, Sydney, 2007, p. 21.

***'Utterly engulfed by a towering world of concrete* ...'** Bob Beale, op. cit., p. 20.

These trees are forest red gums ... Colleen Morris, *The Florilegium – Royal Botanic Gardens of Sydney: Celebrating 200 Years*, Royal Botanic Gardens, Kew, 2017 (first published 2016), p. 22.

According to Beale, they germinated in the early 1700s ... Bob Beale, op. cit., p. 21.

When the Wattle Starts to Bloom

***'A husky, slow tone of voice* ...'** Kate Williams, *Josephine: Desire, Ambition, Napoleon*, Hutchinson, London, 2013, p. 32.

***'Nowhere, except on the field of battle* ...'** Louis de Bourrienne, cited in Terry Smyth, *Napoleon's Australia: The Incredible Story of Bonaparte's Secret Plan to Invade Australia*, Ebury Press, Penguin Random House, 2018, p. 46.

Prickly tea-tree* ... *grew alongside swamp paperbark ... Information on the flora of Malmaison comes from Jill, Duchess of Hamilton, *Napoleon, the Empress and the Artist*, Simon & Schuster, East Roseville, 1999, and Etienne Pierre Ventenant, *Jardin de la Malmaison*, Imprimerie de Crapelet, Paris, 1803, available on Biodiversity Heritage Library, biodiversitylibrary.org/bibliography/70396

While Napoleon was vanquishing Rome ... These letters are referenced in Terry Smyth, op. cit., p. 41.

'To you, to you alone ...' Napoleon, cited in Kate Williams, op. cit., p. 264.

'I should have done better to have stayed in Egypt ...' Andrew Roberts, *Napoleon: A Life*, Viking, London, 2014, p. 781.

'One large flaming red eye ...' Lucia Elizabeth Abell, *Napoleon and Betsy: Recollections of Napoleon on St Helena*, J. Murray, London, 1844, p. 12, available at archive.org/details/recollectionsofe00abeliala

He would lay maps across the floor ... The stories about maps and clouds comes from Lucia Elizabeth Abell, op. cit., p. 119.

'I truly loved her ...' Napoleon, cited in Kate Williams, op. cit., p. 252.

According to art historian ... Eleanor P. DeLorme, 'Her Magical World: Joséphine's Gardens and Conservatory', in Eleanor P. DeLorme (ed.), *Joséphine and the Arts of the Empire*, Getty Publications, Los Angeles, 2005, p. 88.

'Brought golden wattle with him ...' Terry Smyth, op. cit., p. xii.

Governor Beatson refers to Botany Bay willows ... Alexander Beatson, *Tracts Relative to the Island of St. Helena*, W. Bulmer & Co., London, 1816, p. 34.

The species' arrival ... This information comes from Donal McCracken from the University of KwaZulu-Natal, an expert on botanic gardens in the British empire, personal communication with the author, February 2020.

'There are no trees that succeed so well on this island ...' Beatson, op. cit., p. 32.

It is possible Lady Holland, an admirer from England ... Two references for this are: Brian Unwin, *Terrible Exile: The Last Days of Napoleon on St Helena*, Palgrave Macmillan, New York, 2010, p.138, and Jill, Duchess of Hamilton, op. cit., p. 228.

'Look at those dreadful mountains ...' Napoleon, cited in Lucia Elizabeth Abell, op. cit., p. 229.

They have dispersed like weeds ... Information on St Helena's vegetation comes from Q.C.B. Cronk, 'The Past and Present Vegetation of St Helena', *Journal of Biogeography*, vol. 16, no. 1, 1989, pp. 47–64.

They ate the seeds and scrunched up the leaves ... This detail comes from 'Aboriginal Heritage Plants', *Gardening Australia*, ABC-TV, 4 October 2008, abc.net.au/gardening/how-to/aboriginal-heritage-plants/9429182

If Alexander walked to its confluence ... Information on the vegetation of Balcombe Creek comes from the Native Vegetation Information Management

tool, Victoria State Government, environment.vic.gov.au/native-vegetation/
native-vegetation-information-management and personal observation

The first tree to grow after the devastation of Hiroshima ... Maria Hitchcock,
A Celebration of Wattle, Rosenberg Publishing, Kenthurst, 2012, pp. 103–4.

'We stand on the threshold of another Australian spring ...' A.J. Campbell,
Golden Wattle: Our National Floral Emblem, Pranava Books, India, no date
(first published 1921), p. 15.

'What shall we say of the most excellent beauty ...' ibid., p. 28.

'Yellow-haired September ...' ibid., p. 18.

'Rich lemon-yellow flowers ...' ibid., p. 36.

'It expresses all moods ...' Ian Campbell, 'Yellow-haired September: A Reflection
on the National Floral Emblem in A.J. Campbell's Golden Wattle',
Australian Humanities Review, issue 41, 2007, australianhumanitiesreview.
org/2007/02/01/yellow-haired-september-a-reflection-on-the-national-floral-
emblem-in-aj-campbells-golden-wattle1

If eucalypts are coastal, wrote naturalist George Seddon ... George Seddon,
Swan Song: Reflections on Perth and Western Australia, 1956–1995, University of
Western Australia, Perth, 1995, p. 70.

'A picture of illimitable distances ...' Charles Laseron, *The Face of Australia: The
Shaping of a Continent*, Angus & Robertson, Sydney, 1953, p. 33.

The mulga may be long-lived for an acacia ... Information on the mulga comes
from Horst Weber, 'Mulga', Australian Native Plants Society, 1999, anpsa.org.
au/APOL16/dec99-5.html, and Penny van Oosterzee, op. cit., p. 72.

Researcher Roger Oxley writes of gangs of men ... Roger Oxley, *Roger Oxley
Looks at Australian Trees*, ABC Books, Sydney, 1993, p. 46.

When forester Roger Underwood tried to calculate the extent of this clearing
... Victoria Laurie, *The Southwest: Australia's Biodiversity Hotspot*, UWA
Publishing, Perth, 2015, p. 90.

'As well known in the north as the mallee ...' Charles Laseron, op. cit., p. 33.

'Peculiar character to the forest ...' Ludwig Leichhardt, op. cit., entry September
1844.

Only 10 per cent of Queensland's brigalow belt remains ... Leonie Seabrook,
Clive McApline and Martine Maron, 'EcoCheck: Can the Brigalow Belt
bounce back?', *The Conversation*, 6 May 2016.

The view of mulga scrub from Central Mount Stuart today ... Penny van
Oosterzee, op. cit., p. 70.

'*Entrance into hell* ...' Charles Sturt, cited in Jill Waterhouse (ed.), *Journal of the Central Australian Expedition 1844–1845*, Caliban Books, Dover, 1984, p. 74.

Sidmouth Valley

'*Pretty little Table with the Tea and Sugar Cannisters* ...' Lachlan Macquarie, *Journal of Tour of Inspection to Bathurst*, entry 19 December 1821, available on mq.edu.au/macquarie-archive/lema/1821/1821dec.html

'*The same Tree that stood immediately in front of our Sleeping Tent* ...' ibid., entry 20 December 1821.

Today there are manna gums ... Information on the pre-European vegetation around Sidmouth Valley comes from David Goldney, *Cox's Road Dreaming Guide Book: A Natural History of Cox's 1814–1815 Road*, New South Wales Government, Sydney, 2015, and Col Bower, 'The Vegetation of Cox's Road from the Flag Staff in Bathurst to Mount York', an unpublished paper commissioned by Greening Bathurst, Bathurst, 2015. I am grateful to David Goldney's assistance for helping me source the latter.

'*It is impossible to behold this grand scene* ...' Lachlan Macquarie, letter to Government House, Sydney, 10 June 1815, cited in George William Evans, *Two Journals of Early Exploration into New South Wales*, 1916, available on Project Gutenberg, gutenberg.net.au/ebooks13/1300271h.html

'*The most romantic Country I had ever seen* ...' Henry Antill, *Journal of an Excursion Over the Blue or Western Mountains of New South Wales, to Visit a Tract of New Discovered Country, in Company with His Excellency Governor & Mrs. Macquarie and a Party of Gentlemen*, entry 2 May 1815, available on mq.edu.au/macquarie-archive/lema/1815/antill1815.html

'*The longest and soon the most important road* ...' Geoffrey Blainey, op. cit., p. 182.

'*Not a word of ill humour passed* ...' Henry Antill, op. cit., entry 18 May 1815.

'*Rarely has such a low barrier* ...' Charles Laseron, op. cit., p. 108.

'*Sea of harsh trees* ...' Barron Field, cited in John Low, *Blue Mountains: Pictorial Memories*, Atrand, Sydney, 1991, p. 12.

'*Within a distance of ten miles from the site* ...' Lachlan Macquarie, cited in W.G. Semple, 'Native and Naturalised Shrubs of the Bathurst Graintes: Past and Present', *Cunninghamia*, vol. 5, issue 1, 1997, p. 810.

'*Youthful sprightliness and humour* ...' M.H. Ellis, *Lachlan Macquarie*, Angus & Robertson, Sydney, 1978, p. 131.

'*A most excellent traveller* ...' Lachlan Macquarie, cited in ibid., p. 132.

'*Of all women living* ...' Lachlan Macquarie, cited in ibid., p. 134.

'I have spent my time in the manner ...' Elizabeth Macquarie, *Elizabeth Macquarie: 1809 Diary*, entry 13 October 1809, available on mq.edu.au/macquarie-archive/lema/1809em

'Wonderfully well indeed ...' Lachlan Macquarie, *Tour to the New Discovered Country in April 1815*, entry 4 May 1815, available at mq.edu.au/macquarie-archive/lema/1815/1815april.html

'I never saw finer grass ...' William Cox, *Memoirs of William Cox*, entry 1 January 1815, available on Project Gutenberg, gutenberg.net.au/ebooks04/0400191h.html

We have a rich impression of the valley's appearance ... John Lewin's untitled painting is reproduced in David Goldney, 2015, op. cit., p. 27.

'Appeared so tame ...' Henry Antill, op. cit., entry 2 May 1815.

'Beautiful little valley ...' Lachlan Macquarie, letter to Government House, Sydney, 10 June 1815, cited in George William Evans, op. cit.

'Handsome good looking young men ...' Lachlan Macquarie, *Tour to the New Discovered Country in April 1815*, op. cit., entry 10 May 1815.

'In the event of the Natives making the smallest show of resistance ...' Lachlan Macquarie, *The Governor's Diary & Memorandum Book Commencing on and from Wednesday the 10th Day of April 1816 – at Sydney, in N. S. Wales*, entry 10 April 1816, available on mq.edu.au/macquarie-archive/lema/1816/1816april.html

'I think they are watching us ...' George William Evans, op. cit., entry 16 December 1813.

In his depiction of the first camp at Springwood ... see David Goldney, 2015, op. cit., p. 81.

The lack of understorey in Lewin's painting is not natural ... see David Goldney, *Cox's Road Dreaming: The Development of an Innovative Thematic Tourist Package*, Proceedings of the 21st Association of Public Authority Surveyors Conferences, 2016, available on apas.org.au/files/conferences/2016/Coxs-Road-Dreaming-The-Development-of-an-Innovative-Thematic-Tourism-Package.pdf

At the Campbells River crossing ... see David Goldney, 2015, op. cit., p. 22.

'Blaxland, Lawson and Wentworth ...' Bruce McGuinness and Dennis Walker, cited in Penny Olsen and Lynette Russell, *Australia's First Naturalists: Indigenous Peoples' Contribution to Early Zoology*, NLA Publishing, Canberra, 2019, p. 1.

He was a forester, an early colonial term ... Grace Karskens, *Cox's Road: New Histories from Old Legends*, a lecture on behalf of Greening Bathurst and the Cox's Road Dreaming project, 2015, coxsroaddreaming.org.au

'The extreme uniformity of the vegetation ...' Charles Darwin, cited in George Mackaness (ed.), *Fourteen Journeys over the Blue Mountains*, Horwitz-Grahame, Sydney, 1965, p. 228.

'But oft, in lonely rooms ...' William Wordsworth, *Lines Composed a Few Miles Above Tintern Abbey*, On Revisiting the Banks of the Wye during a Tour, 13 July 1798, available on poetryfoundation.org/poems/45527/lines-composed-a-few-miles-above-tintern-abbey-on-revisiting-the-banks-of-the-wye-during-a-tour-july-13-1798

'The roots of the trees here run deep ...' Stan Grant, 'At Poisoned Waterhole Creek I Tell My Son about the Slaughter of Our People', *The Guardian*, 11 October 2015.

Enchanting Edens

'It might turn out that the forests of Gippsland ...' Don Watson, *The Bush*, Hamish Hamilton, Melbourne, 2014, p. 61.

Two hundred years ago ... Information on the pre-European vegetation comes from the Native Vegetation Information Management online tool, op. cit.

He and his brother George ... chopped it down simply to measure its height ... The legend is repeated in a few places, including Jason Alexandra, 'Australia's Plantation Boom has Gone Bust So Let's Make Them Carbon Farms', *The Conversation*, 29 October 2015; 'Site of the World's Tallest Tree', *Weekend Notes*, weekendnotes.com/site-of-the-worlds-tallest-tree-thorpdale; John Stephens, 'Gippsland Giants', *The Habitat Advocate*, 2011, habitatadvocate.com.au/tag/gippsland-giants/page/2/

A substantial forest of mountain ash ... Information on the pre-European vegetation comes from the Native Vegetation Information Management online tool, op. cit.

George Cornthwaite sent a letter ... The letter is available in the journal *The Gum Tree*, September 1925, p. 13. Further details are provided in James Frederick Tilgner, *Recalling 100 Years: A Brief History of Thorpdale and District: 1876–1976*, Thorpdale and District Centenary Committee, Thorpdale, 1976; and John Adams, *So Tall the Trees*, Narracan Shire Council, Narracan, 1978, p. 19.

'Ninety per cent of vegetation in Australia ...' Don Watson, op. cit., p. 300.

One selector recalled nine-tenths of the labour being devoted to felling trees ... W.H.C. Holmes, cited in South Gippsland Development League, *The Land of the Lyre Bird: A Story of Early Settlement in the Great Forest of South Gippsland*, Gordon and Gotch Limited for the Committee of the South Gippsland Pioneer's Association, Melbourne, 1920, p. 55.

'*The giant burns that, they hoped, would turn ...*' Tom Griffiths, *Forests of Ash: An Environmental History*, Cambridge University Press, Melbourne, 2001, p. 35.

'*Enchanting Eden ...*' W. McKenzie McHarg, cited in South Gippsland Development League, op. cit., p. 327.

'*Silent witnesses ... Appealing as it were to heaven ...*' A. Gillan, cited in South Gippsland Development League, op. cit., p. 144.

'*Never more shall I see ...*' W. Johnstone, cited in *The Land of the Lyre Bird*, op. cit., p. 144.

'*Cathedral-like pillars ...*' Tom Griffiths, op. cit., p. 12.

'*He began by making an incision at head height ...*' Oscar Comettant, cited in Shirley Wiencke, *When the Wattles Bloom Again*, S. W. Wiencke, Melbourne, 1984, p. 87.

'*Clearfelling, as the name suggests ...*' Richard Flanagan, 'Out of Control', *The Monthly*, May 2007, p. 20.

'*There is much that broke my heart ...*' Sophie Cunningham, *City of Trees*, Text Publishing, Melbourne, 2019, p. 303.

'*To stand in a tingle forest in even a moderate breeze ...*' Tim Winton, *Island Home*, Hamish Hamilton, Melbourne, 2015, p. 144.

We now know, due to a study ... Details of this study can be found in Summer Allen, '*The Science of Awe*', PhD Thesis, University of California, Berkeley, 2018.

A Tasmanian Romance

'*Trees like this add greatly to the beauty and relaxation of a city ...*' Bob Brown, cited in Peter Solness, op. cit., p. 103.

'*We were filled with admiration ...*' Jacques Labillardière, *Voyage in Search of La Perouse, Volume 1*, John Stockdale, Piccadilly, 1800, p. 96, available on Project Gutenberg, gutenberg.net.au/ebooks12/1203851h.html

By 1905, 4 million feet of blue gum timber supported the wharves ... John Mulvaney, *The Axe Had Never Sounded*, ANU Press, Canberra, 2007, p. 34.

Today, there are around 20 million hectares of blue gum plantations ... John Wrigley and Murray Fagg, *Eucalypts: A Celebration*, Allen & Unwin, Sydney, 2010, p. 229.

The tree has spread to unusual locations ... see Robin Doughty, *The Eucalyptus: A Natural and Commercial History of the Gum Tree*, Johns Hopkins University Press, Maryland, 2000, p. 93, and Danielle Clode, 'Seeing the Wood for the Trees', *Australian Book Review*, no. 366, November 2014.

More than 100,000 objects were on display ... Most of the information in this paragraph comes from Jeffrey Auerbach, *The Great Exhibition of 1851: A Nation on Display*, Yale University Press, New Haven, 1999, and Michael Leapman, *The World for a Shilling: How the Great Exhibition of 1851 Shaped a Nation*, Headline, London, 2001.

'There is nothing picturesque in a sack of wheat ...' John Tallis, *Tallis's History and Description of the Crystal Palace, and the Exhibition of the World's Industry in 1851*, J. Tallis & Co., London and New York, 1852, p. 54.

'Equal to oak as a ship-building timber ...' *Official Catalogue of the Great Exhibition of the Works of Industry of All Nations*, Spicer Brothers, London, 1851, p. 78.

'Unparalleled forestral importance ...' Ferdinand von Mueller, cited in Ashley Hay, *Gum: The Story of Eucalypts & Their Champions*, Duffy & Snellgrove, Sydney, 2002, p. 81.

Brett Bennett asks why native trees planted ... Brett Bennett, 'A Global History of Australian Trees', *The Journal of the History of Biology*, vol. 44, 2011, p. 126.

Little more than a dozen pairs of swifties may remain by 2040 ... this figure comes from Stephen T. Garnett and G. Barry Baker (eds), *The Action Plan for Australian Birds 2020*, CSIRO Publishing, Mulgrave, 2021, p. 429. The current population is estimated at 750, with declines of 79 per cent and 95 per cent expected between 2020 and 2030.

'In 1988, the famous violinist Yehudi Menuhin came out ...' Geoff Law, cited in Peter Solness, op. cit., p. 88.

'Nearly wiped off the face of the earth ...' Lyndall Ryan, *Tasmanian Aborigines: A History Since 1803*, Allen & Unwin, Sydney, 2012, p. xvii.

'Brutal men, capable of extreme, wide-ranging violence ...' James Boyce, *Van Diemen's Land*, Black Inc., Melbourne, 2018 (first published 2008), p. 90.

The open grasslands of central and eastern Tasmania ... James Boyce, ibid., p. 4.

'I am on the island of last things ...' Anna Krien, *Into the Woods*, Black Inc., Melbourne, 2012, p. 297.

A knitted artwork of a blue gum in flower ... *Official Catalogue of the Great Exhibition of the Works of Industry of All Nations*, op. cit., p. 180.

The ghosts of these absences linger ... Anna Krien, op. cit., p. 297.

The Pilliga Forest

'This tree has not had any particular influence ...' Eric Rolls, cited in Peter Solness, op. cit., p. 133.

'An effete Pommy with baby-blue eyes ...' Richard Cooke, 'The Crankhandle of History', *The Monthly*, October 2017.

'An architect's dream-tree ...' P.J. Hurley, *In Search of Australia*, Dymocks Book Arcade, Sydney, 1949 (first published 1943), p. 95.

'Of a most striking character ...' Ludwig Leichhardt, *Journal of an Overland Expedition in Australia*, op. cit., entry 10 September 1845.

'Species names have changed so often ...' Eric Rolls, 'Perfumed Pines: The Exploited and the Exploiter', in John Dargavel, Diane Hart, Brenda Libbis (eds), *Perfumed Pineries: Environmental History of Australia's Callitris Forests*, Centre for Resource and Environmental Studies, Australian National University, Canberra, 2001, p. 196.

'I love cypress pine because it lives life passionately ...' Eric Rolls, ibid., p. 196.

'The spring of 1973 amazed men ...' Eric Rolls, *A Million Wild Acres*, Hale & Iremonger, Sydney, 2011 (first published 1981), p. 269.

A book that was meant to take seven months ... Information on the writing process comes from Tom Griffiths, 'Golden Disobedience: The History of Eric Rolls', *Inside Story*, 9 August 2016.

'It is as long as the good road ...' Eric Rolls, 2011, op. cit., p. 1.

'I could remember the vast tracts ...' Tom Griffiths, 2016, op. cit.

'Hokusai waves in a choppy sea ...' Roger Deakin, *Wildwood: A Journey Through Trees*, Penguin Books, Melbourne, 2008 (first published 2007), p. 276.

'It is difficult ...' Charles Griffiths, cited in Tom Griffiths, 'How Many Trees Make a Forest?', *Australian Journal of Botany*, vol. 50, no. 4, 2002, p. 380.

'I could stand in one place ...' Eric Rolls, 2011, op. cit., p. 247.

'What happened in the Pilliga forest ...' ibid., p. 399.

'Despite the burning of rainforest and cedar brush ...' ibid., p. 402.

Eric Rolls would make the controversial claim ... ibid., p. 1.

This figure changed to six trees ... Eric Rolls, cited in Peter Solness, op. cit., p. 133.

Four older trees and a dozen younger ones ... John Benson and Phil Redpath, 'The Nature of Pre-European Vegetation in South-Eastern Australia', *Cunninghamia*, vol. 5, no. 2, 1997, p. 315.

Four large trees and twenty-five striplings ... Eric Rolls, 'The End, or New Beginning?', in Stephen Dovers (ed.), *Environmental History and Policy: Still Settling Australia*, Oxford University Press, Melbourne, 2000, p. 42.

276

Citing the explorer-cum-artist George Evans ... John Benson and Phil Redpath, op. cit., p. 320.

In 1827, Peter Cunningham did the same ... ibid., p. 319.

Cypress brush west of the Warrumbungles ... John Oxley, *Journal of Two Expeditions into the Interior of New South Wales*, John Murray, London, entry 10 August 1818, available on Project Gutenberg, gutenberg.net.au/ebooks/e00037.html

A forest of small ironbarks ... ibid., entry 18 August 1818.

'In a mosaic fashion ...' John Benson and Phil Redpath, op. cit., p. 296.

The term would find its rightful place fourteen years later ... Bill Gammage, op. cit., p. 2.

One statistic goes to the other extreme ... Corey Bradshaw, 'Little Left to Lose: Deforestation and Forest Degradation in Australia since European Colonization', *Journal of Plant Ecology*, vol. 5, issue 1, 2012, pp. 110–11.

'At night fires glow ...' Eric Rolls, 2011, op. cit., p. 314.

Witjweri

For the Wathaurung people, sitting beneath the crown of a she-oak ... Stephen Murphy, 'The Vegetation of the Barrabool Hills Part 4: Plant Species – Drooping Sheoaks Adorned the Hills', Recreating the Country, 2017, recreatingthecountry.com.au. According to Murphy, a great deal of information comes from personal communication with PhD student Jennifer Dearnaley.

The seed cones, large and heavy, ride with the ocean currents ... For information on the oceanic dispersal, see C. Barry Cox, *Biogeography: An Ecological and Evolutionary Approach*, John Wiley & Sons, Melbourne, 2010, p. 256.

In Tahiti, they call the tree aito ... W. Arthur Whistler, 'Annotated List of Tahitian Plant Names', *Allertonia*, vol. 14, October 2015, p. 14.

He knew the tree as etoa *from his time in Tahiti* ... Banks' observations of the she-oak in Tahiti are from Mel Gooding and David Mabberley, *Joseph Banks' Florilegium: Botanical Treasures from Cook's First Voyage*, Thames & Hudson, Melbourne, 2017, p. 90, and Banks' journal entry, *The Endeavour Journal of Sir Joseph Banks*, 29 June 1769, which recalls the story of the marais.

A tribe in the southern highlands of New Guinea ... Eric Rolls, op. cit., 2011, p. 269.

A word for this sound: witjweri ... Roger Oxley, op. cit., p. 35.

'The tops of the trees are quivering ...' Matthew Condon, 'The Casuarina Forest', *Griffith Review*, edition 2, Summer 2003/2004, p. 38.

'With a lot of small limbs attached to its trunk ...' Albert Facey quotes are from A.B. Facey, *A Fortunate Life*, Penguin Books, Melbourne, 1986 (first published 1981), p. 58.

Planted deliberately to limit bird numbers at the airport ... Belinda Thomson, *A Cost Effective Grassland Management Strategy to Reduce the Number of Bird Strikes at the Brisbane Airport*, PhD Dissertation, Queensland University of Technology, Brisbane, 2007.

Melbourne, where I currently live, was once dominated ... Information on Melbourne's pre-European vegetation comes primarily from Gary Presland, *The Place for a Village: How Nature Has Shaped the City of Melbourne*, Museum Victoria Publishing, Melbourne, 2008; Elizabeth Anthony, *Melbourne's Pre-European Vegetation: A Reconstruction*, Honours Thesis, University of Melbourne, Parkville, available to view at the University of Melbourne; the Native Vegetation Information Management tool, op. cit.; and the 'Flora' page of the eMelbourne website.

The Dhauwurd Wurrung, who inhabited a large stretch ... the term 'gneering' is referenced in the report 'Budj Bim Cultural Landscape: World Heritage Nomination', Department of the Environment and Energy, Melbourne, 2017, p. 37, available as the 'Nomination Test' document on whc.unesco.org/en/list/1577/documents

The Wathaurung call the tree ngarrai or narada ... Stephen Murphy, op. cit.

Children would be encouraged to chew on the immature seed cones ... ibid.

They were healed by a group of Aboriginal women ... Robert Brough Smyth, *The Aborigines of Victoria, Volume 1*, Government Printer, Melbourne, 1878, pp. 465–6.

'One of nature's least charismatic critically endangered species ...' James Woodford, 'Forgotten Tree Is Safe for Now', *The Sydney Morning Herald*, 14 May 2003.

'They're not a very exciting plant ...' Paul Ibbetson, cited in James Woodford, ibid.

A search was made of the remnant vegetation ... Information on the Nielsen Park she-oak comes from NSW National Parks and Wildlife Service, *'Allocasuarina Portuensis* Recovery Plan', 2000, and James Woodford, ibid.

But for others, the pole was a she-oak and the location was near ... Information on these sources comes from Michael Flynn and Gary Sturgess, 'New Evidence on Arthur Phillip's First Landing Place – 26 January 1788', *History: Magazine of the Royal Australian Historical Society*, no. 122, December 2014, pp. 3–5.

'Considered sacred by Governor Macquarie, and the old hands of the colony ...' ibid., p. 3.

Jack remembered the British Flag ... ibid., p. 5.

They may even be the mature suckers ... Doug Benson, 'Oral Histories', interview online at Sydney Oral Histories, 24 April 2012, transcript available on sydneyoralhistories.com.au/doug-benson

The Gadigal word for the swamp oak is guman ... Colleen Morris, op. cit., p. 26.

'If you stand in its shadow by the light of the full moon ...' W. Somerset Maugham, *The Casuarina Tree*, William Heinemann, London, 1922, p. vii.

The Museum of Trees

'An outdoor museum of trees ...' Murray Bail, *Eucalyptus*, Text Publishing, Melbourne, 1998, p. 45.

'Maddeningly nondescript mallee ...' ibid., p. 99.

Dean Nicolle's Currency Creek arboretum ... Other articles on the arboretum include Ashley Hay, 'Gum Grower's Ark', *Nine MSN*, 23 October 2002, and Stephen Orr, 'Ambassadors from Another Time', *Australian Book Review*, no. 395, October 2017.

'No other comparable area of land ...' Tom Griffiths, 2001, op. cit., p. 1.

Ashley Hay asks us to imagine the continent ... Ashley Hay, 2002, op. cit., p. 2.

'No other tree family in the world ...' P.J. Hurley, op. cit., pp. 76–8.

'Of all the eucalypts, the mallees leave me cold ...' Murray Bail, op. cit., p. 119.

Adelaide is the city of eucalypts ... ibid., p. 68.

'More than any other city ...' ibid., p. 76.

For there was indeed a time when the southern part of Adelaide ... Information on Adelaide's pre-European vegetation comes from R.T. Lange, 'Vegetation' in C.R. Twidale, M.J. Tyler and B.P. Webb (eds), *Natural History of the Adelaide Region*, Royal Society of South Australia, Adelaide, 1976, Chapter 7; Phil Bagust and Lynda Tout-Smith, *The Native Plants of Adelaide*, Wakefield Press, Adelaide, 2010, p. 44; and M. Long, *A Biodiversity Survey of the Adelaide Park Lands South Australia in 2003*, Department for Environment and Heritage, South Australia, Adelaide, 2003.

Heroic, resilient and enduring ... Matthew Colloff, *Flooded Forest and Desert Creek*, CSIRO Publishing, Melbourne, 2014, p. 206.

The average person ... had an intricate knowledge ... Alison Page, 'Songlines: The Foundational Australian Story', *Big Ideas*, ABC Radio National, 24 January 2018.

'Part of our mob ...' Jakelin Troy, 'Trees Are at the Heart of Our Country', *The Guardian*, 1 April 2019.

The trees on which the spirits of ancestors ... Diana James, 'Tjukurpa Time' in Ann McGrath and Mary-Anne Jebb (eds), *Long History, Deep Time*, ANU Press, Canberra, 2015, p. 40.

'Wooral addressed the bush ...' Kim Scott, *That Deadman Dance*, Pan Macmillan, Sydney, 2013 (first published 2010), p. 46.

'In English, we give things very static names ...' Jakelin Troy, cited in Georgina Reid, 'Say My Name: On Speaking the Indigenous Names of Plants', *Wonderground*, 11 June 2019, available on wonderground.press/culture/say-name-speaking-indigenous-names-plants

'Stopped being an anonymously shaggy messmate ...' Ashley Hay, op. cit., p. 188.

We have lost the art ... John Fowles, *The Tree*, Vintage, London, 2002 (first published 2000), p. 37.

When people hit its trunk with branches ... this story comes from Dorothy Tunbridge, *Flinders Ranges Dreaming*, Aboriginal Studies Press for the Australian Institute of Aboriginal Studies, Canberra, 1988, p. 46.

Two river reds that have been bisected by a road ... ibid., p. 45.

'You can come to know each tree ...' Paul West, cited in 'Episode 1, Series 1', *Australia's Favourite Tree*, ABC-TV, 2022.

'Scarred and marked by the elements ...' Harold Cazneaux, cited in Bob Beale, op. cit., p. 150.

'See into the life of things ...' William Wordsworth, op. cit.

New Dreamings

Roberts, in a letter to McCubbin after the war ... These are reprinted in Tom Roberts, 'Letters from Tom Roberts to Frederick McCubbin, *La Trobe Journal*, no. 7, April 1971, p. 75.

'It frightened me ...' Hannah Kent, quoted in 'Australian Writers Pick Their Favourite Artworks from the Homeland', *The Guardian*, 21 September 2013.

A country of lost children ... the 'throwaway line' is from Bruce Chatwin, *Songlines*, Vintage, 1998 (first published 1987), p. 116.

'The lost child is the symbol ...' Peter Pierce, *The Country of Lost Children: An Australian Anxiety*, Cambridge University Press, Melbourne, 1999, p. xi.

We are all that McCubbin child ... Tom Wright, 'Picnic at Hanging Rock', presentation at the Wheeler Centre, 18 May 2017.

For three lost children of Daylesford ... The main references for this story are John E. Menadue, *The Story of the Three Lost Children*, Jim Crow Press for the Daylesford & District Historical Society, Daylesford, 1999; 'The Lost Children of Daylesford', *Illustrated Australian News*, Saturday 19 October 1867; and Chris McLennan, 'Almost 150 years Later and the Story of Daylesford's Lost Boys Remains one of the Saddest in Australia's History', *Weekly Times*, 31 January 2014. Jan Smith from the Daylesford & District Historical Society also provided valuable information.

'Colossal wreck, boundless and bare ...' Percy Bysshe Shelley, *Ozymandias*, available on poetryfoundation.org/poems/46565/ozymandias

It may well be a messmate ... This is corroborated by local historian Yvonne Fix in 'The Lost Boys of Daylesford', *History Listen*, ABC Radio National, 16 March 2021.

The boys would have little real hindrance ... John Menadue, op. cit., p. 12.

'So thickly set ...' Ellen Clacy, *A Lady's Visit to the Gold Diggings in 1852–53*, 1853, Chapter 5, entry 'Sunday 12', available on Project Gutenberg, gutenberg.org/ebooks/4054

J.H. Willis, a naturalist who was rumoured to differentiate eucalypt species ... Chester Eagle, *House of Trees: Gippsland's Legends, Places and People Brought to Life*, McPhee Gribble, Melbourne, 1987, p. 82.

The scentbark was its own species ... J.H. Willis and L.D. Pryor, 'A New Victorian (and South Australian) Eucalypt', *Victorian Naturalist*, vol. 71, no. 5, September 1954, p. 125.

They were mainly river red gums ... The full list of trees is catalogued in Ecology & Heritage Partners, 'Western Highway Project, Section 2: Beaufort to Ararat, Victoria – Biodiversity and Habitat Impact Assessment Report – Flora, Fauna and Ecological Communities', VicRoads, Melbourne, August 2012.

'One of the finest examples still in existence ...' This quote and further detail on the trees come from Dr Heather Builth, 'Desktop Report on Culturally Modified Trees Along Planned Roadworks of Southern Deviation Route of Option 1 for the Western Highway Between Ararat and Beaufort, Victoria', unpublished report prepared for Gillian Trebilcock, Daylesford, 2017, p. 26. Another good information resource is Timna Jacks, '"Like Losing my Son": Why Trees Threatened by Western Hwy Are So Sacred', *The Age*, 25 August 2019.

'*Western views of heritage are about static objects from the past …*' Libby Porter, 'Why the Destruction of the Djab Wurrung Tree is So Wrong', *The Fifth Estate*, 3 November 2020.

'*I sat in that tree with my youngest daughter …*' Lidia Thorpe, cited on 'Carving up the Country', *The History Listen*, ABC Radio National, 4 February 2020.

'*Continuity, constancy, balance, symmetry, regularity …*' Bill Stanner, cited in Bruce Pascoe, *Dark Emu*, Magabala Books, Broome, 2018 (first published 2014), p. 201.

'*To sit in a tree that saw your people birthed …*' Nayuka Gorrie, 'The Government Wants to Bulldoze my Inheritance: 800 Year Old Scarred Trees', *The Guardian*, 12 April 2019.

'*A forest is language …*' Murray Bail, op. cit., p. 255.

'*He was at peace with the world again …*' Rolf de Heer, 'A Toxic Mix', *Griffith Review*, edition 16, May 2007.

'*We need to discover new dreamings …*' Matthew Colloff, op. cit., 2014, p. 263.

Epilogue: Saint-Hilaire Trees

'*Of all Australian trees, brush box …*' Inga Simpson, *Understory*, Hachette, Sydney, 2017, p. 4.

'*All the occupations, all the hours …*' Marcel Proust, *In Search of Lost Time, Volume 1: The Way by Swann's*, Penguin Books, Melbourne, 2002 (first published 1913), p. 67.

'*I found a study, admittedly fifteen years old …*' Stephen Frank, Glenn Waters, Russell Beer and Peter May, 'An Analysis of the Street Tree Population of Greater Melbourne at the Beginning of the 21st Century', *Arboriculture & Urban Forestry*, vol. 32, no. 4, 2006, pp. 155–63.

'*Tis true we have no mouldering monasteries …*' Gibbs, Shallard and Co's *Illustrated Guide to Sydney*, 1882, cited in Doug Benson and Jocelyn Howell, *Taken for Granted*, Kangaroo Press in association with the Royal Botanic Gardens Sydney, Kenthurst, 1990, p. 33.

'*No association of the past …*' John Sherer, cited in Robert Hughes, op. cit., p. 599.

'*The land is alive …*' Anne Poelina, 'The Marlaloo Songline', Australian Institute of Aboriginal and Torres Strait Islander Studies, Canberra, 25 May 2022, aiatsis.gov.au/explore/marlaloo-songline

Notes

1   In the words of Robert Hughes.
2   The surface of jarrah wore down more slowly than other timbers and did not soak up horse urine to the same degree. Jonathan Drori, author of *Around the World in 80 Trees*, writes that softwoods 'would soak up the swill of equine urine and ordure and, under pressure from a heavy wheel, squirt it out at passers-by'.
3   On the other side of the continent, *Melaleuca lanceolata* is referred to as moonah.
4   There has long been controversy over whether one of our most common trees should be spelt 'tea-tree' or 'ti-tree'. A 1929 *Queenslander* article reflects that 'the weight of evidence seems to be in favour of the former … In 1898 a dictionary of Australasian words was issued … The tea-tree is very comprehensively dealt with there, the references covering six columns. The references open as follows:— "Tea-tree,n. (Very frequently, but erroneously, spelt 'Ti-tree,' and occasionally, more ridiculously still, 'Ti-tri,'). A name given in Australia, New Zealand, and Tasmania to several species of trees and shrubs, whose leaves were used by Captain Cook's sailors, by escaped convicts, and by the early settlers as a ready substitute for the leaves of the Chinese Tea-plant (*Thea chinensis*) for making tea … The spelling 'ti-tree' is not only erroneous as to the origin of the name, but exceedingly misleading, as it confuses the Australian 'tea-tree' with another ti in Polynesia (*Cordyline ti*) … As to the species of the Australian tea-tree, that first used by Cook's sailors was either *Leptospermum scoparium* or *L. lanigerum* … In New Zealand the Maori name Manuka is more generally used than tea-tree, and the tree denoted by it is the original one used by Cook's sailors." The article laments, 'The majority of newspapers in Australia appear to have adopted the spelling [ti-tree], probably from misapprehension, while the botanists and scientific writers adhere to the "tea" form … in the course of time [it has] almost invariably become grafted on the language … it is unlikely that the original and correct spelling will ever regain a footing.' Perhaps an illustration of the influence of this spelling is the Northern Territory town of Ti-Tree, where in the 1980s residents successfully petitioned the state's legislative assembly to change the name from 'Tea-tree'. Yet the Australian Tea-Tree Industry Association holds firm to the logic that 'tea-tree' refers to a wider range of trees. Indeed, the most confusing aspect of tea-tree is that it refers to both *Melaleuca* and *Leptospermum spp.*, and early settlers blithely used the term without precision.
5   It is believed the last major assembly gathered at Mount Mowbullan in 1875.
6   While they may resemble the pines of Canada or the spruces of Siberia, they are a separate branch of the order Pinales, lacking the needles and winged seeds of true pine trees, and bearing cones that unravel as they fall to the ground.
7   Particularly the species *Calophyllum tomentosum*.

8 The scales are essentially a protective cover for the seeds. It is the interlocking pattern of these scales that gives the cones of *Agathis* and *Araucaria* species their distinctive look.

9 The trees had been observed by European eyes even earlier than this. In personal communication with John Leslie Dowe, I discovered a crocodile hunter used to camp beneath the trees as far back as the 1950s.

10 Yiithuwarra is the collective name, meaning 'saltwater people', for the traditional custodians of Cape Melville and Flinders islands.

11 Ludwig Leichhardt is believed to be the first European to record the tree growing in Australia; hence its common name. The species, however, grows naturally throughout South-East Asia and was already known to Western science by the mid-eighteenth century. Carl Linnaeus assigned the tree its scientific name.

12 The photo is titled *Emmie Tipiloura Rests in the Mangroves During a Hunting Trip, Bathurst Island* (1988).

13 There was an application in 1996 to remove the Old Jarrah Tree in order to extend the existing shopping centre. Locals protested and, after eighteen months, the state government awarded the tree heritage status and forced the design of the shopping centre's extension to accommodate the tree. On the evening of victory, the members of the action group congregated around the tree with champagne bottles in hand. But they were shocked to discover a vandal had taken a meat cleaver to the trunk. The tree was thought dead, but it has miraculously survived, with epicormic leaves growing along the northern side of the trunk.

14 It is still not clear whether they are two trunks sprouting from the same hidden root system or two siblings growing from the seeds of one parent.

15 This refers to the Maritime pine (*Pinus pinaster*).

16 The swamp mahoganies (*Eucalyptus robusta*), which still cradle the old wall, were planted at her request.

17 The painting is simply titled *Springwood* (1815).

18 The painting is titled *Campbell's River Crossing* (1815).

19 At least, the largest tree from a reliable source. William Ferguson, the Inspector of State Forests, claims to have measured a tree near the Watts River in Healesville that was 132 metres tall, but such an extraordinary height seems unlikely.

20 This account, incidentally, contradicts the plaque, saying the tree was cut down in 1885, not 1884.

21 The painting is called *In Adventure Bay, Van Diemen's Land*.

22 The sketch is titled *Arbuthnot's Range from the West*. It was redrawn by Major Taylor and included within the publication of Oxley's journals.

23 Specifically, the coast banksia (*Banksia integrifolia*) and the north coast wattle (*Acacia leptocarpa*).

24 Possibly a narrow-leaved peppermint (*Eucalyptus radiata*), given the location.

25 While it is assumed the forest took its name from the black gum, it is unclear how abundant the species was at the time. Potentially, the narrow-leaved peppermint was the dominant species, giving the forest a slightly blackened appearance.

26 It is not easy to age eucalypts as, unlike the deciduous trees of Europe, they do not exhibit annual growth spurts every summer, but grow as and when water becomes abundant. Trees we think could be 700 years old may be 400 or they could be 1000.